The Failure of the
Franklin National Bank

Institute of War and Peace Studies,
Columbia University

COUNCIL ON FOREIGN RELATIONS BOOKS

The Council on Foreign Relations, Inc., is a nonprofit and nonpartisan organization devoted to promoting improved understanding of international affairs through the free exchange of ideas. The Council does not take any position on questions of foreign policy and has no affiliation with, and receives no funding from, the United States government.

From time to time, books and monographs written by members of the Council's research staff or visiting fellows, or commissioned by the Council, or (like this book) written by an independent author with critical review contributed by a Council study or working group are published with the designation "Council on Foreign Relations Book." Any book or monograph bearing that designation is, in the judgment of the Committee on Studies of the Council's board of directors, a responsible treatment of a significant international topic worthy of presentation to the public. All statements of fact and expressions of opinion contained in Council books are, however, the sole responsibility of the author.

THE FAILURE
of the FRANKLIN
NATIONAL BANK

Challenge to the
International Banking
System

JOAN EDELMAN SPERO

Columbia University Press
New York 1980

Published for the Council on Foreign Relations

*Joan Edelman Spero is Assistant Professor
of Political Science at Columbia University*

Library of Congress Cataloging in Publication Data
Spero, Joan Edelman.
  The failure of the Franklin National Bank.

  Bibliography: p. 211
  Includes index.
  1. Franklin National Bank.   2. Banks and banking,
International.   I. Title.
HG2613.N54F756   332.1′223′0973   79-18851
ISBN 0-231-04788-6

Columbia University Press
New York   Guildford, Surrey

Copyright © 1980 by Columbia University Press
All Rights Reserved
Printed in the United States of America

To Michael

Contents

PREFACE

IT WOULD NOT have been possible to carry out this study without the generous support and assistance of a number of institutions and individuals. The International Affairs Fellowship Program of the Council on Foreign Relations and the Institute for World Politics enabled me to take a year's leave of absence from Columbia University to conduct my research. My year as the holder of the Ira D. Wallach Chair of World Order Studies of the Institute of War and Peace Studies, School of International Affairs, Columbia University enabled me to complete my research and writing.

The Federal Reserve Bank of New York where I spent six months as a visiting scholar opened its doors and its resources to me. I am especially grateful to David Willey who originally suggested the possibilities in a study of the Franklin National Bank, who encouraged and assisted my research, and who offered comments on my manuscript; to Peter Fousek who arranged for my stay at the Reserve Bank; to James Oltman whose advice and assistance I frequently sought and always received; to Walker Todd who was undaunted by my constant requests for documents and who helped me unravel many of my research problems; to Stephen Clarke who gave me the benefit of his wisdom on the politics of international banking and whose enthusiasm for my work gave me constant encouragement; to William Brustein who helped me decipher Franklin's financial statistics; to Jean Deuss, Emily Trueblood and Joan Breitbart of the Research Library who cheerfully helped me with even my most obscure requests; and to the many members of the research department who listened to my daily detective reports and encouraged my quest.

The Council on Foreign Relations not only helped fund my research but also made it possible for me to have that research evaluated by scholars and practitioners in the field of international banking. I am especially grateful to William Diebold for his comments on my manuscript and for organizing and chairing a meeting on my study held at the Council on Foreign Relations. The comments and criticisms at that meeting were of invaluable assistance in preparing the final version of my study. I would like to thank those who took time to read my study and to spend a day discussing it and those who were unable to attend the meeting but gave me their comments on the manuscript: David O. Beim, Henry S. Bloch, Miriam Camps, Stephen V. O. Clarke, Ann Crittenden, Franklin R. Edwards, Jessica P. Einhorn, Charles R. Frank, Jr., Benjamin M. Friedman, George J. W. Goodman, Catherine B. Gwin, Burton A. MacLean, Jr., Barbara Stallings, Helena Stalson, Lawrence A. Veit, Paul A. Volcker, Alfred H. von Klemperer, Henry C. Wallich, Philip A. Wellons, and H. David Willey. Patricia Feldman's transcript of the meeting was most helpful.

My study also benefited from the comments of Robert Keohane who forced me to think harder about the theoretical implications of my findings, C. F. Muckenfuss who encouraged me to look critically at the purposes and future of bank regulation, and Philip Wellons who helped me analyze the systemic implications of the Franklin episode.

The Institute of War and Peace Studies and the Institute on Western Europe of Columbia University made it possible for my research to become a manuscript. I am especially grateful to

Warner Schilling, William T. R. Fox, and Donald Puchala for their guidance and comments on my work; to Peter White for his meticulous research assistance; to Martha Bloomstrom and Wayne Storey who helped to translate Italian documents; to Brian Burkhalter, Miriam Levy, Patricia Murphy, and Georgia Kanary who typed the manuscript; to Gary Pickholz who assisted in the preparation of the bibliography; and to Anna Hohri who coordinated it all. I would also like to thank Bernard Gronert, Leslie Bialler, and Joan McQuary of Columbia University Press, who made it possible for the manuscript to become a book.

Very special thanks must go to the many participants and close observers of the Franklin National Bank events who generously agreed to share their recollections, evaluations, and wisdom with me. Because so many of the interviews covered the same events, I have not cited interviews as the source of information in many instances, but instead have listed my informants in the bibliography. Without them, there could have been no study of the Franklin National Bank crisis.

Finally, I am grateful to C. Michael Spero who served as editor, legal consultant, and constant supporter.

Joan Edelman Spero
May 1979

The Failure of the
Franklin National Bank

1

INTERNATIONAL BANKING, INTERNATIONAL STABILITY, AND THE FRANKLIN NATIONAL BANK

INTERNATIONAL BANKING HAS become a central thread in the increasingly complex web of international interdependence. In little more than one decade the structure of banks, the nature of international financial markets, and the relationship among international banks have changed dramatically.

Banks throughout the world have been transformed into multinational corporations. They have established international networks of foreign branches, subsidiaries, and joint ventures and have dramatically expanded their international business. U.S. banks have been in the forefront of international expansion. In 1965, 13 U.S. banks had 211 overseas branches; by 1975, 126 American banks had 762 foreign branches. In 1965 overseas branches of U.S. banks held $9.1 billion in assets while in 1975 they held $145.3 billion.[1] For many of the world's largest banks, international business has become a vital source of earnings. In 1970 international earnings accounted for well

1

under one-fourth of the total earnings of 12 major U.S. banks; by 1975 they accounted for almost half of all earnings of these banks.[2]

The growth of international financial markets has been as dramatic as the growth of international banking networks. The Eurocurrency market, which is primarily an interbank market and which is the focus of much of the international activity of banks, grew from $14 billion in 1965 to over $380 billion in 1977.[3] With the advent of floating exchange rates foreign exchange markets also expanded. A dearth of figures makes it impossible to measure the growth of foreign exchange markets. We do know, however, that in 1971 foreign branches of twelve major American multinational banks bought and sold about $16 billion of United States and foreign currencies and in 1974 bought and sold about $33 billion in foreign exchange markets.[4]

Through these international financial markets international banks have become closely linked with each other. Multinational banks operating in the Eurocurrency interbank market have become connected by networks of mutual deposits and credits. In 1977, for example, 42 percent of all Eurocurrency liabilities were between Eurobanks.[5] If liabilities between Eurobanks and other banks were included, the share of interbank transactions would be much higher. Banks trading in foreign exchange are similarly linked by networks of spot and forward foreign exchange contracts. Such interbank connections have created a truly interdependent international banking system.

International Banking and the Stability of the Banking System

While there is much evidence of the spectacular growth of international banking, there is little certainty about the nature of the economic and political changes wrought by the new system. The emergence of the new international financial system has generated much debate about its advantages and disadvantages, its strengths and weaknesses. Debate has focused on issues such as the system's contribution to growth and development and to exchange rate instability, its effect on national monetary policy, and its role in international inflation.[6]

One of the central issues in the debate is the impact of international activities on bank soundness and on the stability of the banking system. The problem of instability and crisis is hardly a new theme in the history of banking. The last century has been one of frequent bank panics: the crisis of 1873, which centered on the collapse of banks in Vienna and New York; the 1890 crisis, sparked by the threatened failure of the venerable Baring Brothers and Company of London; the crisis of 1907, which began in New York; and, of course the collapse in 1931 of the Credit Anstalt of Austria, which led to bank crises in Germany, England, and the United States. Most of these banking panics were part of larger financial crises and economic recessions of international dimensions.[7]

Despite the lessons of history, concern with bank soundness and financial stability receded in the three decades following World War II. The world economy and the banking system were remarkably stable and prosperous. Public policy enlightened by economic analysis seemed to have found a way to explain, predict, and manage economic behavior. In the United States, economic policy was supplemented by bank regulatory and supervisory methods which seemed to have brought the banking system under effective control. It was in this stable and prosperous environment that banks expanded their international activities.

In the 1970s, however, the issue of bank stability once again became an important problem and issue of public concern. From prosperity and stability the world economy slipped into recession and instability. Double-digit inflation and negative growth rates, a collapse of the international monetary order, and the OPEC shock— all the economic difficulties of the 1970s put severe strains on the world's financial institutions. A number of banks including some very large institutions found themselves in serious trouble and, for the first time since the Depression, some very large banks actually collapsed.

The causes of the bank difficulties of the 1970s are numerous, complex, and difficult to disentangle. Some grew out of the precarious economic environment, some out of domestic activities such as real estate loans, some out of sheer and outright fraud. Some of the most important problems of the big banks also were related to their international activities.

Several dramatic developments in the 1970s raised the issue of the stability of the international banking system from obscurity to public attention and official concern. First, in 1974, came the failures of the German Bankhaus I. D. Herstatt and of the Franklin National Bank of New York. The collapse of these two banks occurred in the very midst of the world economic crisis: the oil shock, the tottering of the international monetary system, reported and rumored troubles in banks throughout the world. The important role of foreign exchange losses in the demise of Herstatt and Franklin and the foreign exchange troubles of a number of other banks highlighted the vulnerability of banks to foreign exchange losses in the new era of floating exchange rates.[8] Furthermore, because both Herstatt and Franklin had important links to the international banking system, their demise sent shock waves throughout international financial markets. Foreign exchange trading ground to a halt and Eurocurrency activity dropped significantly; rates in foreign exchange and Eurocurrency markets became severely tiered and a number of banks were actually excluded from these markets. The turmoil in international financial markets put further strain on many banks and revealed the vulnerability of the interdependent international banking system to the failure of one of its members.

In 1974 the seeds were being sown for another set of potential problems. Following the quadrupling of the price of petroleum in late 1973 and early 1974, commercial banks assumed a central role in recycling funds from oil-surplus to oil-deficit countries. They accepted large deposits from oil-producing states and made important loans to both developed and developing countries which were used to finance balance-of-payments deficits. While such recycling was vital to the functioning of the international monetary system and the world economy, it placed an important burden on commercial banks. Public debate began to focus on the new risks assumed by banks in making loans to countries which might not be able to repay or service their debts. Technical defaults in a number of Third World states—Indonesia, Peru, Zaïre—focused attention on the vulnerability of banks to a number of new political and economic risks associated with country loans and once again highlighted the interdependence of the international financial system and its vulnerability to weaknesses in one or more of its parts.[9] At the same time the importance of oil-country deposits to multinational banks raised concern about the political and economic risks associated with deposit concentration.[10]

Risk and Management

Underlying the public debate about international banking stability are two central issues: the nature and degree of risk associated with international banking and the lack of public control of the international activities of banks.

Some argue and others contest that, in going international, banks have assumed important new risks which threaten the soundness of individual banks and the viability of the system as a whole. Some of these risks have already been mentioned: foreign exchange trading in an era of floating exchange rates, which may lead to losses and to dangerous speculation and fraud; the dramatic growth of loans to foreign countries that may be unable or unwilling to repay their debts; massive Eurodollar placements by oil-surplus countries, which may make Eurobanks vulnerable to real or threatened deposit withdrawal.

Observers have pointed to a host of other potential problems: excessive reliance on short-term Eurodollar placements to fund long- and medium-term loans; excessive competition in Euromarkets, which leads to unwise policies such as dangerously low interest rates and loans to borrowers whose credit-worthiness is questionable;

linkage to the international interbank market, which makes banks vulnerable to the weakness of other institutions in the system.[11]

A second, closely related dimension of international banking stability is the lack of public control over the international activities of banks and the possibility that, as a result, public authorities may be unable to prevent international bank crises or to control them once they erupt. Since the Depression and the financial crises of the 1930s, governments in the developed market economies have devised a variety of methods for stabilizing the banking system. In Europe the focus has been on economic management through a mixed economy supplemented by bank regulation and supervision; the Japanese rely on an informal system of government-business-banking cooperation; in the United States there has been greater emphasis on bank regulation and supervision. In the 1970s governments are discovering that management methods designed for a banking system with national boundaries may be inadequate for a banking system no longer limited by territorial borders.[12]

In some countries the problem of public management of international banking has arisen in part from the inadequacy of bank supervisory and regulatory methods generally. In the United Kingdom, for example, a bank supervisory method which relied on informal exchanges of information among a network of bankers who knew each other well and who came from similar socioeconomic backgrounds no longer sufficed in an era when bank activities became increasingly complicated and when bankers no longer came from the same class.

In the United States the problem of public control of international banking is complicated by another problem: the diffusion of supervisory and regulatory responsibility among a host of federal and state authorities. The degree of overlapping and divided jurisdiction of bank management in the United States is awesome. Banks, for example, may be chartered by the federal government through the Office of the Comptroller of the Currency (which is part of the Treasury) or by individual states.

All nationally chartered banks are supervised by the Comptroller but are required to join the Federal Reserve. State-chartered banks may also join the Federal Reserve System and, if they do, are supervised by the Federal Reserve. The Federal Deposit Insurance Corporation supervises state-chartered banks which are not members of the Federal Reserve. While banks are chartered by the Comptroller or state authorities, bank holding companies are authorized and supervised by the Federal Reserve.

Responsibility for supervision and regulation of international activities of American banks is equally complex and diffuse. Most multinational banks are nationally chartered and thus are supervised by the Comptroller. Foreign branches of these banks are authorized by the Federal Reserve but supervised by the Comptroller. The Federal Reserve authorizes the formation of and supervises Edge Act corporations, which are subsidiaries of national banks organized for the purpose of international activities. The Federal Reserve also authorizes the formation or acquisition of foreign subsidiaries by bank holding companies or member banks. Foreign activities of bank holding companies are supervised by the Federal Reserve while foreign subsidiaries of national banks are supervised by the Comptroller, and foreign subsidiaries of state member banks are supervised jointly by the Federal Reserve and state authorities.

The diffusion of supervisory and regulatory responsibility for international banking makes jurisdiction and responsibility ambiguous. For example, in acting on an application by a national bank to open a foreign branch or to set up a foreign subsidiary, the Federal Reserve must evaluate the condition of that bank. The primary supervisor, however, is not the Federal Reserve but the Comptroller. Such a situation creates a need for cooperation and coordination, and also opens the door to bureaucratic differences. The Comptroller and the Federal Reserve, for example, have developed different standards for evaluating bank soundness and for minimum standards required for a bank to be permitted to engage in international finance.

A more important problem of managing international banking is the absence of regulation. Banks operating outside their home countries are in important instances regulated and supervised neither by the home nor the host government. American banks abroad, for example, are exempt from U.S. regulations on reserve requirements and interest-rate ceilings and from U.S. domestic restrictions on geographical spread and the nature of activities in which banks may engage. Foreign banks operating in such an important international financial center as London need not conform to regulation that applies to banks chartered there, and banks operating in bank and tax havens such as the Bahamas or the Cayman Islands are subject to virtually no local regulation. Indeed, the system has grown and prospered largely because of this lack of regulation. Profits in the Eurodollar market, for example, are attractive because banks operating there are not burdened by costly regulatory requirements.

Supervision of the international activities of banks is also incomplete. The Comptroller supervises foreign branches of U.S. banks, but other regulatory agencies such as those of Italy and West Germany do not regularly supervise offshore operations of their banks. In other cases, such as Switzerland or Luxemburg, national laws prevent inspection by or release of records of banks operating there to foreign banking authorities.

Another form of public management of banking, especially important in the United States, is deposit insurance. The Federal Deposit Insurance Corporation (FDIC), established in 1933, protects small depositors (since 1974 those with up to $40,000 of deposits) and has been an important factor in deterring bank runs and liquidity crises such as those of the 1930s. It is also empowered to and frequently does arrange for federally assisted acquisitions of all or some of the assets and liabilities of insolvent banks, thus helping to maintain confidence in the banking system. The increasing reliance of banks on large uninsured deposits including Eurodollars weakens the FDIC deterrent. Furthermore, FDIC insurance does not cover foreign branch deposits or deposits in foreign banks operating in the United States. And many countries have no deposit insurance at all. The international spread of banks also greatly complicates the role of the FDIC in disposing of the assets and liabilities of insolvent banks.

A final form of public management of banking is the maintenance of the stability and liquidity of national financial markets through the "lender of last resort" responsibility. In the United States, for example, the Federal Reserve has the authority to determine when the failure of a bank could endanger the nation's financial system and when the resources in the discount window of the Reserve banks will be used to prevent a failure or to delay an insolvency until an acceptable solution can be found.

The mushrooming of offshore subsidiaries has confused and complicated this role and allowed many banking institutions to fall into the cracks. Because branches are integral parts of the parent bank, responsibility of the parent and its central bank for foreign branches seems clear. Responsibility for other subsidiaries, however, is far from clear. Take, for example, the case of a separately incorporated English subsidiary of an American bank. The Bank of England claims it is not responsible for supporting foreign-owned banking institutions incorporated in the United Kingdom. The parent bank is not legally responsible for supporting a separately incorporated subsidiary, and therefore the Federal Reserve claims it is not responsible as lender of last resort for such subsidiaries. To complicate matters, the parent bank may feel it must shore up a troubled subsidiary because the parent's reputation and the market's confidence in its performance may be closely linked with its subsidiary. What, then, happens if the parent runs into trouble because of its aid to—or failure to aid—its foreign affiliate?

For all these reasons, internationalization has weakened national management of banking. Yet, at least until 1974, international management did not develop to fill the gaps. Neither formal institutions nor informal processes existed which could stabilize the international banking system.

The rapid growth of international banking took place without international efforts to establish formal institutions, rules, and regulations for international banking. While in many other areas of international economic relations there are international organizations and some rudimentary rules of behavior—for example, the Articles of Agreement of the International Monetary Fund (IMF) and the General Agreement on Tariffs and Trade (GATT)—international banking is subject to no international organizations and to no international rules. To be sure, some rules of the IMF, such as exchange control provisions, influence international banking; and some activities of the Bank for International Settlements, in particular its collection and analysis of data on the Eurodollar market, bear on international banking. But beyond these tangential rules and activities there has been no effort to create institutions or to codify rules to manage key dimensions of international banking. There were no efforts, for example, to define the lender of last resort and the primary supervisor in international banking and to regulate the Eurodollar market.

There were also no informal means of managing the international banking system. Informal processes—consultation, coordination, exercise of leadership functions—have been as important as formal institutions and rules in the management of postwar international economic relations. The pivotal leadership role of the United States and the consultation of major economic powers through meetings and dialogue of ministers and central bankers, for example, were as central to the functioning of the international monetary and international trading systems as the IMF and the GATT. For years, international banking was not subject to such informal methods of management. Central bankers discussed economic policy but not bank regulatory policy; bank supervisory authorities did not know their counterparts in other countries and had little knowledge of supervisory and regulatory practices in other countries. Not until the bank crisis of 1974 did national authorities even recognize that there was a problem which required national reform and international cooperation.

This study seeks to shed light on the impact of international banking on the two dimensions of international financial stability: the economic and the political. Through a case study of one bank, the Franklin National Bank of New York, and the international banking crisis of 1974 which Franklin helped to create, the study will explore some of the new risks created by international banking for both individual banks and for the system as a whole. It will also focus on the political management of these new risks by examining the reaction of public authorities in the United States and abroad to the Franklin crisis.

The Franklin National Bank of New York

Franklin National Bank, once the twentieth largest bank in the United States, was an ambitious, growth-oriented Long Island bank which expanded rapidly in the 1960s and early 1970s. It grew up with retail banking on Long Island, then moved into New York City and wholesale banking in the early 1960s. Beginning in 1969 Franklin joined the movement abroad. It established foreign branches in Nassau, the Bahamas, and in London; became heavily involved in Eurodollar activities and foreign exchange trading; and even acquired a foreign owner, the Italian financier Michele Sindona. By 1973 Franklin had assets of over $5 billion. It also had a variety of problems: weak management, a bad domestic loan portfolio, poor investments, heavy reliance on very short-term borrowings to finance long-term loans.

In May 1974 Franklin became part of the first, and since then the only, crisis of the new international banking system. Because of a concatenation of difficulties which were largely domestic but included important international problems, Franklin was suddenly faced with the threat of insolvency. The possibility of the precipitous collapse of one of the largest banks in the United States posed grave threats to the United States and the international banking system. Because of the importance of Franklin National Bank within the United States and because of Franklin's links to the international banking system, the crisis forced U.S. and foreign regulatory authorities to devise new ways to avert an international banking crisis. The crisis of 1974 also served as a catalyst for later efforts to bring international banking under public management.

In examining the Franklin case the study will seek answers to the following questions:

Why and how did Franklin become involved in international banking? By exploring the economic and political factors which led Franklin abroad, we hope to shed light on the reasons for the dramatic growth of international banking in the 1960s and 1970s and especially the reasons for the internationalization of American banks.

To what extent and in what way was Franklin's demise caused by its international activities and to what extent were Franklin's problems sui generis *or indicative of larger, systemic problems?* By examining the role of international activities in the Franklin crisis we hope to understand better some of the new risks encountered by banks in their international activities.

In what way did the insolvency of Franklin threaten the international banking system? In examining the links between the Franklin crisis and the banking crisis of 1974, the study will explore the nature of the interdependence of the banking system and the possible threats to the stability of that system arising from that interdependence.

How did U.S. regulatory authorities attempt to manage the Franklin crisis, and, in particular, what innovative steps were they forced to take to manage the international dimensions of the Franklin crisis? By examining the regulatory response in the Franklin case we hope to learn more about the gaps in national management and the process of national policy innovation in a crisis situation.

To what extent were U.S. regulators unable to manage the Franklin crisis alone and to what extent were they forced to seek assistance from other national authorities? The answer to this question should shed some light on the limits of national management and the possibilities for international cooperation.

What, if any, have been the more lasting effects of the Franklin crisis on the management of international banking both at the national level and at the level of international cooperation? The international banking crisis of 1974 was the first crisis of the new international banking system and thus an interesting test of the political response to the new system. The answer to this last question should enable us to evaluate the political processes which have developed in an effort to manage this new form of interdependence.

2

THE INTERNATIONALIZATION OF THE FRANKLIN NATIONAL BANK

FRANKLIN NATIONAL BANK was part of the international revolution in banking. Between 1969 and 1974, Franklin opened two foreign branches, dramatically increased its foreign borrowing and lending, developed a massive foreign exchange trading operation, and acquired a foreign owner who controlled over one-fifth of the stock of the bank holding company which owned Franklin. This chapter will examine how and why Franklin, in the space of five years, became an international bank. In order to understand the Franklin case, however, we must first describe the setting in which the internationalization of Franklin National took place.

The International Banking System

The movement of Franklin National Bank into international banking was part of a much larger process. Banks throughout the world had long been involved in international activities. But in the 1960s and 1970s the quantity and quality of international banking activities changed dramatically.

Many banks, in these years, became multinational corporations: the number of foreign affiliates and the amount of foreign business increased dramatically and foreign operations became a central element of bank activity and bank earnings. United States banks used a variety of forms to establish or expand their foreign operations (see table 2.1). The most important means was the foreign branch. In 1965, 13 American banks had 211 overseas branches; by 1975, 126 banks had 762 overseas branches in foreign countries. In 1965 American branches abroad held $9.1 billion in assets while by 1975 they held $145.3 billion.

Important concentrations of these branches were in London and Nassau, the Bahamas. In 1964, 10 American banks operated 17 branches in London; by the end of 1973, 37 banks operated 52 branches there. In 1964 only 2 American commercial banks had Nassau branches; in September 1974, 84 banks operated 90 branches in the Bahamas.[1]

Representative offices, Edge Act and Agreement corporations,[2] joint ventures, and direct investments in foreign financial institutions also grew rapidly. In 1965, for example, American banks had 41 Edge Act and Agreement corporations with total assets of $1.0 billion. By 1975 there were 116 such subsidiaries with assets of $9.1 billion. Because of capital controls, loans from U.S. offices of American banks grew at a slower rate during this decade of rapid expansion. At the end of 1965 outstanding loans extended by U.S. offices to foreigners amounted to $9.7 billion; by the end of 1973, the last full year of capital controls, that figure had risen to $17.3 billion. At the end of 1974, with the freeing of controls, bank credit to foreigners jumped to $29.0 billion.

In the late 1960s and early 1970s non–U.S. banks also experienced an important surge of growth in international operations. In 1965, for example, 19 foreign banks had 36 branches and 26 agencies in the United States holding $5 billion in assets. By 1974 there were 39 foreign banks with 57 branches and 49 agencies and a total of $42 billion in assets.[3]

International operations, once peripheral to domestic operations, grew as a percentage of total bank business and became a vital activity for many important banking institutions. Because the foreign business of American commercial banks expanded at a rate far greater than that of domestic business, foreign operations assumed a greater role in overall bank operations. In 1960 foreign assets (assets at foreign branches and loans to foreigners from the head office) of all American commercial banks accounted for less than 3 percent of total assets. By the end of 1975 they represented almost 19 percent of total assets.[4] For large multinational banks, which include the major American banks, the figures are much higher. In 1974 assets and liabilities of foreign branches of 12 major American multinational banks accounted for 32.9 percent of total assets and liabilities.[5] Foreign earnings became crucially important to such banks. In 1971 net foreign income represented 22.7 percent of total net income for these 12 multinational banks. By 1975 net foreign income for these banks accounted for 62.0 percent of total net income.[6]

The internationalization of banks coincided with the development of a *truly international financial market* which operates across national boundaries and outside the control of any state and whose participants come from all over the world. That market is, of course, the Eurocurrency market.

The Eurocurrency market is an international money market for currencies deposited and re-lent outside their countries of origin. While there is a Euromarket for many currencies, including German marks, Swiss francs, and the pound sterling, the principal Eurocurrency is the Eurodollar, that is, dollars deposited in banks outside the United States including the foreign branches of American banks. The Eurodollar market grew from an estimated $14 billion in 1964 to almost $380 billion in 1977 (see table 2.2).[7] The major participants in this wholesale market are banks from many countries located in Europe, especially in London, the most important center of the market.[8] Because the currencies and banks in the Eurocurrency

TABLE 2.1   International Operations of U.S. Banks:
Selected Indicators, 1960–1978 ($ billion)

Category	1960	1964	1965	1966	1967	1968
I. U.S. offices:						
Bank credit to foreigners[a]	N.A.	$9.4	$9.7	$9.6	$9.8	$9.2
Deposits of foreigners, other than due to foreign branches[b]	$9.3	$13.4	$13.6	$15.9	$17.5	$19.9
II. Overseas branches of banks:						
Number of banks with overseas branches	8	11	13	13	15	26
Number of overseas branches	124	180	211	244	295	373
Assets of overseas branches[c]	$3.5	$6.9	$9.1	$12.4	$15.7	$23.0
III. Edge Act and Agreement corporations:						
Number	15	38	41	45	51	61
Assets	N.A.	$0.9	$1.0	$1.4	$1.5	$2.5
Memorandum—All commercial banks in the United States:						
Total assets	$257.6	$346.9	$377.3	$403.4	451.0	$500.7
Total deposits	$229.8	$307.2	$332.4	$352.3	$395.0	$434.0

All data shown are for end of period.
N.A. indicates data not available.

[a]Bank credit to foreigners is comprised of 1) two types of short-term claims on foreigners reported by banks in the U.S.: a) total loans payable in dollars and b) acceptances, payable in dollars, made for foreigners; and 2) one type of long term claim on foreigners reported by banks in the U.S.: total loans payable in dollars.

[b]Deposits of foreigners is comprised of short-term demand and time deposits (excluding negotiable time certificates of deposit) held by all foreigners (excluding the International Monetary Fund), payable in dollars.

[c]Figures on overseas branch assets before 1969 include interbranch balances. Figures on overseas branch assets since 1969 are net of interbranch balances.

market are outside the country of origin they have been largely exempt from national regulation.

Eurodollar deposits are short-term deposits placed by central banks or monetary authorities, commercial banks, large corporations, or insurance companies. These institutions hold large amounts of dollars which they prefer to deposit outside the United States for a variety of reasons: higher yields, avoidance of national controls

1969	1970	1971	1972	1973	1974	1975	1976	1977	1978
$9.3	$9.7	$11.6	$13.5	$17.3	$29.0	$32.7	$40.7	$44.8	$46.1[d]
$27.3	$21.8	$15.6	$13.9	$18.2	$24.0	$23.8	$28.2	$30.5	$30.1[d]
53	79	91	107	125	125	126	130	130	N.A.
460	532	577	627	699	732	762	731[e]	730	N.A.
$31.8	$39.6	$55.1	$72.1	$108.8	$127.3	$145.3	$174.5	$203.1	$223.9
68	75	85	92	103	117	116	117	122	N.A.
$3.5	$4.6	$5.5	$6.1	$6.9	$10.1	$9.1	$11.1	N.A.	N.A.
$530.7	$576.2	$640.3	$739.0	$835.2	$919.6	$964.9	$1030.7	$1166.0	$1240.5[f]
$435.6	$480.9	$537.9	$616.0	$681.8	$747.9	$786.3	$838.2	$934.2	$959.4[f]

[d]Preliminary figure for April 1978.

[e]The net decline of 31 branches from 1975 to 1976 was due primarily to the conversion of 30 branches in Colombia into subsidiaries to conform with Colombian banking laws.

[f]Preliminary figure for November 1978.

SOURCES: Various issues of the Federal Reserve *Bulletin* and the Federal Reserve *Annual Report*. Federal Reserve *Annual Statistical Digest* and Federal Reserve *Banking and Monetary Statistics, 1941-1970*. Source for data on overseas branch assets before 1969, and Edge Act and Agreement corporation assets before 1971 is Jane d'Arista, "U. S. Banks Abroad," in FINE: *Financial Institutions and the National Economy*, Compendium of papers prepared for the FINE study, Book II, p. 812. 94th Congress, 2d. Sess., June 1976.

including taxation, political concerns. These deposits are transformed by Eurobanks into large credits, ranging from tens to hundreds of millions of dollars, mainly to prime customers: other banks, large corporations, public entities, or governments. Such loans are used to finance both trade and domestic transactions. Their terms range from "call" to ten years and their interest rate in recent years has been a floating rate linked to the London Interbank Offered

TABLE 2.2   Size of Eurocurrency Market and of Interbank Portion of Eurocurrency Market ($ billion)

Size	1970	1971	1972	1973	1974	1975	1976	1977
Gross size including inter-Eurobank transactions	111	145	200	303	370	457	559	660
Net size	65	85	110	160	215	250	310	380
Inter-Eurobank market	46	60	90	143	155	207	249	280
Inter-Eurobank market as percentage of gross size	41%	41%	45%	47%	42%	45%	45%	42%

SOURCE: Morgan Guaranty Trust Company, *World Financial Markets* (March 1978), p. 6, and *ibid.* (September 1978), p. 12. Used by permission.

Rate (LIBOR).[9] Because of the size of the loans and U.S. statutory limitations on loans to any one borrower, virtually all large Eurodollar loans are syndications in which a number of banks purchase participations from a lead bank.

The *growth of the international interbank market* is closely related to foreign expansion and the proliferating Eurocurrency market. Since the mid-1960s the practice, long common in national banking systems, of placing deposits with and extending credits to other banks has spread to the international banking system. Banks have increasingly chosen not to rely on external deposits to balance demand, and have turned to other banks to borrow or deposit funds. As a result there now exists an international network of commercial banks which hold each other's deposits and extend credits to each other.[10]

The Eurocurrency market is dominated by such interbank transactions (see table 2.2). In 1977, for example, $280 billion or 42 percent of all Eurocurrency liabilities were inter-Eurobank transactions. If transactions among Eurobanks and non-Eurobanks were included, the figures for the interbank market would be even higher.[11]

The activity of foreign branches of American banks, which is to a great extent centered on the Eurodollar market, reflects the significance of the interbank market (see tables 2.3 and 2.4). On December 31, 1973, for example, the foreign interbank market accounted for 53.7 percent of the sources of funds for foreign branches of American banks and for 46.3 percent of the uses of those funds. By the end of 1974, when, as we shall see later, a crisis in confidence led to the contraction of the interbank market, foreign branches of American banks still relied on the interbank market for 43.2 percent of funds and for 39.7 percent of all uses.

Banks throughout the developed world have become linked not only by mutual deposits and credits but also by a network of spot and forward foreign exchange contracts. With the growth of world trade and the advent of floating exchange rates in 1973, foreign exchange operations of banks mushroomed. Motivated not only by a rise in their own and their customers' needs but also by the temptations of profits to be made from speculation in a floating exchange regime, commercial banks greatly expanded their trading activity.

A dearth of data prevents the precise measurement of the growth of foreign exchange trading by banks. Governments do not regularly collect statistics on the volume of trading and banks consider their trading activities highly confidential. Several studies, however, reveal the huge dimensions of such operations. One study of the foreign exchange contracts of the foreign branches of twelve major American multinational banks was conducted for the House Committee on Banking, Housing and Currency. It revealed that the number of contracts to buy rose from almost 16,000 in 1971 to almost 33,000 in 1974. The aggregate value of these contracts rose from about $16 billion in 1971 to about $33 billion in 1974. Contracts to sell of these same foreign branches rose from almost 15,000 in 1971 to 42,000 in 1974. The value of sales contracts rose from just under $15 billion in 1971 to over $42 billion in 1974.[12]

Another study of foreign exchange trading in the United States was conducted by the Federal Reserve Bank of New York. A survey of forty-four financial institutions participating in the American foreign exchange market—banks, Edge Act corporations, and agencies and branches of foreign banks—revealed that gross foreign currency

TABLE 2.3 Sources and Uses of Funds of Foreign Branches of U.S. Banks ($ million)

Sources and uses of funds	Sept. 30, 1969 Percentage distribution			Sept. 30, 1971 Percentage distribution			Sept. 30, 1973 Percentage distribution		
	Amount	Sources	Uses	Amount	Sources	Uses	Amount	Sources	Uses
Internal system:									
U.S. parent:									
Source: Liabilities to U.S. parent	704	2.4		501	0.9		1,178	1.1	
Use: Claims on U.S. parent	11,783		39.4	2,969		5.4	1,917		1.8
Net position	*11,079*			*2,468*			*739*		
Branches in other countries:									
Source: Liabilities to branches	2,779	9.3		7,853	14.2		15,150	13.9	
Use: Claims on branches	2,847		9.5	7,930		14.3	15,092		13.8
Net position	*68*			*77*			*−58*		
Foreign Inter-bank market:									
Source: Liabilities to foreign banks	16,894	56.5		28,489	51.5		58,734	53.7	
Use: Claims on foreign banks	6,839		22.9	22,305		40.3	49,312		45.1
Net position	*−10,055*			*−6,184*			*−9,422*		
Foreign official institutions:									
Source: Liabilities to foreign official institutions	1,781	6.0		5,476	9.9		8,769	8.0	
Use: Claims on foreign official institutions	445		1.5	1,164		2.1	2,242		2.1
Net position	*−1,336*			*−4,312*			*−6,527*		
External market:									
Source: Liabilities to private foreign depositors	4,894	16.4		8,440	15.3		16,221	14.8	
Use: Claims on private foreign borrowers	5,438		18.2	15,736		28.5	32,274		29.5
Net position	*544*			*7,296*			*16,053*		
Residual market:									
Source: all other liabilities	2,871	9.5		4,782	8.2		9,278	8.5	
Use: all other claims	2,456		8.2	5,030		9.1	7,733		7.1
Net position	*−393*			*248*			*−1,545*		
Total resources	29,923	100.0	100.0	55,541	100.0	100.0	109,330	100.0	100.0

Sources and uses of funds	Dec. 31, 1973 Amount	Percentage distribution Sources	Uses	June 30, 1974 Amount	Percentage distribution Sources	Uses	Dec. 31, 1974 Amount	Percentage distribution Sources	Uses	June 30, 1975 Amount	Percentage distribution Sources	Uses
Internal system:												
U.S. parent:												
Source: Liabilities to U.S. parent	1,642	1.3		3,009	2.0		5,809	3.8		12,197	7.5	
Use: Claims on U.S. parent	1,886		1.5	4,093		2.8	4,464		2.9	2,341		1.4
Net position	244			1,084			-1,345			-9,856		
Branches in other countries:												
Source: Liabilities to branches	18,213	14.9		24,234	16.4		26,941	17.7		30,347	18.7	
Use: Claims on branches	19,177		15.7	25,020		17.0	27,559		18.1	30,830		19.0
Net position	964			786			618			483		
Foreign Inter-bank market:												
Source: Liabilities to foreign banks	65,389	53.7		71,956	48.8		65,675	43.2		64,933	40.0	
Use: Claims on foreign banks	56,368		46.3	64,434		43.7	60,283		39.7	63,709		39.3
Net position	-9,021			-7,522			-5,392			-1,224		
Foreign official institutions:												
Source: Liabilities to foreign official institutions	10,330	8.5		13,681	9.3		20,185	13.3		21,104	13.0	
Use: Claims on foreign official institutions	2,693		2.2	3,610		2.4	4,077		2.7	4,824		3.0
Net position	-7,637			-10,071			-16,108			-16,280		
External market:												
Source: Liabilities to private foreign depositors	17,683	14.5		22,456	15.2		20,169	13.3		20,713	12.8	
Use: Claims on private foreign borrowers	33,736		27.7	41,889		28.4	46,795		30.8	51,021		31.5
Net position	16,053			19,433			26,606			30,308		
Residual market:												
Source: all other liabilities	8,549	7.1		12,129	8.3		13,106	8.7		12,913	8.0	
Use: all other claims	8,006		6.6	8,419		5.7	8,727		5.8	9,482		5.8
Net position	-543			-3,710			4,379			-3,431		
Total resources	121,866	100.0	100.0	147,465	100.0	100.0	151,905	100.0	100.0	162,207	100.0	100.0

SOURCE: D'Arista, "U.S. Banks Abroad," pp. 819–20.

TABLE 2.4 Percentage Breakdown of Financial Assets and Liabilities of Foreign Branches of U.S. Banks by Location and Nature of the Entities Owing and Owed

	Dec. 31, 1972		Sept. 30, 1973		Sept. 30, 1974		Sept. 30, 1975	
	Assets (on)	Liabilities (to)	Assets (on)	Liabilities (to)	Assets (on)	Liabilities (to)	Assets (on)	Liabilities (to)
Claims on (and to) U.S. entities	4.0	4.2	4.4	4.4	4.2	6.8	3.95	11.36
Parent banks	1.5	1.0	1.7	1.1	2.5	3.4	1.96	6.49
Others	2.5	3.2	2.7	3.3	1.8	3.3	1.99	4.87
Claims on (and to) foreigners	92.1	91.6	91.3	91.0	91.6	88.7	92.23	84.90
Other branches of parent bank	15.8	14.9	15.5	15.4	17.8	17.8	18.97	18.25
Other banks	45.8	53.9	44.6	53.1	41.5	42.4	39.14	42.52
Official institutions	2.1	8.3	2.0	7.9	2.5	11.8	2.92	11.88
Non-bank foreigners	28.4	14.5	29.2	14.6	29.7	14.3	31.18	12.21
Miscellaneous claims	3.9	4.2	4.3	4.6	4.2	4.6	3.31	3.73
Total	100.0	100.0	100.0	100.0	100.0	100.0	100.00	100.00

SOURCE: d'Arista, "U.S. Banks Abroad," p. 818.

transactions during April 1977 totaled $106.4 billion, or over $5 billion each business day. A similar survey conducted by the Reserve Bank in March 1969 revealed total transactions of $17 billion for the month, or less than $1 billion per day. The Reserve Bank study does not reveal how many of the total transactions were among banks. It does show, however, that 92 percent of all spot transactions resulted from interbank trading and that spot transactions accounted for 55 percent of all transactions.[13]

A third private study of the worldwide foreign exchange market in 1977 yielded more dramatic results. It found an average daily trading volume for all foreign exchange markets of $120 billion or $30 trillion for the year. The study estimated that this $120 billion was roughly a 20 percent decline from the high reached in the middle of 1974 (see fig. 4.2). Of the $120 billion traded in 1977, 80 percent was accounted for by interbank trading—managing positions, seeking to profit from forecasts, arbitrage—and 15 percent by interbank commercially related trading. Much of the foreign exchange trading was found to be centered in Europe. Approximately 87 percent was traded in Europe, including 29 percent traded in London and 24 percent in West Germany. The United States accounted for 7 percent.[14]

In sum, during the latter half of the 1960s and the first half of the 1970s, commercial banks expanded their activities beyond national confines and, in the process, greatly expanded their links with one another. Franklin National was one of these banks.

Nassau and London Branches

Franklin, following the vogue of the period, established a branch in Nassau, the Bahamas, in 1969, opened a representative office in London that same year, and expanded that office to a full-fledged branch in 1972. The reasons for Franklin's move to Nassau and London shed some light on the forces behind the movement of many banks to these two Eurodollar centers.

Growth and Profit

Franklin's move abroad can be explained in part by its pursuit of growth and profit. These traditional economic motives took on a special character and intensity in American banking in the 1960s. The emergence of a new generation of bankers, the growing needs of a dynamic economy, and the encouragement of the Comptroller of the Currency led to a significant change in U.S. commercial banking. The twin goals of high earnings and rapid growth replaced the conservative emphasis on safety and asset quality; bank structure changed through mergers, acquisitions, and the creation of bank holding companies; banks expanded activities such as real estate, municipal and consumer finance, and foreign operations (which were often more risky); and these new activities were financed not by traditional sources of lendable funds such as checking and savings deposits but by the issuance of short-term liabilities such as negotiable certificates of deposit, Federal funds, and Eurodollar placements and by greater leveraging through long-term debt of the new bank holding companies. Franklin National Bank, one of the fastest growing American commercial banks in the 1960s and early 1970s, was part of this revolution in banking. Franklin's growth policy and quest for higher profits were the necessary, though not the sufficient, condition for Franklin's move abroad.

Incorporated in 1926, Franklin National Bank remained for almost forty years a Long Island retail bank.[15] Operating in a rich and growing region, protected by state law from competition from the big New York City banks (see below), and moved by the aggressive growth strategy and liberal loan policy of its chairman, Arthur Roth, Franklin prospered and grew. The bank's assets rose from $71 million in 1950 to $1.2 billion in 1962.[16]

By 1961 Franklin's management concluded that the bank was ready for a major change. Franklin had reached important limits to its growth on Long Island. Although it continued to dominate retail banking in Nassau and Suffolk counties, it was facing increasing competition from big New York banks, which in 1960 had been permitted to establish branches in what had once been Franklin's protected domain (see below). If rapid growth were to continue, Franklin would have to find other green pastures. Chairman Roth thought he saw them in the wholesale market in New York City.[17]

In September 1961 Franklin's Board of Directors voted to apply for permission to establish a branch office in New York City, and permission from the Comptroller of the Currency was granted in November 1961.[18] After much delay, Franklin opened its first branch in New York City and began its venture into wholesale banking in 1964. Other branches followed. In 1967 Roth made what he saw as a major advance in his movement into the New York wholesale market through a merger with the Federation Bank and Trust Company and the acquisition thereby of thirteen new branches.

In order to establish a position and to continue its rapid growth in the highly competitive New York market, Franklin made loans to companies which had low credit ratings and which found it difficult to obtain credit from the major New York banks. Despite the lower quality of these loans, Franklin charged rates other banks were charging prime customers and required lower compensating balances than other major banks.[19] These new assets were financed primarily by the purchase of Federal funds and the sale of certificates of deposit.

As a result of its liberal lending policy, Franklin's assets expanded rapidly. In 1964 Franklin had assets of $1.5 billion; by 1969 assets had doubled to $3 billion. Its earnings and the quality of its loan portfolio, however, suffered. Net income as a percentage of total operating income declined (see table 2.5), and classified and criticized loans as a percentage of total capital rose (see table 2.6).

The third step in Franklin's expansion was its move abroad. Franklin had begun modest international activities when it opened its first New York City branch in 1964. By the end of June 1968 Franklin's international division held foreign deposits of almost $12 million and had loans outstanding of $20.4 million and acceptances of $28.3 million.[20] In July 1967 Franklin organized an Edge Act subsidiary, the Franklin International Corporation, which had remained relatively unimportant.[21] By 1969 Franklin was eager to expand this small international activity.

One of the reasons was the attraction of the Eurodollar market. For many of the larger American banks which established foreign branches in the early 1960s or before, the economic incentive had

TABLE 2.5   Franklin New York Corporation Net Income as Percentage of Total Operating Income

1964	11.5%
1965	8.7
1966	5.5
1967	8.9
1968	10.3
1969	11.0
1970	9.9
1971	8.8
1972	6.6
1973	3.7

SOURCE: U.S. House, Committee on Government Operations, *Oversight Hearings into the Effectiveness of Federal Bank Regulation (Franklin National Bank Failure). Hearings before a Subcommittee on Government Operations,* 94th Cong., 2d sess., 1976, p. 255.

TABLE 2.6   Franklin National Bank Loans Classified and Criticized by Examiners ($ million)

Examination date	Loss	Doubtful	Sub-standard	Total loans classified	Special mention	Total loans classified and criticized	Percent of loans classified and criticized to— Total loans	Percent of loans classified and criticized to— Total capital
June 15, 1964	$ 3.1	$14.9	$25.1	$ 43.1	$ 16.6	$ 59.7	8.1	48.4
Apr. 26, 1965	7.6	13.2	35.3	56.1	21.2	77.3	8.4	63.3
Jan. 10, 1966	5.7	9.5	32.7	47.9	42.2	90.1	8.6	72.4
Oct. 3, 1966	6.4	—	48.5	54.9	75.0	129.9	10.9	100.8
Sept. 25, 1967	5.9	—	36.7	42.6	62.0	104.6	7.9	66.8
Sept. 30, 1968	4.8	1.7	30.6	37.1	56.9	94.0	7.3	53.7
Sept. 29, 1969	1.4	3.7	24.6	29.7	57.0	86.7	5.4	47.5
Aug. 31, 1970	6.0	10.3	90.4	106.7	126.6	233.3	12.7	128.0
May 17, 1971	12.4	20.7	72.5	105.6	100.4	206.0	12.7	102.2
Mar. 6, 1972	9.3	15.4	92.3	117.0	94.1	211.1	11.6	91.2
Dec. 11, 1972	6.8	21.7	77.3	105.8	83.6	189.4	9.3	82.1
Nov. 14, 1973	10.4	39.5	90.1	140.0	148.6	288.6	11.2	126.3
May 14, 1974	13.4	36.6	97.2	147.2	155.7	302.9	11.6	120.7

SOURCE: House Committee on Government Operations, *Oversight Hearings*, p. 237.

arisen from the increase in foreign trade and foreign investment by their customers and the resultant desire of the banks to establish foreign offices to serve the growing international activities of these clients. In applying to Federal regulatory authorities for permission to open foreign branches, Franklin cited its desire to service its customers.[22] In fact, as was demonstrated by its later loan activity, Franklin had virtually no customers with international needs and no local business in foreign countries which would justify the opening of foreign branches. The primary economic incentive for Franklin was the Eurodollar market.

For a bank interested in rapid growth and high-yielding assets, the Eurodollar market looked like an excellent source of new customers and lucrative loans. For a bank like Franklin, which faced a decline in earnings following its movement into New York, Eurodollar profits were particularly attractive. The demand for Eurodollar financing was growing rapidly. Although rate spreads were low, the size of Eurodollar transactions; the low cost of managing large loans; the absence of costly reserve, insurance, and interest rate requirements; and the apparently risk-free nature of interbank transactions and prime borrowers made Euromarket business extremely attractive to Franklin as well as to many other American banks.[23]

Franklin considered a move to London—the center of the Eurodollar market—as early as 1967, and in that year went so far as to meet with Bank of England officials to discuss the possibility of opening a London branch.[24] Despite the advantages of locating in London (the proximity of other Eurobanks, access to market information, greater ease of dealing with other members of the market, and lower rates on borrowing) start-up costs in London (the costs of renting office space and hiring the required personnel) were quite high. Thus, as of 1967, Franklin officials decided that a London branch was too costly.

Instead, Franklin decided to open a representative office in London and a branch in Nassau, where taxes, rents, and personnel costs were much lower. In 1968 the bank requested permission from Federal authorities to open a "shell" branch with the exclusive intent of obtaining access to the Eurodollar market. From there it hoped to attract deposits and make loans solicited in part from the London representative office.[25]

In 1970, feeling the limits to growth in Nassau, Franklin decided to open a London branch. Such a branch, it argued to Federal authorities, would enable Franklin to obtain funds at lower rates, serve as lead bank for syndicated Eurocurrency loans, take care of customers' needs in the United Kingdom, solicit business within the United Kingdom, receive a greater number of offers from other banks in London to participate in Eurocurrency loans, increase foreign exchange and Eurocurrency dealing in order to become more competitive, and establish correspondent bank relationships with continental banks, which are hesitant to deal through the Bahamas.[26]

The Federal Reserve approved the London branch in late 1971, and it opened in 1972. The volume of foreign operations expanded dramatically. Almost overnight foreign branch activity became a central element of Franklin National Bank. Foreign branch deposits as a percentage of total deposits soared from 7.7 percent in 1969 to 30.5 percent in 1973, and foreign branch loans increased from 2 percent of total loans in 1969 to 19.8 percent in 1973.[27]

TABLE 2.7   New York Clearing House Association Members: Total Deposits, Assets, and National Ranking by Deposits ($ million, rounded to nearest hundred thousand)

Bank		1960	1962	1964	1967	1968
Bank of New York	Deposits	554.6	634.8	675.9	1,109.5	1,301.9
	Assets (rank)	635.4 (47)	740.7 (44)	780.8 (46)	1,301.4 (36)	1,520.8 (34)
Bankers Trust	Deposits	2,703.1	3,390.9	3,783.3	5,094.5	6,016.1
	Assets (rank)	3,051.0 (9)	3,847.9 (8)	4,358.7 (9)	5,945.1 (7)	6,850.9 (7)
Chase Manhattan	Deposits	7,526.3	8,875.8	10,696.1	13,751.0	15,760.2
	Assets (rank)	8,471.9 (2)	10,051.9 (2)	12,118.2 (2)	16,007.8 (2)	18,012.9 (2)
Chemical	Deposits	3,711.2	4,352.7	5,023.6	6,140.8	7,091.8
	Assets (rank)	4,314.5 (4)	5,046.9 (5)	5,831.0 (5)	7,277.3 (6)	8,365.7 (6)
Citibank	Deposits	7,103.6	8,371.8	10,424.9	12,939.6	15,201.2
	Assets (rank)	8,123.2 (3)	9,530.0 (3)	11,797.7 (3)	15,065.5 (3)	17,497.3 (3)
Franklin National[a]	Deposits	612.5	821.9	1,079.1	1,638.1	2,171.5
	Assets (rank)	669.6 (39)	904.8 (37)	1,272.8 (26)	1,942.9 (19)	2,625.9 (18)
Irving Trust	Deposits	1,674.0	2,266.4	2,382.2	3,219.5	3,523.3
	Assets (rank)	1,920.0 (14)	2,530.8 (12)	2,495.0 (15)	3,801.6 (13)	4,076.4 (13)
Manufacturers Hanover	Deposits[b]	—	5,521.1	5,578.3	6,786.7	8,026.2
	Assets (rank)	—	6,322.1 (4)	6,064.8 (4)	7,728.7 (4)	9,171.6 (4)
Marine Midland	Deposits	603.9	769.6	826.5	1,368.9	1,637.7
	Assets (rank)	680.3 (40)	875.6 (37)	932.8 (36)	1,620.5 (26)	1,920.9 (23)
Morgan Guaranty	Deposits	3,363.0	4,135.6	4,492.8	6,445.2	7,284.1
	Assets (rank)	4,109.8 (5)	5,221.8 (6)	5,641.0 (6)	7,863.7 (5)	9,168.4 (5)
U.S. Trust	Deposits	166.8	193.9	206.0	270.9	303.6
	Assets (rank)	203.7 (167)	243.8 (167)	250.0 (177)	323.2 (172)	362.8 (169)

SOURCE: *Polk's World Bank Directory: North American Editions*, figures for December 31 of previous year. Used by permission.
[a] Franklin National joined the Clearing House Association in 1971.
[b] In 1960 Manufacturers Trust and the Hanover Bank were separate institutions.

Bank		1969	1970	1971	1972	1973	1974ᶜ
Bank of New York	Deposits	1,550.3	1,537.0	1,679.7	1,717.9	1,869.6	2,085.7
	Assets (rank)	1,723.6 (30)	1,808.3 (29)	1,966.2 (32)	2,008.3 (37)	2,218.5 (39)	2,500.9 (41)
Bankers Trust	Deposits	6,827.7	7,809.8	8,806.4	8,905.7	10,634.8	17,215.4
	Assets (rank)	7,653.0 (7)	9,069.2 (7)	9,272.1 (7)	10,150.6 (7)	12,635.6 (7)	20,211.1 (6)
Chase Manhattan	Deposits	16,709.9	18,998.7	21,227.8	20,373.8	24,998.6	35,156.3
	Assets (rank)	19,265.8 (2)	22,145.0 (2)	24,473.7 (2)	24,422.5 (3)	30,351.6 (3)	42,453.1 (3)
Chemical	Deposits	7,640.5	7,882.7	8,981.5	10,527.9	12,514.1	16,523.6
	Assets (rank)	8,967.7 (6)	9,739.5 (6)	10,979.5 (6)	12,624.5 (6)	15,267.6 (6)	20,449.8 (7)
Citibank	Deposits	16,643.2	19,148.0	21,085.5	24,368.6	27,750.6	41,438.9
	Assets (rank)	19,621.1 (3)	22,843.3 (2)	25,218.9 (3)	28,713.1 (2)	33,543.8 (2)	51,575.1 (2)
Franklin National	Deposits	2,301.2	2,060.3	2,567.1	2,840.1	3,460.4	2,085.3
	Assets (rank)	2,868.3 (18)	3,002.3 (21)	3,454.1 (19)	3,505.5 (20)	4,366.3 (20)	4,151.7 (42)
Irving Trust	Deposits	4,413.0	5,000.3	4,621.1	4,434.3	5,205.8	8,499.2
	Assets (rank)	5,070.3 (13)	5,744.1 (11)	5,427.5 (14)	5,233.9 (16)	6,154.6 (15)	9,734.8 (12)
Manufacturers Hanover	Deposits	9,202.4	10,444.5	11,072.8	12,210.4	13,994.1	21,738.9
	Assets (rank)	10,439.2 (4)	11,965.3 (4)	12,664.8 (4)	14,277.2 (4)	16,230.4 (4)	25,193.8 (4)
Marine Midland	Deposits	2,280.8	2,266.7	2,790.4	3,975.4	4,842.5	7,473.8
	Assets (rank)	2,533.0 (19)	2,797.7 (18)	3,542.0 (18)	4,598.1 (18)	5,533.0 (17)	8,375.5 (15)
Morgan Guaranty	Deposits	8,211.7	9,019.3	9,589.1	10,670.3	12,838.9	18,309.1
	Assets (rank)	10,370.0 (5)	11,425.1 (5)	11,152.6 (5)	13,615.0 (5)	16,458.6 (5)	23,882.0 (5)
U.S. Trust	Deposits	381.0	418.4	388.2	387.5	489.6	439.7
	Assets (rank)	439.6 (156)	488.7 (138)	484.1 (169)	506.7 (186)	633.8 (175)	583.4 (195)

ᶜFigure for 1974 is for midyear 1974.

Market Structures

Franklin National Bank's expansion abroad was also shaped by its position in the markets in which it was competing. In moving into New York wholesale banking in 1964, Franklin entered a market dominated by the ten members of the Clearing House Association (see table 2.7), which are among the largest banks not only in the United States but in the world (see table 2.8).

Surrounding and competing with the big banks were a large number of smaller banks and thrift institutions. Until 1964 Franklin was one of these fringe competitors; after 1964 Franklin's strategy was to become part of the dominant group. Franklin's size—in 1964 it was the twenty-sixth largest bank in the United States, larger than three of the Clearing House members—and its ambitions for continued growth led to an attempt to join the big league.

Franklin took a number of steps to establish a sizable position in the New York wholesale market. As we have seen, it attempted to establish a position by taking less attractive credits at less attractive rates. It sought to establish a visible presence in New York by opening a large number of elegantly furnished branches including offices in a building it constructed on Park Avenue.[28] Franklin also sought to offer the same sophisticated wholesale banking services offered by the other big banks and to emulate their structure by setting up the Franklin New York Corporation, a one-bank holding company it hoped to use to diversify and expand its activities. By 1971 Franklin had become sufficiently important to be admitted to membership in the Clearing House Association.

Franklin National Bank's expansion abroad was part of its competitive behavior in the New York market. The New York banks Franklin sought to emulate were not only among the largest banks in the United States, they were also among the most important American multinational banks. Seven of the Clearing House banks were among the twelve top American multinational banks (First National City Bank, Chase Manhattan Bank, Manufacturers Hanover Trust Company, Morgan Guaranty Trust Company, Chemical Bank,

TABLE 2.8 The Largest Banks in the World

Bank	Head Office	Total Assets					Total Deposits			
		1971 $m	1971 £m	1970 $m	1970 £m	1971 m	1971 £m	1971 $m	1970 $m	1970 £m
1 BankAmerica Corp. (Bank of America)	San Francisco	33,412	13,103	28,863	12,045	—	11,401	29,073	25,643	10,711
2 First National City Corp.	New York	28,741	11,271	25,337	10,583	—	9,514	24,260	21,013	8,777
3 Chase Manhattan Corp.	New York	23,953	9,393	24,227	10,137	—	7,989	20,373	21,303	8,913
4 Barclays Bank Group	London	18,658	7,317	15,809	6,615	—	6,385	16,282	13,833	5,778
5 Dai-ichi Kangyo Bank	Tokyo	17,515	8,869	14,907	6,224	¥5,512,216	5,294	13,499	9,719	4,058
6 National Westminster Bank	London	16,952	6,648	13,250	5,544	—	6,068	15,473	12,019	5,029
7 Groupe BNP (Banque Nationale de Paris)	Paris	15,491	6,075	10,032	4,441	Fr80,858	5,266	13,428	9,460	3,958
8 Deutsche Bank	Frankfurt	15,224	5,970	10,521	4,402	DM49,788	4,234	10,797	8,787	3,670
9 Banca Nazionale del Lavoro	Rome	14,736	5,779	12,075	5,044	L8,758,075	5,116	13,046	10,676	4,459
10 Manufacturers Hanover Corp.	New York	13,840	5,427	12,257	5,120	—	4,788	12,210	11,072	4,625
11 Crédit Lyonnais	Paris	13,755	5,394	9,621	4,017	Fr71,791	4,694	11,970	8,351	3,487
12 JP Morgan (Morgan Guaranty)	New York	13,269	5,204	11,776	4,919	—	4,184	10,670	9,576	4,000
13 Western Bancorp (United California Bank and others)	Los Angeles	13,142	5,154	11,254	4,701	—	4,319	11,014	9,692	4,048
14 Westdeutsche Landesbank Girozentrale	Dusseldorf	12,798	5,019	10,490	4,382	DM41,859	4,081	10,407	8,717	3,641
15 Fuji Bank	Tokyo	12,767	5,148	9,704	4,046	¥4,283,491	4,059	10,066	7,456	3,123
16 Dresdner Bank	Frankfurt	12,682	4,973	7,720	3,223	DM41,478	3,611	9,208	7,090	2,960
17 Chemical New York Corp.	New York	12,446	4,881	10,865	4,546	—	4,129	10,528	9,023	3,775
18 Royal Bank of Canada	Montreal	12,390	4,976	10,667	4,463	Can$12,474	4,696	11,693	10,093	4,223
19 Sumitomo Bank	Osaka	12,348	4,979	9,423	3,946	¥4,142,411	4,008	9,940	7,339	3,074
20 Mitsubishi Bank	Toyko	12,183	4,912	9,400	3,937	¥4,087,107	3,871	9,600	7,166	3,001
21 Sanwa Bank	Osaka	11,609	4,681	9,222	3,862	¥3,894,636	3,641	9,030	6,868	2,876
22 Lloyds Bank	London	11,447	4,489	7,657	3,197	—	4,105	10,468	6,890	2,877

TABLE 2.8 (Continued)

Bank	Head Office	Total Assets					Total Deposits			
		1971		1970		1971	1971		1970	
		$m	£m	$m	£m	m	$m	£m	$m	£m
23 Midland Bank Group	London	11,393	4,468	8,834	3,692	—	10,371	4,067	7,953	3,322
24 Société Générale	Paris	11,087	4,348	8,096	3,382	Fr57,875	8,894	3,488	6,522	2,724
25 Canadian Imperial Bank of Commerce	Toronto	11,001	4,418	10,524	4,422	Can$11,046	10,378	4,168	9,972	4,190
26 Bankers Trust New York Corp.	New York	10,739	4,211	9,748	4,079	—	9,440	3,702	8,592	3,595
27 Banca Commerciale Italiana	Milan	10,164	3,986	8,639	3,609	L6,040,757	9,647	3,783	8,051	4,177
28 Banco di Roma	Rome	10,157	3,983	7,638	3,189	L6,036,493	8,820	3,459	6,658	2,780
29 Bank of Montreal	Montreal	9,874	3,958	8,273	3,469	Can$9,914	9,412	3,772	7,850	3,291
30 Conill Corp. (Continental Illinois National Bank & Trust Co.)	Chicago	9,833	3,856	8,662	3,618	—	8,456	3,316	7,154	2,988
31 Union Bank of Switzerland	Zurich	9,738	3,819	7,007	2,932	SwFr38,153	7,296	2,861	4,905	2,049
32 Security Pacific National Bank	Los Angeles	9,710	3,808	8,012	3,347	—	8,540	3,349	7,033	2,938
33 Cassa di Risparmio delle Provincie Lombarde	Milan	9,558	3,748	7,694	3,214	L5,680,577	4,933	1,934	3,862	1,613
34 Industrial Bank of Japan	Tokyo	9,526	3,841	7,339	3,074	¥3,196,005	8,660	3,492	6,652	2,795
35 Commerzbank	Frankfurt	9,244	3,625	5,671	2,369	DM30,230	7,313	2,868	4,728	1,975
36 Swiss Bank Corporation	Basle	9,208	3,611	6,508	2,718	SwFr36,078	7,936	3,112	5,605	2,341
37 First Chicago Corp. (First National Bank of Chicago)	Chicago	9,153	3,589	7,974	3,336	—	7,188	2,189	6,289	2,631
38 Marine Midland Banks Inc.	Buffalo, N.Y.	9,002	3,530	7,506	3,135	—	7,615	2,986	6,231	2,607
39 Credito Italiano	Milan	8,998	3,529	7,278	3,040	L5,347,700	7,686	3,014	6,658	2,781
40 Tokai Bank	Nagoya	8,669	3,496	7,717	3,223	¥2,908,268	6,854	2,764	5,417	2,263
41 Banco do Brasil	Brazil	8,527	3,344	7,948	3,320	Cr47,815	3,805	1,492	3,303	1,380
42 Daiwa Bank	Osaka	8,459	3,411	6,666	2,792	¥2,838,276	7,274	2,933	4,472	1,873
43 Mitsui Bank	Tokyo	8,123	3,275	6,592	2,761	¥2,725,144	6,337	2,555	4,811	2,015
44 Swiss Credit Bank	Zurich	7,931	3,110	6,494	2,713	SwFr31,072	6,686	2,622	5,606	2,342

45	Wells Fargo & Co.	San Francisco	7,754	3,041	6,158	2,572	—	6,383	2,503	5,254	2,195
46	Bank of Tokyo	Tokyo	7,326	2,950	5,866	2,457	¥2,449,082	3,498	1,410	2,434	1,019
47	Long Term Credit Bank of Japan	Tokyo	7,187	2,898	5,464	2,296	¥2,411,142	6,618	2,669	5,044	2,120
48	Mitsubishi Trust and Banking Corp.	Tokyo	7,130	2,875	5,134	2,157	¥2,392,039	6,659	2,685	4,798	2,016
49	Bank of Nova Scotia	Toronto	6,795	2,729	6,078	2,543	Can$6,847	6,383	2,563	5,762	2,411
50	Hessische Landesbank-Girozentrale	Frankfurt	6,569	2,576	4,716	1,970	DM21,482	6,337	2,485	4,555	1,906
51	Bayerische Hypotheken-und Wechsel-Bank	Munich	6,547	2,568	4,811	2,009	DM21,413	6,077	2,383	4,451	1,858
52	Sumitomo Trust & Banking Co.	Osaka	6,488	2,616	4,836	2,032	¥2,176,455	6,093	2,457	4,529	1,903
53	Crocker National Corp.	San Francisco	6,480	2,541	6,005	2,508	—	5,372	2,107	4,843	2,023
54	Mellon National Bank & Trust Co.	Pittsburgh	6,433	2,523	5,710	2,384	—	5,221	2,047	4,748	1,987
55	Algemene Bank Nederland	Amsterdam	6,360	2,494	5,445	2,274	F22,261	3,361	1,318	3,020	1,261
56	Toronto Dominion Bank	Toronto	6,242	2,507	5,186	2,170	Can$6,268	5,914	2,375	4,928	2,062
57	Mitsui Trust & Banking Co.	Tokyo	6,170	2,488	4,551	1,912	¥2,069,734	5,838	2,354	4,258	1,789
58	Amsterdam-Rotterdam Bank	Amsterdam	6,089	2,388	4,563	1,906	F19,808	3,490	1,369	1,125	470
59	Standard & Chartered Group	London	6,081	2,513	5,529	2,294	—	5,738	2,371	5,230	2,170
60	Commonwealth Banking Corp.	Sydney	6,013	2,495	5,488	2,283	A$5,356	5,794	2,404	5,296	2,203
61	Charter New York Corp. (Irving Trust and others)	New York	5,936	2,328	6,160	2,577	—	5,186	2,034	5,269	2,200
62	Banco di Napoli	Naples	5,732	2,248	4,861	2,034	L3,406,200	4,077	1,599	3,530	1,474
63	Kyowa Bank	Tokyo	5,731	2,311	4,368	1,829	¥1,922,595	4,868	1,963	3,651	1,529
64	National Bank of Detroit	Detroit	5,666	2,222	5,175	2,162	—	4,666	1,830	4,423	1,851
65	Norddeutsche Landesbank Girozentrale	Hanover	5,567	2,183	4,300	1,799	DM18,206	5,288	2,074	4,101	1,716
66	Deutsche Genossenschaftskasse	Frankfurt	5,447	2,136	4,030	1,686	DM17,812	4,593	1,801	3,466	1,450
67	Société Générale de Banque	Brussels	5,388	2,113	4,397	1,836	BFr241,614	4,888	1,917	3,899	1,628

TABLE 2.8 (Continued)

Bank	Head Office	Total Assets					Total Deposits			
		1971		1970		1971	1971		1970	
		$m	£m	$m	£m	m	$m	£m	$m	£m
68 Istituto Bancario San Paolo di Torino	Turin	5,363	2,103	4,071	1,700	L3,185,675	4,284	1,680	3,442	1,438
69 Crédit Industriel et Commercial (6)	Paris	5,330	2,090	4,170	1,742	Fr27,821	4,593	1,801	3,569	1,491
70 Bayerische Vereinsbank	Munich	5,307	2,081	4,323	1,806	DM17,358	4,993	1,958	4,032	1,684
71 American Express Co.	New York	5,213	2,044	4,665	1,949	—	1,080	424	908	379
72 Monte dei Paschi di Siena(1)	Siena	5,138	2,015	3,691	1,542	L3,053,055	4,062	1,593	3,149	1,315
73 First Bank System (First National Bank)	Minneapolis	5,073	1,989	4,407	1,840	—	4,197	1,646	3,684	1,539
74 Northwest Bancorp (Northwestern National Bank of Minneapolis)	Minneapolis	5,056	1,983	4,342	1,814	—	4,331	1,698	3,739	1,562
75 First National Boston Corp. (First National Bank of Boston)	Boston	5,038	1,976	4,662	1,947	—	4,032	1,581	3,624	1,514
76 Banque de Paris et des Pays-Bas	Paris	4,941	1,938	3,046	1,272	Fr25,799	3,601	1,412	2,211	923
77 Bank of Kobe	Kobe	4,708	1,899	3,658	1,532	¥1,579,555	3,820	1,540	2,869	1,202
78 Bayerische Gemeindebank-Girozentrale	Munich	4,574	1,794	3,660	1,529	DM14,960	4,311	1,690	3,469	1,449
79 Hongkong & Shanghai Banking Corp.	Hong Kong	4,547	1,783	3,695	1,546	HK$25,986	3,917	1,536	3,203	1,338
80 Tokyo Trust & Banking Co.	Tokyo	4,509	1,818	3,368	1,415	¥1,512,643	2,930	1,182	2,181	917
81 Nippon Fudosan Bank	Tokyo	4,469	1,802	3,300	1,382	¥1,499,549	4,082	1,646	2,723	1,140
82 Yasuda Trust & Banking Co.	Tokyo	4,412	1,779	3,311	1,387	¥480,296	3,648	1,471	2,799	1,176
83 Bank of New South Wales	Sydney	4,409	1,778	3,757	1,573	A$3,818	4,097	1,652	3,523	1,475
84 Australia & New Zealand Banking Group	London	4,385	1,768	3,867	1,622	A$3,805	3,496	1,410	3,168	1,329

85 Co-operatieve Centrale Raffeisen Bank	Utrecht	4,335	1,700	3,305	1,380	F14,104	4,103	1,609	3,123	1,304
86 Banco di Sicilia	Palermo	4,287	1,681	3,549	1,482	L2,547,417	3,629	1,423	3,046	1,272
87 Bank für Gemeinwirtschaft	Frankfurt	4,204	1,649	3,231	1,352	DM13,750	3,965	1,555	3,045	1,274
88 First Pennsylvania Corp.	Philadelphia	4,095	1,606	3,288	1,373	—	2,895	1,135	2,516	1,051
89 Deutsche Girozentrale/ Deutsche Kommunalbank	Frankfurt	4,052	1,589	3,286	1,375	DM13,256	2,043	801	1,740	728
90 Banco Espanol de Credito	Madrid	3,960	1,553	3,560	1,487	P260,846	3,445	1,351	2,702	1,129
91 Lloyds & Bolsa International Bank	London	3,866	1,559	NA	NA	—	3,209	1,294	NA	NA
92 Saitarna Bank	Urawa	3,859	1,556	3,055	1,279	Y1,294,752	3,355	1,353	2,602	1,090
93 Svenska Handelsbanken	Stockholm	3,848	1,509	3,431	1,433	Kr18,714	3,302	1,295	2,968	1,240
94 Franklin New York Corp.	New York	3,460	1,357	3,410	1,424	—	2,839	1,113	2,567	1,072
95 National & Commercial Banking Group	Edinburgh	3,452	1,392	2,964	1,240	—	2,909	1,173	2,488	1,041
96 Banque de Bruxelles	Brussels	3,417	1,414	2,920	1,213	BFr169,573	3,054	1,263	2,602	1,081
97 Banco Hispano Americano	Madrid	3,392	1,330	2,955	1,234	P223,775	2,736	1,073	2,236	934
98 Taiyo Bank	Tokyo	3,360	1,355	2,572	1,077	¥1,127,125	2,988	1,205	2,264	948
99 Skandinaviska Banken(2)	Stockholm	3,320	1,302	3,031	1,268	Kr16,149	2,433	954	2,065	864
100 Hokkaido Takushoku Bank	Sapporo	3,291	1,327	2,662	1,115	¥1,104,342	2,884	1,163	2,230	934
101 Bank of New York Co.	New York	3,281	1,287	3,121	1,304	—	2,861	1,122	2,717	1,135
102 State Bank of India(3)	Bombay	3,261	1,279	2,335	975	Rp24,260	2,958	1,160	1,902	794
103 Banco Central	Madrid	3,236	1,269	2,449	1,023	P213,553	2,953	1,158	2,216	926
104 Unionamerica Inc. (Union Bank)	Los Angeles	3,225	1,265	2,574	1,077	—	2,776	1,089	2,213	926
105 Banca Nazionale dell'Agricoltura	Rome	3,068	1,203	2,680	1,051	L1,822,663	2,563	1,005	2,082	870
106 Bank of Yokohama	Yokohama	3,059	1,234	2,335	978	¥1,026,300	2,738	1,104	2,084	873
107 Banco de Bilbao	Bilbao	3,045	1,194	2,343	979	P200,905	2,206	865	1,719	718
108 Cooperatieve Centrale Boerenleenbank	Eindhoven	2,927	1,148	2,323	970	F9,520	2,802	1,099	2,223	928
109 Bank Leumi le-Israel	Tel Aviv	2,919	1,145	2,311	971	I£12,302	2,454	962	1,955	817
110 Republic National Bank of Dallas	Dallas	2,892	1,134	2,579	1,077	—	2,196	861	1,770	739

SOURCE: *The Banker*, (June 1972) 122 (556): 813–21. Used by permission.

Bankers Trust Company and Marine Midland Bank), and six were among the thirty largest banking organizations in the world (all the foregoing except Marine Midland Bank; see table 2.8). Virtually all of these banks had established a presence abroad and in the Eurocurrency market by the time Franklin entered the New York wholesale market, and their international activities grew rapidly during the 1960s (see table 2.9). By the late 1960s and early 1970s international operations came to represent a significant percentage of total earnings for Franklin's competitors. For example, by 1972, when Franklin opened its London branch, international earnings accounted for 54 percent of the total earnings of First National City Bank's holding corporation, for 35 percent of the earnings of J. P. Morgan's holding corporation, and for 34 percent of the earnings of Chase Manhattan's holding corporation (see table 2.10).

The mushrooming foreign operations of its rivals were an important force leading Franklin to Nassau and London. Franklin officials felt that without a foreign presence it was at a competitive disadvantage in attracting and maintaining domestic customers. One of the reasons that Franklin's rivals had established foreign branches was to service the growing international needs of their domestic customers. The ability to service these international needs of borrowers in the New York wholesale market was part of the sophisticated banking service offered by Clearing House banks. Foreign branches, Franklin officials hoped, would enable it to offer those services and thereby enhance its competitive position.

Foreign branches gave Franklin's rivals a competitive advantage beyond service. With foreign branches they had greater access to funds for use both at home and abroad. For example, when credit became less available to banks in the late 1960s due to the Federal Reserve's anti-inflation policy, banks with foreign branches were able to use those branches to borrow funds that were transferred to the head office for use within the United States.[29] Furthermore, the higher profit on foreign operations enhanced the ability of Franklin's rivals to compete with Franklin in New York. Finally, foreign branches gave Franklin the same status as its domestic rivals, a psychological factor of great importance to Franklin officers.

Table 2.9 New York Clearing House Association Members: Foreign Branches, Representative Offices

Bank	60-61	61-62	62-63	63-64	64-65	65-66	66-67	67-68	68-69	69-70	70-71	71-72	72-73	73-74	74-75
Bank of New York	0,0	0,0	0,0	0,0	0,0	0,0	0,0	1,0	1,0	1,0	1,0	1,0	1,0	1,0	3,0
Bankers Trust	2,2	2,2	2,2	2,2	2,3	2,4	2,6	2,9	2,9	3,11	3,11	3,12	4,13	5,14	7,21
Chase Manhattan	26,9	23,6	25,7	26,6	27,11	37,6	37,7	43,6	47,6	53,6	63,7	71,7	90,9	99,13	98,14
Chemical Bank	1,0	1,0	1,0	1,0	1,3	2,4	2,4	2,4	2,7	2,9	3,9	5,11	5,11	8,14	8,14
First National City	84,1	79,0	91,0	96,0	89,1	99,0	114,1	132,1	167,1	198,2	230,2	236,2	233,2	234,1	249,3
Irving Trust	0,0	0,0	0,0	0,2	0,2	1,3	1,3	1,3	1,3	1,3	1,9	1,11	2,11	4,9	6,7
Manufacturers Hanover	2,6	2,6	2,7	2,7	2,9	2,10	2,10	2,11	3,13	3,15	3,15	4,13	4,14	5,14	8,18
Marine Midland	0,0	0,0	0,0	0,0	1,0	1,1	1,3	1,3	1,4	2,6	2,6	3,11	3,14	5,12	6,14
Morgan Guaranty	4,1	4,0	4,3	4,3	4,3	6,3	6,5	7,5	6,6	8,5	9,5	12,6	12,6	11,6	11,6
United States Trust	0,0	0,0	0,0	0,0	0,0	0,0	0,0	0,0	0,0	0,0	0,0	0,0	0,0	0,0	0,0
Franklin National	0,0	0,0	0,0	0,0	0,0	0,0	0,0	0,0	0,0	1,1	1,1	1,1	2,0	1,1	—

SOURCE: *Bankers Almanac & Year Book.* Used by permission.

TABLE 2.10 International Earnings Growth 1970-75 ($ million)

	1970	% of Total Earnings	1971	% of Total Earnings	1972	% of Total Earnings
Bank America Corp.	$ 25.0E[a]	15.0E	$ 33.9E	19.0E	$ 39.7E	21.0E
Citicorp	58.0	40.0	72.3	43.0	110.0	54.0
Chase Manhattan Corp.	30.7	22.0	42.8	29.0	50.4	34.0
Manuf. Hanover Corp.	11.4	13.0	19.4	24.0	24.0	29.0
J. P. Morgan & Co.	25.5	25.0	31.8	28.9	41.9	35.0
Bankers Trust NY Corp.	7.8E	14.5E	10.7E	19.1E	18.7E	31.0E
Chemical NY Corp.	7.7	10.0	12.4	17.0	9.0	14.2
First Chicago Corp.	1.2	2.0	4.6	7.0	8.6	11.0
Continental Illinois Corp.	(.1)	(.2)	2.1	3.0	13.0	17.0
Charter New York Corp.	3.7E	12.0E	5.4E	20.0E	7.8	28.0
First National Boston Corp.	3.3	8.0	4.0	8.8	5.1	12.1
Wells Fargo & Co.	2.9	9.0	4.8	14.0	5.9	15.0
Security Pacific Corp.	.2	.4	1.1	2.0	2.9	5.0
Total	$177.3	16.7%	$245.3	22.1%	$337.0	28.2%

SOURCE: Salomon Brothers, *United States Multinational Banking: Current and Prospective Strategies* (New York: Author, 1976), p. 13. Used by permission.
[a]E = estimated figure.

In sum, Franklin officials felt the bank needed foreign branches in order to compete in the New York wholesale market. As one former Franklin official described it: "Franklin's move to London began when it decided to buck the New York market. Franklin's standing in the United States required that it have access to the Eurodollar market, and that eventually meant that it had to have a London branch."[30]

The structure of another market—the Eurodollar market—and Franklin's position in it help to explain the rapid growth of foreign operations after the establishment of the London branch. By the time Franklin entered the Eurodollar market at the end of the 1960s, that market had become highly competitive due to the influx of large numbers of American as well as Japanese and European banks. Confronting a highly competitive market without any customers of its own, Franklin's strategy was twofold.

1973	% of Total Earnings	1974	% of Total Earnings	1975	% of Total Earnings	Compound Annual Growth Rate 1970-1975	Growth 1974-1975
$ 52.6E	24.0E	$ 74.4	29.0	$123.7	41.0	37.7%	66.3%
152.0	60.0	193.0	62.0	243.6	70.0	33.2	26.2
68.0	39.0	89.0	47.0	101.0	56.0	26.9	13.5
35.9	36.0	59.9	47.2	67.5	49.5	42.7	12.7
68.0	45.9	80.0	45.0	115.1	60.0	35.2	43.9
26.4	40.0	37.0	52.0	39.6	62.0	38.4	7.0
13.0	18.5	31.3	34.0	44.4	45.0	42.0	41.9
11.0	12.0	3.0	3.0	35.9	34.0	97.0	1,096.7
17.3	20.0	3.8	4.0	15.5	13.0	64.9	307.9
13.4	41.9	25.0	63.0	26.6	59.0	48.4	6.4
5.2	10.0	5.0	9.5	6.8	16.0	15.6	36.0
7.5	17.0	6.0	12.0	7.7	13.7	21.5	28.3
7.2	12.0	8.9	16.0	8.5	13.0	112.0	(4.5)
$477.5	34.2%	$616.3	37.8%	$835.9	47.7%	36.4%	35.6%

First, it sought to develop its own customers and to become the lead bank in some Euromarket syndications. For the most part, this effort, like that of other newcomers, failed. Franklin was able to lead only four small syndications: a $4.7 million loan to Banco Nationale de Costa Rica, a $40 million loan to the Bulgarian Foreign Trade Bank, a $20 million loan to the Republic of Gabon, and a $30 million loan to Petróleos Mexicanos (Pemex). The Mexican syndication suggests the degree to which Franklin was desperately trying to secure a visible position in the market. The loan to Pemex was organized not by Franklin but by Loeb Rhoades and Company, an investment banking firm. Because investment banks cannot act as agents and lead banks, they select a commercial bank to manage loans they syndicate. So eager was Franklin to show that it could head a syndicate that it agreed with Loeb Rhoades to a nominal fee for its management services in return for the prestige of being named as agent and lead bank.[31]

Unable to assume a leadership role in the competitive Eurodollar market, Franklin decided to establish a place in the market by participating in virtually every possible syndication organized by other banks. The rapid growth in Franklin's portfolio suggests that it turned down virtually no participation offered it. Franklin also made some nonsyndicated Eurodollar loans to little-known borrowers. These loans, however, represented only a small part of its international portfolio.

It is important to note that in seeking to buy a place in the Eurodollar market, Franklin did not offer lower rates or lend to less credit-worthy borrowers than other banks. Most of the bank's portfolio consisted of syndications. Franklin could not offer lower rates than other participants in the syndications, which included the major international banks. While Franklin may not have had the pick of the most attractive syndications arranged by the large Eurobanks, the fact that major banks were partners with Franklin indicates that in the foreign area, at least, Franklin was not taking on loans that other established banks rejected. In the Eurodollar market Franklin's effort to buy a place led to the massive size of the portfolio but not to greater credit risks or lower interest rates than those prevailing at the time throughout the market.

Government Policy

The final important factor in Franklin National Bank's foreign expansion was government policy. United States balance-of-payments policies, especially the Voluntary Foreign Credit Restraint Program (VFCR), were a crucial influence. The VFCR, in effect from early 1965 until January 1974, was an effort to ameliorate U.S. balance-of-payments deficits by limiting capital outflows in the form of credits extended by American banks to foreigners. The 1965 guidelines requested banks to limit foreign credits to 105 percent of credits outstanding at the end of 1964. The revised guidelines of 1968 asked banks to reduce the level of outstanding foreign credits and to make no new term loans to Western European countries except for the financing of American exports.[32] While the law blocked foreign loans from bank offices in the United States, it did not prevent

American banks from making loans from foreign branches using funds, including dollars, acquired outside the United States. Thus the VFCR virtually pushed American banks into offshore operations to borrow funds in the Eurodollar market in order to extend credits abroad.

The incentive to move abroad created by the VFCR was reinforced by the Foreign Direct Investment Program (FDIP) and by the Interest Equalization Tax (IET). The FDIP, instituted as a voluntary program in 1965 and made mandatory in 1968, constrained American corporations from increasing foreign investment by exporting capital from the United States and thereby created a demand by these bank customers for offshore financing. The IET, established in 1963, discouraged foreign borrowing in the United States by making it more expensive. Initially the IET applied only to foreign securities with maturities over one year. In 1965, however, it was extended to foreign loans from both domestic and foreign branches of American banks with maturities over one year. In 1967 lending by foreign branches was exempted from the IET, a move which gave great incentive to American banks to increase loan activity at foreign branches.

The VFCR discriminated in favor of large multinational banks. For banks with existing foreign branches and access to the Eurocurrency market, the VFCR imposed few limitations on international operations. For middle-sized and regional banks without branches and Eurocurrency access, the program was a major constraint on existing international activity and on hopes for foreign expansion.

In order to compensate for this discriminatory effect, the Federal Reserve, which administered the VFCR and which is responsible for approving the establishment of foreign branches by all member banks, adopted a policy of permitting smaller banks to open "shell" branches in Nassau.[33] These branches offered only limited services, had no contact with the Bahamian economy, and were directed by their head offices or in some cases by other foreign branches. They were simply bookkeeping operations which enabled banks to escape at low cost the constraints of the VFCR and to finance foreign

business through borrowing abroad, primarily through the Eurodollar market. The Bahamas were particularly attractive for this
purpose because of the absence of regulation and taxation and the
low cost of operating such a shell branch.

The VFCR was an important reason for Franklin's move to
Nassau. As the bank put it in its letter of application to the Board of
Governors of the Federal Reserve System:

The growth of the [International] Department and its ability to be effectively
competitive with other New York City banks has, of course, been seriously impeded
by compliance with the voluntary credit restraint program designed to improve the
balance of payments of the United States. Under the guidelines established by the
Board, we cannot expand our foreign lending even to finance U.S. exports without
access to Eurodollars that may be used for this purpose.[34]

The letter goes on to say that without an overseas branch, Franklin
can obtain Eurodollars only in limited amounts by selling loans to
European banks, and that it was primarily for the purpose of
obtaining Eurodollars through deposits that it was requesting
permission to establish a branch in Nassau.[35]

Another crucial political factor in Franklin's expansion abroad
was bank regulatory policy. Franklin's movement abroad was
critically influenced by the laws of both the Federal government and
New York State and by the policies of Federal regulatory agencies.
Those laws and policies created a political environment which made
it more difficult and in some ways less attractive for a growth-
oriented bank like Franklin to expand within the United States and
relatively easy and in ways more attractive for it to expand abroad.

The strict regulation of domestic banking activity and the relative
lack of regulation of international activity created important incen-
tives for Franklin to establish foreign branches. The way in which
Franklin chafed under Federal regulations in seeking to develop its
international banking business was expressed in a "white paper"
written by Howard D. Crosse, vice chairman of the Board of
Directors of Franklin and the officer in charge of building Franklin's
international department in the late 1960s. In November 1968 Crosse
wrote that:

In the international field . . . Federal regulations and the administration of the balance of payments guidelines work to stifle competition. Entry into this rapidly expanding market is made costly, if not impossible, while those larger banks which have been in this market a long time are able to continue their growth and secure an even larger share of the market. The basic reason for this is that Regulation Q governing interest rates, and Regulation D, governing reserve requirements, do not apply to deposits of foreigners held in the overseas branches of American banks.[36]

Regulation Q prevents American banks from paying interest on domestic demand deposits and establishes ceilings on interest rates paid on domestic time deposits of less than $100,000, but does not apply to deposits held in foreign branches of American banks. Thus American banks with such branches could attract demand deposits by paying interest and could use foreign branches to attract time deposits by paying higher interest rates than those allowed at home. Regulation D, which requires that a portion of domestic deposits be held as reserves which earn no income, does not apply to foreign deposits. Regulations thus enable banks to avoid the cost of maintaining reserves on foreign deposits and enable them to pay interest rates on demand deposits to attract funds and to earn higher profits abroad. Furthermore, Crosse points out, banks with foreign branches could borrow abroad outside Regulations Q and D and place these funds with head offices to be used for domestic lending and investment.[37] In addition, he noted, deposits received by foreign branches and lent or invested abroad were exempt from balance of payments guideline ceilings. "Thus," he concludes, "a bank with branches abroad has access to the vast Eurodollar market and the ability to expand its foreign lending free from the competition of smaller but often energetic banks, which would like to participate in this business but cannot or, at least, not to the extent or with the ease they would like."[38] As a result, he says, there has been "a rash of new American branches in London," branches which are much more costly for a moderate-sized bank with a smaller volume of deposits. Some banks, Crosse says, have found a branch in the Bahamas less costly than a branch in London but, "while such an office can be a useful facility—a way to participate moderately in the market—it certainly cannot be fully competitive with branches in London, Paris or Frankfurt."[39]

Law and regulatory policy regarding branching also had a crucial influence on Franklin.[40] One of the fundamental elements of United States banking regulation, designed to prevent concentration of banking power and to protect local banks from out-of-state competition, is to restrict the geographical spread of banks.[41] American banks, whether chartered by the Federal government or by states, cannot branch across state lines. Thus Franklin could not expand into, say, Connecticut or New Jersey.

New York State laws imposed further restrictions on Franklin's geographical spread.[42] During the period of Franklin's initial growth on Long Island, the bank was well protected by a 1934 New York State banking law which limited branching within the state. This law prevented New York City banks from encroaching on Franklin's lucrative Nassau-Suffolk market and prevented Franklin from moving to Manhattan.

A new banking law enacted in 1960 had a significant effect on Franklin. The Omnibus Banking Act permitted New York City banks to branch into contiguous counties, including Nassau, and allowed suburban banks like Franklin to enter New York City. The law—which was bitterly fought by Franklin—created competition in Franklin's formerly protected market as New York banks established new branches in Nassau and gave Franklin a motive to seek profits and growth elsewhere. The law also provided an "elsewhere" by opening the formerly prohibited New York City market to Franklin. Thus it was that in September 1961, one year after the enactment of the Omnibus Banking Act, Franklin applied for permission to open a branch in New York City.

While Franklin's branching within the United States and New York State was closely circumscribed, its international branching was relatively uncontrolled by law and policy. Providing it had the permission of the United States government and of the government where it established a branch, Franklin could expand without geographical restriction, and U.S. and foreign approvals were easily obtained.

Franklin National Bank was within the jurisdiction of two

principal regulatory agencies in the fragmented American bank regulatory system. As a nationally chartered bank Franklin's primary supervisor was the Office of the Comptroller of the Currency, a division of the Treasury which administers national banks. The Comptroller was responsible for examining all of Franklin's branches, including its foreign branches, and for approving expansion into new domestic activities, including the opening of all domestic branches. The Federal Reserve was the authorizing agency for all of Franklin's overseas branches and was the supervisor of activities of Franklin's holding company, the Franklin New York Corporation. As a member of the Federal Reserve System, like all national banks, Franklin was also required to follow the rules of that system, including the maintenance of reserves at the Federal Reserve Bank of New York. As a member it was eligible for assistance from the Federal Reserve's discount window, a privilege that became crucially important when crisis erupted.

The Comptroller of the Currency played an important role in the banking revolution of the 1960s and 1970s. Under Comptrollers James J. Saxon, William B. Camp, and James E. Smith, U.S. national banks were encouraged to grow at home and to compete abroad.[43] The Comptroller encouraged growth through mergers and the creation of bank holding companies within the United States. The Comptroller also was an advocate of foreign expansion. The following exchange between James J. Saxon and Senator Jacob Javits during Saxon's confirmation hearing in 1962 is illustrative:

MR. SAXON: I believe we need more education and more purposeful efforts by the authorities on a sound, sane basis to amplify the participation of the American banking system abroad, particularly in the light of the enormous expansion of the Common Market.

I foresee the day, perhaps not 15 years from now, when the resources of the large banks of the country now operating in the foreign area will be doubled on account of such operations.

. . . banking resources committed abroad will be very substantial in relation to total resources.

. . . it is a very surprising reflection, I think, on the extent of U.S. participation in this growing area, that this richest and greatest of all countries should even at this stage have such a limited participation. I think this participation inevitably must grow substantially, and one of the purposes of this inquiry is to see if by changes in law and changes in administrative procedure and policies the activity of more banks in this area can be properly expanded.

SENATOR JAVITS: Is it the clear implication of your view then that you will, as far as you can within the ambit of your authority, seek to forward that concept—greater participation by the American banking system and a moving outward of our Nation's economy throughout the world?

MR. SAXON: Yes, sir.[44]

During his tenure Comptroller Saxon encouraged foreign expansion by proposing two important changes in banking laws, both of which were adopted: the liberalization of the Federal Reserve Board's regulations to expand the activities in which a foreign branch could engage, and the authorization for U.S. banks to establish banking subsidiaries overseas or to acquire directly shares in foreign banks.[45]

The Federal Reserve Board also followed a liberal policy regarding foreign expansion. Board policy was crucial, for its authorization was required for the establishment of foreign branches by member banks.[46] Board policy was summarized in the following statement made in 1973 by Chairman Burns:

The Congress in enacting the Federal Reserve Act in 1913 authorized the establishment of foreign branches by national banks, subject to the approval of the Board and such rules and regulations as the Board might prescribe, on the grounds that such foreign branches would contribute to the furtherance of the foreign commerce of the United States. The Board in carrying out its responsibilities under the statute has sought to foster a strong branch banking system overseas which would afford U.S. commercial and investment interests from all sections of the country access to adequate and alternative sources of financing and financial services for their international transactions. The criteria employed by the Board in approving the establishment of foreign branches have been mainly concerned with the condition of the bank and its ability to operate and manage a foreign branch. . . . Only rarely have other policy considerations been taken into account in acting on an application to establish a foreign branch.

In the past decade, only four applications for overseas branches have been denied by the Board.[47]

Both the Comptroller and the Federal Reserve supported Franklin's expansion abroad—sometimes even in the face of evidence that such expansion was not wise. The Comptroller supported both Franklin's domestic and international expansion. Comptroller Saxon approved Franklin's expansion into New York City, approved the merger with Federation Bank and Trust Company despite serious questions about the condition of Franklin, and continued to approve domestic branch applications even when Franklin was placed on the problem bank list.[48] The Comptroller repeatedly relied on assurances by Franklin's management that problems were being corrected.

Franklin's application for a Nassau branch was made in August 1968 and routinely approved by the Board in February 1969, although since 1965 there had been concern about Franklin's strength.[49] Franklin had been put on the problem bank list by the Comptroller in 1965 but in 1969 was no longer on the list. Furthermore, the Federal Reserve, as has been noted, had recently adopted the policy of permitting banks like Franklin to establish shell branches in order to compete with the big international banks in international finance. The branch was opened in 1969 with Franklin's typical extravagant style, but activity at the Nassau branch remained limited and peripheral to the bank's activities.

Regulatory approval of Franklin's London branch application was not so simple as in the Nassau case, for by late 1970 Franklin had again been classified as a problem bank. The Office of the Comptroller of the Currency played an important role in the Federal Reserve Board's consideration of the London branch application. In this case, as with its domestic regulation of Franklin, the Comptroller chose to rely on the assurances of bank management that problems were being corrected and to permit expansion.

The first reaction of the Comptroller's office had been to recommend against approval of the London application. In a memorandum dated February 12, 1971, Robert A. Mullin, Director of the International Division, concluded that because of the many problems of the bank either Franklin should withdraw its request or the Board should deny the application. However, just two weeks later, on March 1, 1971, Mr. Mullin wrote to the Board of Governors that the Comptroller's office had reviewed Franklin's problems with the Board of Directors and that corrective measures had been initiated by the bank's management. Therefore, wrote Mullin, "we have concluded that we do not object to your approval of the application to open the London branch."[50]

The Board of Governors, concerned about Franklin's rapid expansion and need for consolidation, hesitated. Finally, on December 2, 1971, Harold Gleason, Chairman of the Board, wrote to Arthur Burns, Chairman of the Board of Governors, referring to the delay in approving the London branch application and noting the successful completion of a capital offering of $35 million, of which $30 million had been added to Franklin's capital. On December 31, 1971, the Board of Governors approved the establishment of a London branch. The Board's letter to Franklin noted the Board's concerns and its reliance on the assurances of Franklin's management that changes were being made:

In passing upon your application for this branch, the Board considered the over-all condition of your bank, particularly the large volume of assets classified and specially mentioned by examiners in recent reports of examination in relation to the bank's relatively low capital position. It is the Board's understanding that strenuous efforts are being made by the bank to reduce the volume of problem assets and that the bank's parent holding company has recently contributed $30,000,000 to the bank's surplus account. . . . The Board will have a continuing special interest in the operation of the branch and in the progress made by the bank in reducing the volume of problem assets and in otherwise improving the condition of the bank.[51]

Interestingly, the letter noted, "It is also understood that the proposed branch in London will be moderate in terms of staffing, quarters, and the volume of business to be conducted."[52]

Having passed this first hurdle, Franklin then had to obtain approval from the Bank of England in order to open a branch and to deal in the London interbank market. English regulatory policy was another important political element in Franklin's foreign expansion. The United Kingdom, in its effort to maintain the position of the City of London as a world financial center, had adopted a policy of encouraging the establishment in London of foreign branches dealing in the Eurodollar market. Regulations for offshore activities were limited and permission relatively easy to obtain. American banks had to register as a company to obtain Bank of England authorization to deal in foreign exchange.

Foreign exchange authorization for American banks depends essentially on the Bank of England's confidence in the management of the branch and on the affirmation by American regulatory authorities that a bank is in good standing with United States authorities. British encouragement of foreign branches combined with American support for international activities thus made an environment conducive to moving to London.[53]

Franklin made appropriate application to the Bank of England and went about hiring two people whom the Bank of England knew and of whom it approved, a foreign exchange dealer and foreign exchange controller. Satisfied that Franklin personnel were competent, the Bank of England sought affirmation from United States regulatory authorities that Franklin was in good standing with them. Repeated requests from the Bank of England regarding Franklin's status with United States authorities were followed by repeated evasive responses from the Office of the Comptroller of the Currency. The reasons for such evasion were continuing reports of problems at Franklin. In 1972 the Comptroller's office carried out an examination of Franklin which revealed serious difficulties, including problems in the international division. One of the examiners emphasized that the London branch should not be opened until the international division was operating properly. Once again, however, the Comptroller's office accepted the assurances of the bank's management that corrections were being made and on October 31, 1972, wrote to the Bank of England stating that "we believe Franklin should be recognized in London."[54]

Accordingly, the Bank of England under its usual procedures granted Franklin limited exchange control authorization on June 1, 1972. Branch officials anticipated that if all went well, full authorization would be given in approximately three months. However, in July 1972 a major change occurred in Franklin National Bank, when 21.6 percent of the shares of Franklin New York Corporation were purchased by Michele Sindona. The Bank of England, feeling uncertain about Sindona's resources and intentions, concerned about his colleague, Carlo Bordoni (who had a well-known but poor reputation in foreign exchange markets—see below) and feeling that United States regulatory authorities should be given time to take action on the Sindona acquisition, wrote to the Board of Governors and the Comptroller of the Currency to learn their views. United States authorities responded that they were aware of press comment about Sindona, that they would not be embarrassed if the Bank of England delayed final authorization, and that the Bank should make its own decision about delay. Thus the Bank of England decided to defer approval for three months because of uncertainties about Sindona. In November the Bank of England again raised the issue with United States authorities. By then Franklin had hired Peter Shaddick, who had been employed by and was known to the Bank of England, to head its international department. Ironically, Shaddick would play a key role in illegal activities at Franklin. In November the Comptroller told the Bank of England that Franklin had probably learned a lesson from the fears about Sindona and that the Bank of England could authorize the London branch. This it did in November 1972.[55]

A Foreign Owner

In July 1972 Michele Sindona purchased 21.6 percent of the common stock of Franklin New York Corporation, the holding company which owned Franklin National Bank. Although Sindona was frequently described in the press as a "mysterious Italian financier," he was, in fact, well known in international financial circles.[56] Born in Sicily, Sindona began his career after World War II as a lawyer in Milan, where he specialized in the complexities of Italian tax laws and became active in arranging acquisitions and mergers. After developing a sizable practice helping others to expand their holdings, Sindona began to develop his own financial empire. He created Fasco A.G., a wholly owned holding company incorporated in Lichtenstein, and began to acquire a vast and varied network of companies. Much later, after the Sindona empire was in ruins, authorities uncovered over 125 companies in 11 countries (see figure 2.1). They ranged from banks to manufacturers of photographic equipment, from real estate companies to offshore corporations engaged in foreign exchange speculation. All were connected to Sindona through a complex set of holding companies located in tax haven countries such as Lichtenstein and Luxemburg, and Fasco A.G. of Lichtenstein at the apex.

Through Fasco, Sindona had a controlling interest in at least five banks: Banca Privata Finanziaria, Milan; Banca Unione, S.P.A., Milan; Banca de Messina, Messina; Banque de Financement (Finabank), S.A., Geneva; and Bankhaus Wolff A.G., Hamburg. He also reportedly had control of Amincor Bank, Zurich.

Through Fasco, his banks, and his consulting work Sindona had close relations with a number of important European and American banks. For example, Continental Illinois National Bank and Trust Company of Chicago, in 1972 the ninth largest bank in the United States, and Hambros Bank Ltd. of London, a leading British merchant bank, were substantial shareholders in Banca Privata Finanziaria, and Banca Privata in turn owned a significant interest in Banca de Messina and Banque de Financement. Sindona also had close relations with the important French bank, Banque de Paris et des Pays Bas. In 1963, for example, Sindona joined with that bank to buy a controlling interest in Libby, McNeill and Libby, the American food processing company.[57]

These major banks were Sindona's clients as well as his partners. In the 1960s and early 1970s he helped them and other non-Italian groups acquire control of Italian corporations. For example, Sindona reportedly helped Hambros acquire La Centrale Finanziaria Generale, one of Italy's largest industrial and financial private holding companies and helped Banque de Paris et des Pays Bas acquire a share in Sviluppo, another large Italian holding company. He reportedly tried but failed to acquire yet another Italian giant, Bastogio, for a syndicate which included Hambros.[58]

Other of Sindona's clients were large corporations, one of the most important of which was Gulf and Western, the American conglomerate. He sold Gulf and Western his control of Brown Company, a paper producer, and helped the company acquire stock in Societa Generale Immobiliare (SGI), a giant Italian real estate development

Figure 2.1. Corporate Structure of

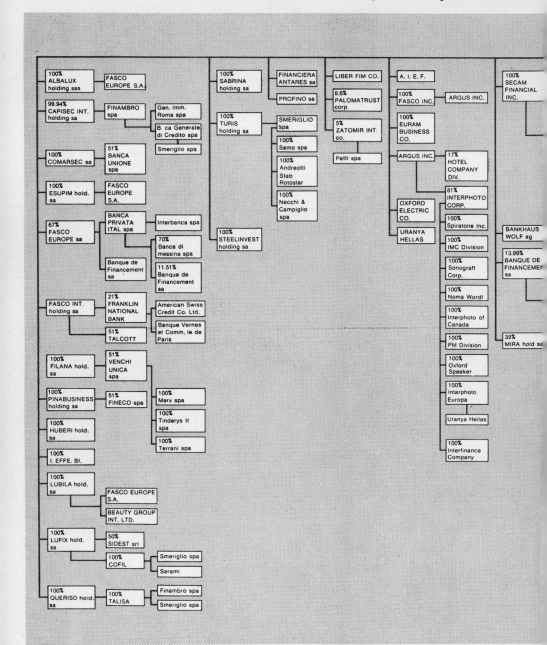

asco A. G. (*Il Moneo*, July 21, 1976).

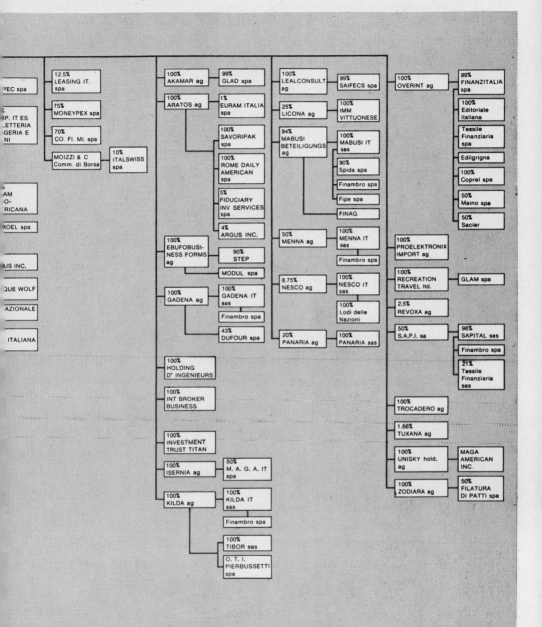

company which counted the Washington Watergate complex among its many holdings.[59] Another shareholder in SGI, and a Sindona client, was the Istituto per le Opere de Religione—the financial arm of the Vatican.

Interestingly, Sindona remained involved in many of the acquisitions he helped to arrange. He became a member of the Board of La Centrale Finanziaria Generale after the Hambros acquisition and later acquired control of both Sviluppo and SGI.

Through these partners and clients Sindona developed excellent connections throughout the world of banking and finance. As he himself put it: "Banking is a matter of connections. . . . I have personal connections in all important financial centers. Those who do business with Michele Sindona will do business with Franklin National."[60]

One such connection was David M. Kennedy, Chairman of the Board and Chief Executive Officer of Continental Illinois Bank from 1959 to 1969, Secretary of the Treasury of the United States from 1969 to 1971, United States Ambassador at Large from 1969 to 1971, and Ambassador to the North Atlantic Treaty Organization from 1971 to 1973. Kennedy knew Sindona from Continental Illinois days and saw him frequently then and later when Kennedy went into government. In April 1973, after leaving government, Kennedy joined the Board of Fasco International and served as an adviser to Sindona, providing him with connections to public and private banking officials in the United States and abroad. According to Kennedy, Sindona offered him the job of chief executive of Franklin National in 1973, an offer Kennedy declined. He nonetheless advised Sindona on Franklin matters and served as a sort of ambassador for the bank in Europe and the Far East. Kennedy has also testified that he received a $200,000 loan from Sindona in early 1974, which Kennedy reported he fully repaid.[61] As we shall see, Kennedy would also play a minor role in the settlement of the Franklin affair.

While Michele Sindona was well known in international financial circles, he remained "mysterious" in one important sense: no one knew where his money came from. The story behind the construction of the Sindona empire would not be known until that empire including Franklin National Bank was in ruins.

Sindona wanted very much to expand his empire to the United States. Before 1972 he had had, at various points, significant holdings in a number of American companies including Libby, McNeill and Libby; Brown Company; Oxford Electric; Interphoto; and Argus. He had, however, sold all his American holdings except for these last three, which represented only a very minor part of the Sindona empire. By 1972, however, Sindona had decided to expand his American holdings in a significant way. When a block of shares in Franklin came on the market, he jumped at the opportunity without, it seems, investigating the strength of the bank. After all, Franklin was a large American bank and a member of the New York Clearing House Association, and was noted for its growth. It probably seemed a perfect vehicle for establishing a foothold in both the United States and the international financial system. It also turned out to be a useful vehicle for Sindona's international financial manipulations. So eager was Sindona to acquire the shares that he paid $40 per share, $8 above the market price.

Sindona's purchase of the Franklin New York Corporation shares caused a stir in the financial press and in Congress, in particular with Wright Patman, Chairman of the House Committee on Banking and Currency. On July 19, 1972, Chairman Patman wrote to Chairman Burns raising the issue of the Sindona purchase.[62] The Bank of England, as has been noted, delayed final authorization of the London branch due to the acquisition. Although American regulatory authorities, in particular the Federal Reserve, might have sought through the Bank Holding Company Act, to prevent the Sindona acquisition or to limit his activities as owner of such a large bloc of Franklin New York Corporation stock, they failed to do so.

The Federal Reserve, Fasco, and the Bank Holding Company Act

Under section 2 of the Bank Holding Company Act of 1956 as amended in 1970, a company is conclusively presumed to be a bank holding company if it controls 25 percent of any class of voting shares or if it controls in any manner the election of a majority of directors or trustees of a bank or a bank holding company. A company may also be defined as a bank holding company if the Board of Governors of the Federal Reserve system determines, after notice and the opportunity for a hearing, that a company directly or indirectly exercises controlling influence over the management or policies of a bank or company. According to Federal Reserve regulations a company may be presumed to constitute a holding company if it owns, controls, or has power to vote more than 5 percent of any class of voting shares and if (1) one or more of the company's directors, trustees, or partners or officers or employees with policymaking functions serves in any of these capacities with the bank or other company, and (2) no other person owns, controls, or has power to vote as much as 5 percent of any class of voting securities. A company may also be presumed to have control if it enters into a management contract which gives it policymaking power. These conditions are termed "rebuttable presumptions" of control, i.e., they may be contested by the company.

In 1971, 21.6 percent of the outstanding common stock of Franklin New York Corporation was owned by Loews Corporation, and the Chairman of Loews, Laurence A. Tisch, held one seat on the Board of Directors of both the holding company and the bank. Under United States law and Federal Reserve regulations, therefore, there existed a "rebuttable presumption" that Loews Corporation controlled Franklin New York Corporation. If the Federal Reserve Board had found that Loews did control Franklin, Loew's would have been declared a "bank holding company" and would have come under federal regulation and surveillance. Among other requirements, such regulation would have forced Loews to divest itself of its significant and profitable nonbanking holdings. After the Board of Governors undertook to investigate the possibility that it held a controlling interest in Franklin New York Corporation, Loews sold its share of the holding company in July 1972.[63]

The new owner of 21.6 percent of Franklin New York Corporation's common stock was Fasco International Holding, S.A., a

Luxembourg holding company. On July 11, 1972, the law firm White & Case wrote to the Federal Reserve Bank of New York on behalf of and with the knowledge of Michele Sindona informing the Bank that Fasco International was wholly and directly owned by Michele Sindona and was formed for the sole purpose of holding Franklin stock for Sindona and that its only assets were Franklin stock. White & Case sent the Federal Reserve Bank a chart which it said was prepared by Sindona showing that Sindona also owned another holding company, Fasco A.G., incorporated in Lichtenstein, which in turn held one Swiss and two Italian banks and three United States manufacturing companies: Oxford Electric Corporation, Argus Corporation, and Interphoto Corporation. Sindona's lawyers informed the Federal Reserve Bank of New York that they had advised Sindona that in their view neither Fasco International nor Fasco A.G. had the requisite control over Franklin New York Corporation to be declared a bank holding company.[64]

Officials of the Federal Reserve Bank of New York agreed. Although Fasco International held over 5 percent of Franklin New York stock and although no other stockholder held such a bloc of stock, Fasco did not control a directorship or other policymaking function. Thus the rebuttable presumption did not apply.

In August 1972, however, Sindona and his close associate Carlo Bordoni, a director of Fasco International and a managing director of Banca Unione, a Sindona-owned bank, were elected to the Board of Directors of Franklin New York Corporation. The election of two Fasco directors to the Board of Franklin New York Corporation meant that the rebuttable presumptions of the Federal Reserve regulations could have been applied. Nonetheless the Reserve Bank did not recommend action. Apparently, lawyers interpreted the rebuttable presumptions as necessary but not sufficient conditions. Instead, officials began to seek greater information regarding the role of Sindona and Bordoni in Franklin. The Federal Reserve Bank of New York sent a letter to Sindona's new lawyers, Mudge, Rose, Guthrie, and Alexander, asking for more information.[65]

The response to a letter from the Federal Reserve Bank of

New York revealed that the information originally supplied to the Bank was inaccurate. Fasco A.G., not Sindona, was the owner of Fasco International. Sindona's lawyers said that Sindona "considered Fasco to be his wholly owned subsidiary since he owned all the stock of Fasco A.G." They went on to say that, in that context, the letter from White & Case correctly stated the facts but that "Mr. Sindona did not see the chart attached to the letter and in this respect the chart is in error."[66] The funds used by Fasco International to acquire Franklin New York Corporation stock were supplied by Fasco A.G. and, in fact, represented a capital investment in Fasco International by Fasco A.G. Federal Reserve Bank officials still were not satisfied that a clear case for action existed and continued to acquire more information.

The Talcott Acquisition

Early in 1973 events demonstrated that Fasco and Sindona had control of Franklin New York Corporation. In March and April Sindona through Fasco International acquired a controlling interest in Talcott National, an American financing and factoring company, with the intention of selling that interest to Franklin New York Corporation at cost. Sindona was in effect making policy for Franklin New York Corporation. Although Franklin New York Corporation continued to affirm to the Federal Reserve Bank that no change in control had occurred, the lawyers for the Federal Reserve Bank of New York apparently concluded that the rebuttable presumptions were applicable and that Sindona's role in the Talcott acquisition and much other evidence, including Sindona and Bordoni's close cooperation, their active presence on the Board, and their influence over the growing international operations of the bank, suggested that Sindona, Fasco International, and Fasco A.G. controlled Franklin New York Corporation and should be declared bank holding companies. Even if the development of further evidence through a Board investigation proved that Fasco did not control Franklin, bank officials apparently concluded such an investigation was advisable because of the importance of the issue. Thus, in May 1973, the Federal Reserve Bank of New York recommended to the Board of Governors that a preliminary determination of control be found.

The Board of Governors never declared Fasco International and Fasco A.G. holding companies. Wright Patman, as has been noted, wrote to Chairman Burns on July 19, 1972, raising the issue of the status of Fasco International; and Burns replied on August 2 that the Board was making inquiries.[67] The Board's attention remained at the level of "inquiries" by the Board staff.

A combination of factors led to the Board's inaction. Aside from the Patman inquiry, there was little external pressure to decide. Apparently the Federal Reserve Bank of New York recommendation did not have the strong and active backing of high bank officials. Franklin National Bank was making strong representations to the Reserve Bank and the Board that Sindona did not control Franklin New York Corporation.

Internally, Board lawyers were uncertain about whether a corporation wholly owned by an individual should be considered an individual in terms of the law and thus not subject to Bank Holding Company provisions or a company and subject to the law. Governor Robert C. Holland testified in July 1975 that the Board thought that the issue would be resolved in connection with the Board's decision on the acquisition of Talcott, for if the acquisition had been approved, Sindona's share would have jumped over 25 percent and control would have been presumed. The Board's denial left the issue unsettled.[68] In the absence of pressure to act, the Board did nothing, and the Fasco issue stayed at the bottom of the pile in the Board's legal office.

Much later, on May 14, 1974, after Franklin's troubles had become public knowledge and the role of Sindona in those troubles a public issue, Patman again wrote Chairman Burns chastising him for the Board's delay and requesting an explanation. After much agony and delay at the Board, Chairman Burns responded on June 5, 1974, that determining control in a case when a company controls less than 25 percent of stock is highly complex and time consuming, and difficult because "simple, objective criteria for exercise of control are lacking."[69]

Escape from Surveillance
and Regulation

Because Fasco International and Fasco A.G. were not declared bank holding companies, Sindona was able to avoid U.S. regulation and surveillance.

Because his purchase of shares of Franklin New York Corporation did not require governmental approval, Sindona was able to escape investigation by federal authorities of his merits as an owner of an American bank holding company. Had Fasco been declared a bank holding company its acquisition of Franklin New York Corporation shares would have required approval by the Board of Governors of the Federal Reserve System. In acting on Fasco's application the Board under the Bank Holding Company Act would have examined, among other factors, the financial and managerial resources and future prospects of Fasco. Such an investigation might well have led to the discovery of information about Sindona and his empire which would have justified a denial of the Fasco acquisition.

A report by the Italian Ministry of Finance issued after the debacle revealed that as early as 1972 the Bank of Italy had uncovered widespread irregularities in Sindona's Italian banks, irregularities so serious that a report was made in 1972 and 1973 to the Milan magistrate for possible criminal proceedings.[70] While is is unclear whether officials of the Bank of Italy would have revealed such information to American officials, their position on disclosing information, it seems, was not tested, for there is no evidence that they were asked.

There was virtually no inquiry into Sindona in the U.S. Despite rumors in the press and inquiries from Wright Patman and from the Bank of England in connection with the authorization of the London branch, the Federal Reserve and the Comptroller seem to have done little serious investigation of Sindona. The first evidence of regulatory concern came in February 1974, long after the Franklin and Talcott purchases. On February 1 Alfred Hayes, President of the Federal Reserve Bank of New York, received a call from Chairman Burns. Burns said that he had received a call from Secretary of the Treasury

George P. Shultz informing him that Comptroller Smith would like the Federal Reserve to call the Bank of Italy to ask Governor Guido Carli his personal opinion of Sindona. Burns asked Hayes to make the call but not to inform Carli of the source of the concern. This Hayes did on February 4, 1974. As Hayes expected, Carli was cautious, saying that Sindona was intelligent and endowed with initiative and imagination, that the world needed such people but that the job of central bankers was to place controls on and to build boundaries around such ambitious and explosive persons. By February 1974 it was too late to place controls on Sindona.

The failure to declare Fasco a Bank Holding Company also gave Sindona other liberties. He was able to retain three U.S. commercial corporations engaged in nonbank or bank-related activities which were owned by Fasco A.G. and which, had Fasco been declared a bank holding company, would have violated U.S. law regarding nonbank activities of bank holding companies.

Furthermore, Franklin was able to make loans to Fasco-affiliated companies without being subject to provisions of the Federal Reserve Act, which limits the amount that a bank may loan to its bank holding company or any affiliate and which requires that all such loans be secured by collateral having a value of 120 percent of the loan. Sindona was not obliged to divulge information about the activities of his holding companies. Although surveillance and reporting requirements are less stringent under Federal Reserve regulations for foreign bank holding companies than for domestic bank holding companies, U.S. regulatory authorities would have been more likely to discover or deter some of Sindona's questionable practices had there been such a reporting requirement.

Foreign Exchange

The final international dimension of Franklin National Bank was its massive foreign exchange operation. Many American banks increased foreign exchange trading after the advent of floating exchange rates. Up until that time banks engaged in foreign exchange operation primarily for their own needs or on a customer's account, and it was considered routine sound banking practice to cover all foreign exchange transactions. Floating rates and the wide fluctuations characteristic of the first years of the float, however, created irresistible temptations to make profits by speculating in foreign exchange, and increasingly banks engaged in foreign exchange trading for their own account. One of those banks was Franklin National.

In Franklin's case, the search for profits through foreign exchange speculation was reinforced by the weakness of the bank. By the early 1970s Franklin was suffering from a number of diseases—a bad loan portfolio acquired through excessively rapid growth, poor investment policies, excessive reliance on purchased short-term money—all of which were aggravated by the economic crisis and tight monetary policies of the early 1970s (see below). For Franklin, foreign exchange trading was a way to generate earnings at a time of losses in other divisions. Franklin's vice president in charge of the international division admitted in late 1973 that Franklin was trading for its own account and that such trading was a conscious decision by management to attempt to bolster weak earnings and to make use of tax deductions which it could not otherwise use.[71]

Evidence also suggests that Michele Sindona influenced the decision of management to engage actively in foreign exchange trading (see chapter 3). Sindona's Italian banks reportedly had engaged heavily in such speculation, and it seems Sindona transferred their practices to Franklin. In 1972 he reportedly told Arthur Roth, the former chairman of Franklin and still a substantial stockholder, that "I'm going to make most of my money in foreign exchange. That's the way I do it in my Italian banks."[72] The chief agents in the Franklin foreign exchange operation were Carlo Bordoni and Peter Shaddick. Bordoni, as has been noted, was a close associate of Sindona and a member of the Board of Directors of Franklin New York Corporation. Before coming to Sindona's employ, Bordoni had been a foreign exchange trader with an international reputation for speculating in great volume. Although not on the Board of Directors of the bank itself and although not a member of Franklin's management, Bordoni was in daily contact with Franklin's foreign exchange department giving advice on market conditions and engaging in transactions between Banca Unione, the Sindona bank of which he was managing director, and Franklin National Bank.[73]

Peter Shaddick, once an employee of the Bank of England, met Sindona in the early 1960s when Shaddick was vice president of Continental Illinois Bank. When Continental purchased an interest in Banca Privata Finanziaria, a Sindona controlled bank, Shaddick joined the Board of Directors of that bank and that of another Sindona bank, Banque de Financement (Finabank) in Switzerland. Shaddick continued to see Sindona frequently, even after leaving Continental to go to the Bank of Montreal. In the fall of 1972 Sindona recruited Shaddick to head the international division of Franklin National. According to Shaddick, Sindona told him that a major part of his new job would be to develop Franklin's foreign exchange activity. Shaddick also reported that Sindona gave him carte blanche to run the foreign exchange department and the international division.[74] And, indeed, Shaddick ran the department as a "bank within a bank,"[75] independent of the Franklin's central management. Paul Luftig, president and chief executive officer of Franklin from May 1972 to May 1974, testified that the international division did not report to him.[76] In January 1974 the examiner-in-charge informed officials of the Federal Reserve Bank of New York that the Executive Vice Chairman Peter Shaddick was, "in fact, the chief executive officer operating Franklin in accordance with Mr. Sindona's wishes."[77]

As a result of an explicit bank policy of expanding foreign trading and of a series of illegal foreign exchange activities (which will be discussed in detail later), Franklin foreign exchange trading volume exploded (see table 2.11). On May 17, 1971 Franklin bought and sold a total of $19 million in foreign exchange; by May 14, 1974 that figure stood at $3.3 billion.

Federal authorities failed to discover Franklin's illegal actions or to take measures against the high level of foreign exchange trading.

Illegal actions taken with the consent and cooperation of manage-ment are difficult to detect. Federal authorities were hampered by the absence of regular and current data on Franklin's position and by their own lack of experience in evaluating foreign exchange specu-lation due to the novelty of the phenomenon. Nevertheless, the Comptroller and the Federal Reserve seemed to ignore numerous warning signals. Examiners in the Office of the Comptroller of the Currency, despite their knowledge of chaos in the international division, relied on assurances of the bank's management that controls were being implemented and at several points failed to report or to check for falsification of data.[78] Officers of the Federal Reserve Bank of New York also failed to recognize the seriousness of Franklin's speculations, even when informed of concern and fear of pending crisis by officers of Morgan Guaranty Trust Company. In November 1973, two officers of that bank met with the president and several officers of the Federal Reserve Bank of New York to signal their concern about the volume of foreign exchange trading being done by Franklin. The Morgan officials told the Reserve Bank of-ficers that Morgan and many other banks were so concerned about the extent of Franklin's speculation that they would no longer enter into forward and, in some instances, spot foreign exchange contracts with Franklin National Bank.

TABLE 2.11   Franklin National Bank Foreign Exchange Trading

Foreign Exchange Growth

Date of Examination	Total Foreign Exchange Bought and Sold ($ million)
9-29-69	$ 13.6
8-31-70	10.7
5-17-71	19.0
3-6-72	422.4
12-11-72	1,375.2
11-14-73	3,760.7
5-14-74	3,332.6
8-14-74	1,900.2

SOURCE: *Oversight Hearings,* p. 97.

After the meeting, Reserve Bank officers agreed that the situation was potentially explosive and that further investigation was necessary. The conclusion of that investigation was that the total volume of commitments on Franklin's books did not seem excessive, that foreign exchange speculation was common practice among major banks, and that the size of Franklin's open position relative to the size of the bank did not seem alarming. The Federal Reserve, like the Comptroller, relied on assurances of Franklin's management that the bank would take action soon to improve the situation.[79] However, as a result of the Morgan warning and of its own information about Franklin's problems growing out of the Talcott National investigation, officers of the Federal Reserve Bank became sufficiently concerned about Franklin's condition to consider the possibility that Franklin might need assistance from the Bank's discount window. Thus, in December 1973 the Reserve Bank took the precautionary step of establishing a Franklin task force to monitor Franklin's performance on a weekly basis with a view to making contingency plans in the event Franklin requested a discount window advance.

3

THE
FRANKLIN
CRISIS

ON OCTOBER 8, 1974, after five months of persistent crisis, Franklin National Bank was declared insolvent. Franklin's demise was caused by a number of problems, some arising from troubles at home and some from troubles abroad, some caused by poor judgment and some by outright fraud, some associated purely with Franklin and some linked to the harsh economic conditions of 1973 and 1974. It is difficult to unravel these problems from one another, and it is impossible to identify any one of them as the principal reason for the collapse of the bank.

In this chapter we shall explore the reasons for the Franklin crisis, putting special emphasis on Franklin's international problems. Although Franklin's international activities were not the principal source of the bank's difficulties, they did play a key role in the bank's demise. Foreign exchange problems triggered a crisis of confidence and caused massive deposit losses; Eurodollar operations weakened the earnings of the bank and, when confidence collapsed, accounted for a substantial part of Franklin's liquidity problem; and Franklin's link with Michele Sindona aggravated both the loss of confidence and the liquidity crunch. We emphasize these international problems here because one of the purposes of this study is to explore new risks associated with international operations and because it was Franklin's international operations that linked the bank to the larger international banking system and helped to create the international banking crisis which we will examine in chapter 4.

Domestic Problems

Over a decade of rapid growth and poor management had left Franklin with a number of domestic problems, most importantly an excessive reliance on short-term financing, a dismal earnings record, and illiquidity of its assets. Franklin National Bank was heavily dependent on short-term borrowed money. Instead of financing growth through increased bank equity capital or increased demand, savings and time deposits, Franklin National like many other banks used funds borrowed short-term from other banks or from large lenders. Franklin relied on certificates of deposit with maturities under ninety days and on overnight Federal funds to finance term loans of several years. In 1964 Federal funds and agreements to repurchase accounted for 5 percent of total liabilities, in 1972 for 11 percent of total liabilities, and by 1973 for 16 percent of liabilities.[1] Figures for Franklin's dependence on certificates of deposit (CDs) are less complete. However, a former vice president of the bank testified that, when he joined the bank in August 1973, CDs averaged nearly $600 million or approximately 13 percent of total liabilities for 1973.[2] In April 1974, Franklin issued an average of $446 million in money market CDs or 9 percent of total liabilities at that time (see table 3.1).

At the same time domestic demand, time and savings deposits, as a percentage of total liabilities, declined from 83.5 percent in 1964 to 61.6 percent in 1972 to 51.6 percent in 1974. Franklin's capital base as a percent of total resources also declined. Capital funds accounted for

8.1 percent of total bank resources in 1964, for 5.9 percent in 1969, and for only 4.0 percent in 1973.[3]

Reliance on short-term borrowing instead of on equity or on FDIC-insured deposits made Franklin vulnerable to a loss of money market confidence and a liquidity crisis. Such uninsured funds are highly volatile: in the event of a crisis of confidence, Federal funds could—and did—disappear overnight while CDs could—and did—disappear quickly as they came due.[4]

Reliance on short-term financing also contributed in a major way to a bad earnings record. Not only are such funds more expensive than deposits, they are also highly interest-rate sensitive. Any rise or decline in interest rates was quickly reflected in Franklin's total cost of borrowing. In addition, Franklin, because of doubts about its credit worthiness, was forced to pay a premium for these funds. When interest rates rose to unprecedented heights in 1973 and 1974, Franklin's operating costs soared. Interest on Federal funds purchased and securities sold under agreement to repurchase rose from 11.9 percent of operating expenses in 1972 to 21.3 percent in 1973.[5] The resultant squeeze between the cost of financing and the return on investments was accentuated by a decision of President Paul Luftig in 1973. Calculating that interest rates would decline, Luftig increased the bank's reliance on short-term financing with the expectation that when rates declined he could shift into lower-cost, longer-term financing. Luftig miscalculated, however, and the squeeze tightened.

Another of Franklin's expenses which cut into earnings was rising loan losses. In its program of rapid expansion, as we have seen, Franklin followed a liberal lending policy. Eager to increase assets in a competitive market, Franklin followed questionable lending practices including loans to people of uncertain integrity and dependence on inadequate and unreliable financial statements and supporting data. As a result, Franklin acquired a high proportion of bad loans. On September 29, 1969, 5.4 percent of Franklin's loans were listed as classified or criticized by national bank examiners; by May 14, 1974, 11.6 percent of all Franklin's loans were classified or criticized. On May 14, 1974, classified loans represented 58.7 percent of total

TABLE 3.1   Franklin National Bank Comparative Statements of Condition, Various Dates–1974 ($ million)

	April (Avg.)	May 3	May 8	May 10	May 13	May 17
Assets						
Cash and due from banks	$ 666	$ 710	$ 575	$ 492	$ 566	$ 367
Commercial loans	1,529	1,515	1,520	1,531	1,538	1,580
Other domestic loans	568	505	504	507	503	501
Subtotal	2,763	2,730	2,599	2,530	2,607	2,448
Investments	860	877	880	878	890	897
Trading account	63	47	42	43	47	56
Subtotal	923	924	922	921	937	953
Other assets	157	153	144	151	153	148
Foreign branch investments	389	333	288	289	282	272
Foreign branch loans	589	590	587	588	590	587
Subtotal	978	923	875	877	872	859
Total assets	$4,821	$4,730	$4,540	$4,479	$4,569	$4,408
Liabilities						
Domestic demand deposits	$1,226	$1,237	$1,166	$1,082	$1,128	$ 858
Domestic time and savings	825	811	833	831	817	797
Subtotal	2,051	2,048	1,999	1,913	1,945	1,655
Foreign branch deposits	982	926	883	882	872	759
Secured Federal funds	0	0	0	0	0	0
Money market CDs	446	468	464	459	436	331
Federal funds (net)	591	520	334	329	57	0
Repurchase agreements	333	350	344	346	291	294
FRB borrowings	0	0	110	135	550	960
Subtotal	1,370	1,338	1,252	1,269	1,334	1,585
Other liabilities	216	217	205	215	217	207
Capital accounts	202	201	201	200	201	202
Total liabilities	$4,821	$4,730	$4,540	$4,479	$4,569	$4,408
Memo item: Head office support of foreign branches	NA	NA	NA	NA	NA	NA

capital while criticized loans represented 62.0 percent of total capital. Franklin suffered from heavy loan losses which increased from $1.4 million of a total of $1.6 billion on September 29, 1969, to $13.4 million of a total of $2.6 billion on May 14, 1974. From December 11, 1972, to November 14, 1973, alone, loan losses rose 54 percent.[6]

May 24	May 31	June 7	June 14	June 21	June 28	July 5	July 12	July 26
$ 376	$ 346	$ 338	$ 330	$ 312	$ 309	$ 299	$ 233	$ 238
1,531	1,514	1,501	1,475	1,449	1,426	1,416	1,416	1,389
498	494	504	505	508	500	513	508	511
2,405	2,354	2,343	2,310	2,269	2,235	2,228	2,157	2,138
901	898	900	896	897	796	776	777	774
38	41	47	54	51	42	42	40	36
939	939	947	950	948	838	818	817	810
142	179	161	160	159	180	186	149	145
269	272	227	219	205	192	158	190	160
588	588	589	590	586	591	593	595	586
857	860	816	809	791	783	751	785	746
$4,343	$4,332	$4,267	$4,229	$4,167	$4,036	$3,983	$3,908	$3,839
$ 788	$ 797	$ 770	$ 718	$ 742	$ 785	727	652	608
797	775	741	730	700	643	618	580	571
1,585	1,572	1,511	1,448	1,442	1,428	1,345	1,232	1,179
705	665	616	586	543	508	485	462	409
0	0	0	200	200	200	200	201	226
267	232	200	181	170	151	140	131	114
0	4	(4)	(2)	(16)	(55)	(17)	(21)	(10)
261	271	277	280	239	186	160	147	166
1,130	1,170	1,260	1,135	1,190	1,235	1,310	1,400	1,410
1,658	1,677	1,733	1,794	1,783	1,717	1,793	1,858	1,906
195	285	276	273	273	211	191	189	183
200	133	131	128	126	172	169	167	162
$4,343	$4,332	$4,267	$4,229	$4,167	$4,036	$3,983	$3,908	$3,839
NA	NA	NA	NA	$ 267	$ 304	$ 307	$ 337	$ 362

Franklin was not the only bank facing serious problems in the difficult year of 1974. A confidential report prepared by the Board of Governors of the Federal Reserve System in 1975 and leaked to the press in 1976 revealed the difficulties of a number of state-chartered member banks, including a number of Franklin's rivals (see table

TABLE 3.1   (Continued)

	Aug. 9	Aug. 23	Sept. 6	Sept. 20	Oct. 4	Oct. 7
Assets						
Cash and due from banks	$ 246	$ 211	$ 215	$ 205	$ 213	$ 211
Commercial loans	1,362	1,328	1,314	1,309	1,277	1,272
Other domestic loans	507	508	519	515	520	519
Subtotal	2,115	2,047	2,048	2,029	2,010	2,002
Investments	785	789	811	808	800	800
Trading account	25	24	0	0	0	0
Subtotal	810	813	811	808	800	800
Other assets	150	147	153	149	159	161
Foreign branch investments	145	149	144	138	105	103
Foreign branch loans	584	582	580	579	584	584
Subtotal	729	731	724	717	689	687
Total assets	$3,804	$3,738	$3,736	$3,703	$3,658	$3,650
Liabilities						
Domestic demand deposits	584	557	568	559	538	548
Domestic time and savings	584	575	563	568	572	564
Subtotal	1,168	1,132	1,131	1,127	1,110	1,112
Foreign branch deposits	360	320	296	278	225	222
Secured Federal funds	227	226	226	226	0	0
Money market CDs	100	93	88	77	63	63
Federal funds (net)	3	0	(2)	(2)	2	0
Repurchase agreements	163	162	158	126	166	166
FRB borrowings	1,420	1,445	1,481	1,527	1,723	1,722
Subtotal	1,913	1,926	1,951	1,954	1,954	1,951
Other liabilities	198	196	192	183	198	195
Capital accounts	165	164	166	161	171	170
Total liabilities	$3,804	$3,738	$3,736	$3,703	$3,658	$3,650
Memo item:						
Head office support of foreign branches	$ 412	$ 433	$ 451	$ 452	$ 476	$ 477

SOURCE: Call reports. Franklin National Bank. At FRBNY.

3.2). The classified loans of Marine Midland–New York, for example, represented 128.1 percent of total capital; those of Chemical Bank, 84.3; those of Manufacturers Hanover Trust 65.7; those of Bank of New York 51.6; and those of Irving Trust 48.5 percent. In 1974 Manufacturer's Hanover had actual loan losses of $40 million out of a total of $16.7 billion in outstanding loans; Chemical Bank that year had $16.8 million in loan losses out of a total of $12.3 billion.[7]

Not only did Franklin face soaring operating costs, it also was saddled with low income on its loans and investments. One of the major problems was Franklin's investment in state and municipal securities, which amounted to $312.6 million or 60 percent of total investment securities in 1970 and to $281.1 million or 40 percent of total investment securities in 1973.[8] These low-yield, tax-free securities were a good investment when the bank had taxable income, but made little sense when taxable income declined. Franklin's municipals were yielding an average of only 4 percent in 1974, while the bank's average cost of money was 7.5 percent.[9]

TABLE 3.2   Bank (and National Ranking on June 30, 1975) Ratio of Classified Loans to Total Capital (Percent)

	1974	1973
Marine Midland-New York (18)	128.1	21.5
Union Bank, Los Angeles (22)	99.7	43.0
Chemical Bank, New York (5)	84.3	25.7
Manufacturers Hanover Trust, New York (4)	65.7	23.4
United California Bank, Los Angeles (14)	60.1	32.8
Bank of New York (45)	51.6	8.7
Irving Trust Co., New York (13)	48.5	21.6
Girard Trust Bank, Philadelphia (31)	47.9	19.7
Marine Midland-Western, Buffalo (53)	46.7	37.5
State Street Bank & Trust Co., Boston (74)	45.5	21.1
Manufacturers & Traders Trust Co., Buffalo (73)	45.3	37.8
Bankers Trust Co., New York (7)	28.1	21.5
Trust Company of Georgia, Atlanta (68)	26.9	11.0
Fidelity Bank, Philadelphia (42)	21.9	23.8
Connecticut Bank & Trust Co., Hartford (58)	17.3	18.4
Union Commerce Bank, Cleveland (78)	17.1	9.9
Harris Trust & Savings Bank, Chicago (24)	15.6	6.4
Morgan Guaranty Trust Co., New York (6)	12.1	13.1
Cleveland Trust Co. (25)	8.4	4.1
Detroit Bank & Trust Co. (32)	8.2	4.9
Northern Trust Co., Chicago (27)	5.0	9.1

SOURCE: Michael C. Jensen, "Loans Assessed at Charter Banks—Fed Report Says Portfolio of 1974 Lending Showed Sharp Deterioration," *New York Times*, January 26, 1976; reprinted in U.S., Congress, Senate, *Problem Banks. Hearing before the Committee on Banking, Housing and Urban Affairs*, 94th Cong., 2d sess., 1976, p. 320.

Another problem was Franklin's bond trading account. In late 1973, believing that interest rates would fall and thus that the price of bonds would rise, President Luftig decided to seek a profit by purchasing bonds.[10] As we have seen, instead of sinking interest rates soared and the value of the bank's bond trading portfolio declined.

By the 1970s Franklin was caught in a profit squeeze. The spread of returns on earning assets declined from 2.6 percent in 1971 to 1.00 percent in 1973. At one point in 1974, the yield on loans was less than the bank's costs of acquiring liabilities to cover them. Net income declined from $21,636,000 in 1970 to $17,488,000 in 1971, to $13,228,000 in 1972, to $12,815,000 in 1973. Net income as a percentage of total assets declined from 0.9 in 1970 to 0.3 in 1973. At the same time, other money market banks' net income as a percentage of total assets rose from 0.7 to 0.8.[11]

While many of Franklin National Bank's problems were domestic in origin, it was an international activity, foreign exchange trading, that triggered the loss of confidence in Franklin which eventually led to the bank's demise.

Foreign Exchange

As we have seen, one of the reasons for Franklin's heavy foreign exchange trading was its search for profits to compensate for losses in other divisions. Ironically, however, losses in foreign exchange trading pushed the bank over the brink into disaster.

While exchange trading under floating exchange rates offered the enticement of large profits, it also entailed the risk of significant losses. In the period from March 1973, when the system of generalized floating began, until May 1974, when the Franklin crisis erupted, exchange markets fluctuated significantly and rapidly (see fig. 3.1). Differing balance of payments trends, interest rate developments, capital flows, and inflation rates created exchange rate expectations and speculative pressures which were not moderated by coordinated governmental intervention.

As a result there frequently were significant day-to-day and week-

Figure 3.1. Exchanges, Rates and International Liquidity.

Spot Exchange Rates against the U.S. Dollar
January 1973–June 1975 (May 1970 = 100)

Source: International Monetary Fund, *Annual Report, 1975*, p. 25.

to-week movements in exchange rates. In June and July 1973, for example, sharp speculative pressure led some European currencies to appreciate against the dollar by as much as 4 percent on a single day, and by as much as 10 percent in little more than a week. During one week in early January 1974, the dollar appreciated by over 6 percent against certain European currencies, only to depreciate quite rapidly thereafter.[12]

Longer-term swings were equally volatile. Not only did exchange rates move significantly and rapidly over the period of a few months, they also reversed direction rapidly and dramatically. The case most important for Franklin National Bank was that of the dollar. After experiencing a precipitous decline of 9 to 18 percent against major currencies from May to July 1973, the dollar rose dramatically from

October to January, reflecting the market's judgment that the United States was better able to deal with the disruptive effects of the oil crisis than the other developed countries. From October 1973 to January 1974 the dollar gained 14 percent against continental European currencies and 10 percent against the pound sterling and the yen. In the early weeks of January—just as Franklin National traders began speculating heavily on the dollar—the U.S. currency looked strong, but toward the end of the month, it began a serious decline. The termination of U.S. capital controls and the easing of restraints on capital inflows abroad led to a reversal in the exchange markets. From January to May 1974 the dollar depreciated vis-à-vis major currencies, losing between 9 and 11 percent in relation to the six currencies in the European "snake" (the German mark, the Dutch guilder, the Belgian franc, the Danish and Norwegian krone, and the Swedish krona). Ironically, on May 14, just as Franklin's troubles erupted, the announcement of the German, Swiss, and American central banks that they would intervene to counter excessive speculation against the dollar and the relative increase in short-term interest rates in the United States led to yet another reversal, the rise of the dollar, and the recovery of most of the losses the dollar had suffered earlier in the year.[13]

It was in this volatile and unfamiliar environment that Franklin's foreign exchange traders, inexperienced in dealing with the new world of floats and the unpredictable exchange market behavior, began to speculate heavily. For them, as for traders in many other banks whose careers are built on foreign exchange speculation, the floating rates were an irresistible temptation. As we shall see, floating rates were also an irresistible temptation for Franklin's management which pressed for trading as a source of profits and a way to balance other losses. In January 1973 Franklin's traders, expecting a continual rise in the dollar, began to take significant short positions in various currencies: they sold for future delivery more foreign currencies than they purchased in the expectation that the value of the currencies sold short would decline vis-à-vis the dollar before the delivery date and that Franklin would purchase the currencies for less than the sale price and make a substantial profit. On December 11, 1972, Franklin had a net short position of $5.2 million; by November 14, 1973, the bank had a net short position of $62.6 million; and by May 14, 1974, its net short position was $232.6 million.[14]

Much of this enormous speculation was unauthorized by senior bank management. Some of Franklin's traders were able to engage in unauthorized trading because of the cooperation and encouragement of two high level officials (Peter Shaddick, executive vice chairman and head of the international division, and Carlo Bordoni, director of Franklin New York Corporation) and because of inadequate controls on the trading operation.

Peter Shaddick had managed foreign exchange trading for Continental Illinois Bank and for Bank of Montreal before coming to Franklin. According to Shaddick, Sindona hired him in late 1972, offering, in addition to a five-year contract at $100,000 per year, a $100,000 interest-free loan, which Sindona placed in a secret Swiss bank account. Sindona also provided Shaddick with a personal foreign exchange trading account, which Sindona guaranteed would incur no losses and which, in fact, made a profit of $476,000. This was deposited in the same Swiss bank account. According to Shaddick when he was hired, Sindona told him that one of his main functions would be to develop aggressive foreign exchange activity at the bank in order to generate profits. Shaddick came to Franklin in January 1973 and from that moment the bank began to engage heavily in foreign exchange speculation.

Bordoni, a close associate of Sindona, also had a long background in foreign exchange, albeit a less distinguished one than Peter Shaddick. Bordoni had been asked to resign as a foreign exchange trader at an Italian bank, Monte dei Paschi, because of speculation and because he concealed some of his trading from his employers. He was later asked to leave the Milan branch of First National City Bank after being accused of speculating in foreign exchange and falsely inflating the profits of his branch. After leaving First National City Bordoni went to work for various Sindona entities, always closely involved in foreign exchange activities. He was frequently in touch with Shaddick and Franklin's head foreign exchange trader, Andrew Garofalo, advising them on market conditions and, as we shall see, lending them a hand when necessary.[15]

The rapid expansion of Franklin's foreign exchange trading was not accompanied by an improvement in bank controls on foreign exchange operations. Some Franklin officials were not sensitive to the need for stringent and sophisticated systems of command and control to minimize the increased risks in foreign exchange trading, while others, like Shaddick it seems, did not want them.

Poor controls on foreign exchange trading were not a new problem at Franklin. The weakness of controls had been recognized before the era of the float by examiners from the Office of the Comptroller of the Currency. The Federal examiner assigned to the international division in the March 6, 1972, examination reported that the division was in a state of "chaos" and that internal controls were virtually nonexistent. The division had no aggregate limits to control trading; because forward contracts were not prenumbered or controlled, it was possible for such contracts to remain unrecorded until they were executed; there were no minimum accounting procedures or formalized records. As a result the examiner found unrecorded contracts, mispostings, and other errors which made position records of traders inaccurate.[16]

The examiner-in-charge and the Comptroller's Director of International Operations met with Franklin officers, requested corrective action, and were assured that appropriate changes would be instituted. Franklin's management then commissioned a management consulting firm to create a program to improve controls. Informed by letter—but not by on-site inspection—of the new system, the Comptroller's office reported that it was satisfied.

In December 1972 an on-site examination noted substantial improvements in procedures but also found control deficiencies such as the absence of trading limits. The bank then instituted limits. For example, in August and November 1973, George A. Hermann of the international division established foreign exchange position limits for traders and ordered that they be "strictly maintained."[17] Any excess was to be referred to Hermann or Peter Shaddick for approval. The November 1973 examination report found no significant control problems in foreign exchange operations, although it noted the risks of Franklin's large open positions.[18] What the report did not reveal, however, was that Shaddick had established an audit division for foreign exchange and international banking which reported exclusively to him.[19]

In fact, since January 1973, which was when Shaddick joined the bank, some of Franklin's foreign exchange traders had been entering into unauthorized futures contracts and had, with the cooperation of processing clerks in the foreign exchange department and of Shaddick and Bordoni, exceeded limits set by senior management. Traders entered into contracts without actually filling in one of the prenumbered contracts which all traders were to complete and submit to processing clerks in the foreign exchange department. Such contracts, literally hidden in drawers, would have been discovered quickly had it not been for the cooperation of certain clerks in the processing department who were in charge of filling out and signing confirmation forms to be sent to the other party to the contract. The clerks simply filled out confirmation forms without a written contract. The deception might also have been uncovered in the daily position sheets submitted to George Hermann and Peter Shaddick. However, traders and clerks again cooperated to submit false position sheets.[20] Shaddick also frequently encouraged the head trader Garofalo to be "less conservative" in his monthly re-evaluations of Franklin's foreign exchange, that is, to inflate the value of the book.[21]

Had Franklin's traders gambled successfully, the bank might have made substantial profits. But from the beginning they gambled and lost (see table 3.3). So great were the trading losses that Franklin's traders and clerks, as well as Shaddick and Bordoni, desperately tried to conceal them. One method of concealing losses was to enter into numerous foreign exchange contracts with two Sindona-owned banks—Banca Unione of Milan and Amincor Bank, A.G., of Zurich—which appeared profitable for Franklin but which were

TABLE 3.3 Franklin National Bank Reported and Actual Foreign Exchange Profit/(Losses)

Date	Foreign Exchange Profit/(Losses)	
	As Stated	Correct
1/73	$ 69,000	$ (436,000)
2/73	83,000	(703,000)
3/73	(104,000)	(420,000)
4/73	144,000	693,000
5/73	241,000	(3,643,000)
6/73	363,000	(791,000)
7/73	193,000	193,000
8/73	732,000	3,801,000
9/73	1,519,000	(244,000)
10/73	(336,000)	172,000
11/73	3,848,000	7,165,000
12/73	423,000	593,000
1/74	3,822,000	5,688,000
2/74	(2,469,000)	(16,936,000)
3/74	1,024,000	(19,390,000)

SOURCE: USDC, Southern District, Indictment S. 75 Cr. 948, *U.S. v. Carlo Bordoni, Peter R. Shaddick, Andrew Garofalo, Arthur Slutzky, Donald Emrich, Martin Keroes, Michael Romersa and Paul Sabatella.*

actually fictitious. At the end of an unprofitable quarter, Franklin would buy or sell currencies from Banca Unione or Amincor Bank at nonmarket, favorable rates, enabling Franklin's foreign exchange department to show a profit in its quarterly report. After submitting profit reports, the foreign exchange department would engage in a transaction reversing its purchase from or sale to Unione or Amincor at the same rate.

Another method of concealment was the actual transfer of money from Sindona banks to Franklin. This was made possible by false foreign exchange transactions arranged by Shaddick and Bordoni. In September 1973, during a quarter when Franklin suffered actual foreign exchange losses of $4.8 million, the foreign exchange department entered into contracts with Amincor at nonmarket rates favorable to Franklin. The effect of these transactions was the gift or loan to Franklin of $2 million, which was shown as an operating profit in the foreign exchange income account of the bank.[22] According to testimony by Shaddick, he arranged this transaction through Bordoni at the request of Michele Sindona.

In March 1974 similar nonmarket transactions arranged by Shaddick and Bordoni were carried out between Franklin on the one hand and Amincor and Banca Unione on the other. These transactions created another fictitious $2 million profit for Franklin. Chairman Gleason has been convicted of involvement in the March transaction. According to Shaddick's testimony at Gleason's trial, Franklin's Chairman asked Shaddick to arrange for a profit in foreign exchange to conceal losses incurred not only in foreign exchange but also in the bank generally. By that time Franklin's problems were so serious that Gleason, President Luftig, and Senior Vice President J. Michael Carter were also desperately trying to conceal losses. Luftig and Carter have been convicted of falsely valuing securities to cover losses in the bank's bond trading department.[23]

A final way of concealing losses was by falsifying profit and loss reports. From January to May 1974, in a quarter in which the bank lost over $30 million in foreign exchange trading, the foreign exchange traders inserted false rates in the bank's profit and loss sheets in order to disguise these massive losses (see table 3.3). Clerks in the processing and auditing departments relied on the false rates and did not check them against actual market rates. In the few cases when auditors noted a discrepancy and questioned traders, they were told not to worry.[24]

Franklin's excessive foreign exchange trading was a crucial element in the collapse of confidence in the bank. In 1973 major American and foreign banks became increasingly concerned about Franklin's high levels of trading, and many refused to enter into or limited significantly their forward foreign exchange contracts with Franklin. As early as May 1973, for example, Morgan Guaranty Trust Company became reluctant to do forward foreign exchange contracts with Franklin because of what Morgan saw as Franklin's excessive trading and its taking unprofitable positions. By the fall of that year Morgan and many other banks were so concerned about the extent of Franklin's speculation that they would no longer enter into forward foreign exchange transactions with Franklin. In some instances banks refused even spot contracts with Franklin. By the fall of 1973, for example, the Deutsche Bank of Frankfurt would no longer clear for Franklin and the Commerzbank of Frankfurt was considering refusing to deal with Franklin. Other European banks were questioning Franklin's credit worthiness.[25]

In November 1973 Morgan officials met with Shaddick and then with Shaddick and Gleason to express concern about the extent of foreign exchange activity.[26] By November 1973, as was noted in chapter 2, Morgan officials were also sufficiently concerned to take the unusual step of reporting declining market confidence in Franklin to officers of the Federal Reserve Bank of New York. In a meeting with the president and high-level officers of the Reserve Bank, two Morgan officers revealed the concern about Franklin developing in foreign exchange markets. They also noted their fear that reluctance to deal with Franklin in foreign exchange might spill over into reluctance by banks to lend Eurodollars to Franklin, a critical problem for a bank as dependent on Eurodollars as Franklin.[27]

News of Franklin's foreign exchange problems came at a time when the Federal Reserve Bank of New York was considering other potential problems of market confidence in Franklin. The Reserve Bank was evaluating the application of Franklin New York Corporation to acquire Talcott National Corporation, a large factoring company which had been acquired by Michele Sindona through Fasco International and which Franklin New York Corporation proposed to buy from Sindona (see above, chap. 2, "The Talcott Acquisition"). In preparing a report for the Board of Governors of the Federal Reserve System, which would make the decision to approve or deny the Talcott acquisition, Reserve Bank officials had become concerned about the overall financial and managerial strength of Franklin National Bank[28] and especially about its lack of liquidity and inadequate capital.

As noted earlier, after the meeting with Morgan officers, the

Reserve Bank officers agreed that the situation was potentially explosive and that further investigation was necessary. A review of Franklin's foreign exchange trading as then known by the Office of the Comptroller of the Currency was conducted. According to the Comptroller's figures, Franklin had a total book of $2.1 billion and net oversold position of $60 million.

David Bodner of the Reserve Bank met with examiners of the Office of the Comptroller, who confirmed that Franklin was trading for its own account and that figures suggested Franklin was being excluded from the forward and forced into the spot market. The examiners also told Bodner that, while they had no standards for measuring the appropriate size of open positions, they were disturbed by Franklin's position. Nonetheless, Bodner concluded that "leaving aside the question of Franklin's low earnings and weak capital position" the total volume of Franklin's book did not seem excessive, that foreign exchange speculation was common practice among major banks, and that the size of Franklin's open position relative to the size of the bank did not seem alarming.[29] Bodner also met with Peter Shaddick and other Franklin officers. According to Bodner:

Shaddick said that their foreign exchange business was almost entirely for their own account and represented a conscious decision of the management to attempt to bolster their weak earning's [sic] position and take advantage of tax loss carry forwards through trading in exchange. The exchange operations had in fact been quite profitable and he expected that their current positions would continue to generate profits for the bank. He did not regard their trading activity as excessive in relation to the size of the bank.[30]

Bodner told Shaddick that he agreed that Franklin's trading position insofar as it had been revealed to him did not seem excessive, but he pointed out that the real issue was whether the volume was excessive in relation to the willingness of other banks to deal with Franklin. Bodner went on to impress upon Shaddick "our concern that the situation was a potentially explosive one and that they ought seriously to consider prompt action to rectify it." Bodner reported that he "left with the feeling that they recognized the nature of the problem that appeared to be facing them and would attempt to take them [sic] in hand soon."[31]

The way Franklin took the situation in hand was to step up speculation. Between January and May 1974 foreign exchange trading, much of it concealed, soared. From November 14, 1973, to May 14, 1974, Franklin's net short position exploded from $62,615,000 to $232,584,000.[32] It was as if Shaddick and Franklin's traders, in a last and desperate attempt to reverse their losses and the growing concern of the market, engaged in a massive gamble. That gamble was on the dollar.

In January 1974 all signs seemed to point to the strengthening of the dollar and the decline of other major currencies. The dramatic rise in oil prices by OPEC had occurred in December 1973. Because of the relative independence of the United States from oil imports and the belief that oil exporters would invest their petrodollars in the United States, those involved in exchange markets believed that the United States' balance of payments would be less affected by the price rise than would the balance of payments of most industrial countries. Franklin's traders, following this logic, developed massive short positions in sterling, Swiss francs, French francs, lire, and guilders.

At first, it looked as if they had gambled correctly. The French withdrew from the European "snake" and the franc fell 5 percent. Pressure on the French franc spilled over into pressure on the lira, which suffered a similar decline. The dollar continued strong. Then exchange markets reversed themselves. The easing of capital controls in the United States and several continental European states made it more likely that countries would be able to finance their payments deficits; short-term and long-term capital flows suggested that the other industrial countries would not suffer as much as predicted from payments deficits; and the United States began to ease its monetary policy, which was incorrectly seen as a future trend. From January to May the dollar depreciated against the world's major currencies.[33] Franklin built up staggering losses, over $33 million for the first quarter of 1974. It was at this time that traders began to enter false reports on profit and loss sheets. But they could no longer conceal their losses.

In early May the Franklin crisis erupted. On May 1 a first blow was dealt to the bank when the Board of Governors of the Federal Reserve System denied Franklin New York Corporation's request to acquire Talcott National Corporation.[34]

The denial could hardly have come as a surprise to Franklin officers. Beginning with the initial discussions about the proposed merger in May 1973, officials of the Federal Reserve Bank of New York and the Board of Governors signalled their concern about the bank's earnings and capital to Franklin officers. Franklin had revised the merger plan a number of times in an effort to satisfy Federal Reserve officials. Initially Franklin's plan was to pay Sindona $30 million in cash for his Talcott shares and to exchange other Talcott shares for Franklin stock. After a number of revisions the plan emerged to offer Sindona Franklin New York Corporation stock, to increase the capital of the bank by borrowing $35 million from another bank and by converting a $30 million debt of the Franklin Bank to Franklin New York Corporation into equity in the bank, and eventually to increase the capital of the holding company through a public stock offering. The latter was deemed impossible in 1973 and 1974 because of depressed stock prices. Despite these changes Federal Reserve officials informed Franklin officers in December and April that the Board might reject the proposal and that Franklin officers might be wise to avoid a denial and the resultant public reaction by withdrawing the proposal. This they refused to do.[35]

The official reason for the Board's denial was the problem status of the bank. The Board noted that the merger would place excessive demands on Franklin's already weak internal structure. Franklin National Bank, the Board said,

has experienced an earnings record in recent years below the industry average, and has recently made a substantial shift in management policies designed to improve performance significantly. As changes in the institution's internal structure and asset composition are pursued, it is the Board's view that the acquisition of Talcott would be a complicating and diversionary factor. As the Board has previously stated on a number of occasions, a bank holding company should be a source of financial and managerial strength for its subsidiary banks. The Board finds that this proposal may constitute an undue claim on Applicant's managerial and financial resources and concludes that this represents an adverse effect.[36]

According to Andrew Brimmer, who was at the time a member of the Board, it, too, was concerned about the growing influence of Michele Sindona in the American financial system, an influence which would have increased under the terms of the proposed Talcott acquisition.[37]

The Talcott decision made Franklin's troubles public and led to a withdrawal of deposits by informed and knowledgeable domestic money market participants. The Board had anticipated such a reaction but apparently felt the bank could withstand it.[38]

On Friday, May 3, however, there began a series of events which Franklin could not withstand. On that day Franklin's London branch, which had been executing foreign exchange operations at the direction of New York, notified headquarters that the National Westminster Bank had objected to the volume of Franklin's sterling clearings through National Westminster's account, which had averaged £40 million–£60 million per day during that week. An inquiry over the next few days revealed unauthorized and hidden foreign exchange transactions not only in sterling but also in other currencies, and the likelihood of significant foreign exchange losses. On Tuesday, May 7, Franklin informed the Comptroller and the Federal Reserve Bank of New York of potentially heavy but as yet undetermined foreign exchange losses.

Franklin officers had been meeting with officers of the Federal Reserve Bank of New York on a variety of problems—the problems growing out of the Talcott decision, their concern about low earnings and an anticipated omission of a dividend, and their anticipated need to use the discount window. Now Franklin officers expressed concern that the revelation of foreign exchange losses would result in an unwillingness of banks to sell Franklin Federal funds, on which, as has been noted, Franklin had become heavily dependent. In the months preceding the May revelation of foreign exchange losses, Franklin had found it increasingly difficult to purchase its daily Federal funds needs, forcing President Luftig to spend a good part of his time urging other banks to deal with Franklin.[39] Yet Luftig had managed to come up with the needed money. Officers now feared he would no longer be able to purchase sufficient funds. Indeed, between May 3 and May 8 Federal funds sold to Franklin declined from $520 million to $334 million (see table 3.1). Franklin officers told Reserve Bank officers that they anticipated a need to borrow $100 million–$200 million for three to four weeks. On May 8 Franklin borrowed $110 million from the Federal Reserve Bank of New York (table 3.1). Franklin's May 7 estimates of the bank's borrowing needs proved to be far too low.

Rumors of Franklin's foreign exchange losses began to fly. The price of Franklin New York Corporation common stock fell from 16½ on April 30 to 9½ on May 10; preferred stock dropped from 25 on April 30 to 12 on May 10.[40] On Friday, May 10, the Securities and Exchange Commission informed Franklin that it would suspend trading immediately if the bank did not issue a statement of its financial condition.

SEC pressure led Franklin's management to announce that same day that it would recommend that the Board of Directors vote not to pay the regular quarterly dividend. The bank also announced that it had requested the SEC to suspend trading in Franklin New York Corporation shares until the Board of Franklin could review and recalculate first-quarter earnings.[41] It was the first time since the Depression that a major American bank had missed a dividend.

The announcement of foreign exchange losses and the resultant suspension of dividends destroyed market confidence in Franklin National Bank. As the Federal Reserve Bank of New York described the situation:

By the close of business on Friday, Franklin National faced the prospect that its own dividend announcement, combined with the news of foreign exchange losses and intensified market rumors about the bank's condition would result during the next week in a virtual drying-up of money market sources of funds and a very real possibility of a run on the bank.[42]

It was clear to bank officers, regulators, and the market that unless something were done on that weekend, Franklin would face a crippling runoff of deposits and would collapse soon after its doors opened on Monday, May 13.

Eurodollar Problems

Although Franklin National Bank's foreign exchange problems were its most visible international problem, the bank's Eurodollar operations proved to be equally life-threatening. By 1973 Eurodollar activities had become an important part of Franklin's total activity. By that year foreign branch loans, consisting primarily of participations in Eurodollar syndications, accounted for 19.8 percent of the bank's total loans.

These Eurodollar loans were among the most attractive of Franklin's assets. A study of the foreign portfolio of Franklin's London and Nassau branches done by an investment banking firm in June 1974 showed a total of $582,786,269 in foreign loans as of April 30, 1974.[43] Of this total only $6,040,000 were fixed interest loans, while the rest were floating rate loans based on a spread over the London Interbank Offered Rate (LIBOR). Thus, at a time of rapidly rising interest rates, Franklin was somewhat protected against such increase.

Rates on these loans approximated then-current market rates. Fixed rate loans ranged from 7 to 12 percent, floating rates from ⅜ to 2¼ percent over LIBOR.[44] In 1973–74 LIBOR ranged from a low of 6 percent to a high of almost 14 percent in August 1974,[45] making Eurodollar loans among the highest yielding in Franklin's portfolio. Franklin was also protected against currency fluctuations. According to FDIC figures for international loans outstanding on October 8, 1974, Franklin had a total portfolio of almost $513 million, of which over $476 million was denominated in dollars.[46]

Franklin's borrowers were also credit worthy. Most loans were to governmental or semi-governmental institutions. There were few loans to those underdeveloped countries which might have little capacity to repay such loans, and there was a good distribution of loans. Franklin had concentrations of loans to Italy, Mexico, Brazil, and Greece, but these concentrations represented relatively small percentages of total loans.[47] Finally, time has proved the strength of the portfolio. In managing Franklin's international loan portfolio since 1974, the FDIC has found it excellent from a credit stand-point. Borrowers have regularly and fully paid interest and amortization on Franklin's loans.[48]

Despite the strength and high yield of the foreign branch assets, Franklin's Euromarket activities proved to be a drain on the bank's earnings. Although Franklin was earning a high rate of return on the assets of its Nassau and London branches, it was also paying a high rate of interest on funds used to finance those assets. Virtually all of Franklin's Eurodollar loans were financed by the purchase of dollars in the interbank market at high interest rates. Franklin's gross yield, in effect, was its spread over LIBOR. That spread was increasingly narrowed as competition grew in the London interbank market. At the end of 1973 the typical spread for prime borrowers ranged from ⅝ to ¾ of one percent over LIBOR. At the end of the first half of 1974 the spread had narrowed to ⅜ to ½ of one percent over the interbank rate.[49]

Banks which had long been active in Euromarkets did not suffer seriously from the narrowing of rates. These institutions had in their portfolios more profitable loans made in earlier periods. Furthermore, many were able to act as lead banks and thereby to earn a management fee above and beyond the interest rate on loans. Thus they were able to increase their actual earnings from loans in the unfavorable market of 1973–74. Franklin, however, was building a portfolio at a time of narrow spreads and, as we have seen, was unable to act as lead bank in Eurodollar syndications. Thus, its earnings were limited to the narrow spread over LIBOR. In addition, because floating rates were recalculated twice a year, Franklin was not protected against the rapid rise of short-term rates on money it borrowed to fund these loans. As rates soared in 1973–74, Franklin was at some points paying more for deposits than it was earning.

Adding insult to injury, as confidence in Franklin weakened in late 1973 following concerns about foreign exchange trading, Franklin was forced to pay a premium over LIBOR for its Eurodollar borrowings. By May 1, 1974, an outside management consultant hired by Franklin to evaluate the bank's overall position warned the president of Franklin that the money spread for London had become a major threat to the bank as a whole.[50] And, finally, Franklin was facing high administrative costs in opening its London branch. According to one estimate, the London branch had accumulated losses of $1.2 million on its loan operations by mid-1974.[51]

Even more vital was the transformation problem: Franklin had relatively long-term loans financed with extremely short-term money. The average maturity of Franklin's foreign branch loans was a long five and a half years. A package of $392 million of Franklin's international loans offered for sale by the FDIC in June 1975 reflected the maturity structure of the entire portfolio: 20.7 percent matured in 1977; 34.3 percent matured in 1978–80; 44.2 percent in 1981–86; and 0.08 percent in 1987–91.[52] These term loans were entirely financed by short-term, uninsured borrowing ranging from overnight Euromarket placements to 30- to 90-day certificates of deposit.[53] In the event of a loss of confidence in Franklin such deposits could be withdrawn as they matured.

Officials of Morgan Guaranty Trust Company expressed the fear of just such a withdrawal during their visit to the Federal Reserve Bank of New York in November 1973. One of their major concerns was that the reluctance of banks to deal with Franklin in foreign exchange might spill over into a reluctance to lend Eurodollars to Franklin.[54] According to David Bodner of the Reserve Bank, Peter Shaddick admitted in November that,

the situation, while merely uncomfortable at the moment, was potentially explosive since there was a risk that banks which now refuse to deal with them on forward contracts could begin to close their Eurodollar lines and even their Federal funds lines to Franklin. Since Franklin uses about $1.2 billion in Eurodollars to fund its London branch operations, a sharp cutback on its ability to get such funds could have serious repercussions on the bank.[55]

The possibility of a Eurodollar runoff was particularly acute in late 1973 and early 1974. World economic conditions were taking a turn for the worse and tight monetary conditions in particular were

TABLE 3.4   Franklin National Bank Funds Flow: May 8, 1974 through October 7, 1974 ($ million)

Outflows: Decreases in Liabilities and Capital	
Federal funds	$ 535
Repurchase agreements	175
Money market CDs	411
Time savings deposits of individuals, partnerships, and corporations	128
Other domestic time deposits	108
Domestic demand deposits	741
Foreign branch deposits	679
Foreign exchange transactions	23
Capital funds[a]	22
Total outflows	$2,822
Inflows: Reductions in Assets	
Loans	$ 227
Investments	113
Foreign branch investments	198
Cash	561
Total inflows	$1,099
Net outflow	$1,723

SOURCE: Information submitted by Chairman Burns for the record of the hearing of the Joint Economic Committee on October 10, 1974, in response to additional questions asked by Representative Reuss in U.S. House, Committee on Banking Currency and Housing, *An Act to Lower Interest Rates and Allocate Credit,* Hearings Before the Subcommittee on Domestic Monetary Policy, 94th Cong., 1st sess., February 4, 5 & 6, 1975, p. 218.
[a]Decrease caused by operating losses and realized losses on securities, loans, and foreign exchange transactions.

putting a squeeze on banks (see chapter 4). Should Franklin lose access to the Eurodollar market, it would be forced to fall back on the American domestic market, where funds were simply not available.

Furthermore, since the failure of United States National Bank of San Diego in October 1973, foreign banks had become acutely sensitive to their vulnerability to the failure of an American bank and more likely to withdraw Eurodollar placements. U.S. National had been declared insolvent and merged with Crocker National Bank as a result of fraudulent activities by its owner, C. Arnholt Smith. Smith had funded some of his illegal activities with letters of credit which were purchased by foreign banks. After the merger Crocker chose not to assume responsibility for the letters of credit, and the FDIC, as receiver of assets not claimed by Crocker, delayed honoring the letters until it could determine whether European suppliers had been aware of the fraud. The refusal of the FDIC automatically to honor the letters of credit was seen by foreign banks as an abdication of responsibility by the United States government and it infuriated and embarrassed foreign bank international departments and top management. As a result these institutions became particularly cautious about dealing with any American bank with a hint of problems.

The worst fears of a runoff of Eurodollar deposits from Franklin National Bank were realized after the announcement of foreign exchange losses. Table 3.4 reveals the type of outflows from Franklin from the onset of the crisis on May 8 to the demise of the bank on October 8. The loss of foreign branch deposits was the second largest outflow from Franklin, accounting for one-fourth of total losses. When broken down by location of outflow, as in table 3.5, foreign branch losses become the largest single outflow. This hemorrhage of Eurodollar deposits was a major cause of the insolvency of Franklin National Bank.

TABLE 3.5   Franklin National Bank Deposit Outflows from May 8, 1974 to October 7, 1974 ($ million)

Location	Demand	Savings	CD and Other Time	Total
Domestic branch	$223	$126	$ 17	$ 366
New York corporate division	46	—	48	94
National division	52	—	14	66
Centralized time deposits (including large and small CDs and municipal time deposits)	—	—	426	426
International division	24	—	14	38
Foreign branch	12	—	667	679
Trust, junior savings	—	2	—	2
Official checks, etc.	390	—	—	390
Total	$747	$128	$1,186	$2,061

SOURCE: Information submitted by Chairman Burns for the record of the hearing of the Joint Economic Committee on October 10, 1974, in response to additional questions asked by Representative Reuss in *An Act to Lower Interest Rates and Allocate Credit*, p. 228.

The Sindona Empire

When Fasco International purchased 21.6 percent of Franklin New York Corporation in 1972, Franklin National Bank became part of Michele Sindona's vast and complex international empire (fig. 2.1). That empire, organized through Fasco A.G., Sindona's Lichtenstein holding company, had three central components. Sindona, as we have seen, controlled several European banks. He also controlled an international real estate, construction, and financial empire based on Società Generale Immobiliare, the giant Italian holding company. Sindona was also developing his American holdings, the most important of which were Franklin National Bank and Talcott National Corporation.

The international spread of his empire enabled Sindona and his associates to engage in transactions which contributed to the demise of Franklin National Bank. Thus the integration of Franklin into the Sindona empire had an important impact on the viability of that bank. The Sindona connection was not the major cause of Franklin's demise, but it did accentuate other problems.

Sindona had an important impact on Franklin's foreign exchange operations. His influence on the policy of increasing trading has already been discussed. By bringing in his own people, particularly Shaddick and Bordoni, Sindona apparently was able to encourage the growth of trading. Sindona and Bordoni have been indicted on criminal charges of having bribed Shaddick "for the purpose of corruptly influencing his conduct at the bank" and of having "encouraged unauthorized speculation in the trading of foreign currencies at the Franklin National Bank."[56]

Sindona's international network of banks also enabled Shaddick, Bordoni, and Franklin's traders to engage in transactions to conceal foreign exchange losses. Sindona has been indicted on criminal charges and has been accused by the Securities and Exchange Commission in a civil action of active participation in these fraudulent schemes. According to the criminal indictment, Sindona and Bordoni were involved in the false foreign exchange transactions which were used to conceal Franklin's massive foreign exchange losses. Sindona's control of Banca Unione and Amincor Bank made possible the

fictitious foreign exchange transactions used to disguise losses in
the bank's quarterly reports and the actual transfer of $2 million
from Amincor to Franklin in September 1973 and from Unione
and Amincor in March 1974, which were used to conceal foreign
exchange losses.[57] Without access to these foreign sources of
funds, Franklin's excessive trading might have been uncovered
much earlier, before it so thoroughly damaged the bank.

Sindona has also been accused in a criminal indictment and
in testimony by Bordoni of looting Franklin of $15 million.
According to these accusations, Sindona and Bordoni arranged for
Franklin to make a time deposit of $15 million in Interbanca, Banca
per Finanziamenti a Medio e Lungo Termine, of Milan. Banca
Privata Finanziaria, a Sindona bank, owned 2.5 percent of
Interbanca, and Sindona was a member of Interbanca's board of
directors. According to the indictment and Bordoni's own testimony,
Bordoni, on behalf of Sindona, then bribed the general manager
of Interbanca $105,000 to transfer the money to Amincor which
in turn transferred it to Banca Unione.[58]

There apparently were other instances of such looting in
Sindona's empire which involved Franklin National Bank. Ac-
cording to the criminal indictments and to testimony by Bordoni,
Sindona and Bordoni took $18 million from the general funds of
Banca Unione and $22 million from Banca Privata Finanziaria to buy
shares of Franklin New York Corporation and Sindona took
$27.18 million from Banca Unione to acquire Talcott National. These
transactions resembled the Franklin-Interbanca arrangement.
Banca Unione and Banca Privata Finanziaria, it is charged,
deposited funds with Amincor and with Privat Kredit Bank of
Zurich which appeared on bank books as interbank time deposits.
Then, Amincor and Privat Kredit Bank under secret fiduciary agreements with Sindona transferred the funds to Fasco International in
New York.[59] Sindona has been charged by Italian authorities with
similar manipulations between his Italian banks and various
Sindona-owned companies.[60]

One other transaction in the Sindona empire involving Franklin
National Bank has come to light. According to an SEC complaint

which has been supported by testimony at the trial of Franklin officers, in December 1973 Shaddick, acting on Franklin's behalf and at Sindona's direction, committed $200 million to the underwriting of a $1 billion issue of eight-year notes of Consorzio de Credito per le Opere Publiche (Crediop), an Italian governmental body engaged in financing public works.[61] This commitment was made without the knowledge of Franklin's key senior executives and despite the fact that Federal lending regulations limited Franklin to the purchase of only $5 million. According to the complaint, Shaddick entered into the commitment only because Sindona gave him oral assurances that he would assume any unsold portion of Franklin's participation.

When Franklin was unable to sell $96.5 million of its participation, Sindona arranged for that portion to be assumed by Edilcentro International Limited, a merchant bank in Nassau. Edilcentro was owned by SGI and thus controlled by Sindona, and its managing director was Carlo Bordoni. At the time Edilcentro had total capital of only $1 million. It was able to assume the $96.5 million because, according to the SEC complaint, Sindona and Shaddick ordered Franklin's London branch to credit the account of Edilcentro with that amount, which it then used to pay for the Crediop participation.

When Franklin's senior officers learned of the transaction, they directed Shaddick and Sindona to find another institution to assume the Edilcentro purchase. This they did through a complex series of transactions worked out by Shaddick, Sindona, and Bordoni. According to the SEC, senior officers did not, however, report this illegal transaction. Although it might have had a serious market impact, the Edilcentro affair in fact did not become public and therefore did not lead to any deposit withdrawals.

In the end, however, Sindona's international network did have an important impact on market confidence in Franklin. Before the Franklin crisis, there had been questions and rumors about Sindona's empire and its practices. The Bank of England, as we have seen, delayed approval of Franklin's London branch after the Sindona acquisition in order to allow United States authorities to investigate his background. The Bank of Italy, as we have noted, knew of irregularities and possible criminal activities in Sindona banks. By 1973 these matters were in the hands of Italian courts. No specific allegations were ever made publicly, and Sindona remained a "murky" and "mysterious" Italian financier. His reputation did not help Franklin but neither did it do the bank significant damage.

However, when Franklin's foreign exchange losses were announced, the Sindona connection began to have a perverse effect on the Sindona empire and, in turn, on Franklin National Bank. The news of Franklin's foreign exchange losses, announced by the Italian press on May 14, 1974, caused a decline in the value of SGI stock and led to rumors that Edilcentro-Sviluppo, the SGI subsidiary of which Carlo Bordoni was managing director, was involved in Franklin's foreign exchange losses. The loss of confidence in Franklin also spilled over into a loss of confidence in and massive deposit withdrawals from Banca Privata Finanziaria and Banca Unione. By June, Sindona informed the Bank of Italy that his Italian banks were facing a liquidity crisis.[62]

At the request of the Bank of Italy, the Banca di Roma lent Sindona's banks the equivalent of $100 million for six months, renewable for a second six months. As collateral Banca di Roma took controlling interests in both Sindona banks and in SGI. It also demanded and obtained from Sindona effective management control of the banks and SGI. In August, according to a plan made in 1973 and approved by the Bank of Italy in July 1974, Banca Unione and Banca Privata Finanziaria merged to form Banca Privata Italiana, one of the largest banks in Italy.

Meanwhile, investigations by the Bank of Italy and by the new managers appointed by Banca di Roma uncovered serious irregularities in the Sindona banks, including foreign exchange losses and irregularities on loans to companies in the Sindona group. The banks' heavy losses, serious irregularities, and liquidity problems created by deposit withdrawals led the Bank of Italy to recommend to the Ministry of the Treasury that Banca Privata be put into forced liquidation. This was done on September 27, 1974. On October 14, just one week after Franklin was declared insolvent, the Court of Milan declared Banca Privata Italiana insolvent. Three big Italian banks including Banca di Roma held its assets in trust for liquidation. SGI was sold shortly thereafter. The Sindona empire had collapsed.[63]

The tribulations of the Sindona empire in Italy in turn had repercussions in the United States. Revelations about Banca Unione and Banca Privata Finanziaria contributed to the loss of confidence in Franklin. The Italian scandal also made a sale or merger of Franklin more difficult. The Sindona connection and in particular the Sindona "taint" on Franklin's foreign exchange book complicated efforts to resolve the Franklin crisis through merger or sale and, as we shall see, lengthened the time required to find a solution to the crisis.

4

THE FRANKLIN NATIONAL BANK
AND THE INTERNATIONAL
BANKING SYSTEM

THE IMPENDING FAILURE of Franklin National Bank posed
a major threat to the international banking system. As we have seen,
large banks have become highly interdependent because of the
development of the Eurocurrency interbank market and the dramatic
rise in interbank foreign exchange trading. The growing interrelationship of banks across national boundaries increasingly
resembles the connections of banks within national boundaries which
are closely knit by a domestic interbank network of deposits and
other money-market instruments. However, unlike the national
interbank market, which is stabilized by a regulatory and supervisory
system, the international interbank market is not subject to a
supervisory or regulatory "order." The Franklin crisis demonstrated
that the interdependence of the international banking system and its
independence from management makes the system a fragile one.

International Interbank Markets and Financial Stability

The interrelationship of banks through the Eurocurrency and foreign exchange markets makes them vulnerable to the failure of an important bank within the system (see chap. 2). The collapse of one bank—especially a collapse in a period of economic uncertainty or difficulty—can lead to a series of chain reactions which threaten other banks within the system.

The transmission of problems through the international banking system may be direct, from the troubled bank to other banks that: (1) have deposits in the troubled bank which may be lost or blocked; (2) are participants in loan syndications with the troubled bank which may be complicated by a failure; or (3) have foreign exchange contracts with the bank which may be blocked or on which there might be a default. The larger the bank and the more extensive its international operations, the more widespread the direct impact of its collapse. While such direct impacts are important, it is unlikely that any one bank in the system will have such a significant amount of business with a troubled bank that a collapse will seriously threaten its viability.

More important is the problem of confidence. The collapse of an important bank within the international banking system can lead to a loss of confidence in banks related or perceived to be related, in banks actually weaker or perceived by the market to be so, and in the markets themselves. A loss of confidence in banks can lead to their exclusion from Eurocurrency and foreign exchange markets or to discriminatory treatment in the form of higher rates in those markets. Because of the interrelationship of banks, a loss of confidence in and market reaction to one bank or group of banks can create a chain reaction which spreads to other banks. A loss of confidence in the international interbank markets can lead to a withdrawal of funds generally and a slowdown or even a paralysis of activity.

The problem of confidence and the threat of panic are more

severe in the international interbank market than in domestic financial markets. Domestic systems are supported by a regulatory and supervisory "order" which encourages confidence, while the international system does not benefit from such an "order." Governments, as we have seen, have developed a variety of tools to assure bank solvency and to manage bank failures and their consequences within national boundaries. In the United States the Office of the Comptroller of the Currency, the Federal Reserve System, and the Federal Deposit Insurance Corporation, as well as state banking agencies, regulate and supervise banks. One of the central functions of these authorities is to assure that banks remain solvent. Regulations such as entry restrictions and interest rate ceilings seek to assure solvency by restricting competition and increasing profits. Regulations such as capital and liquidity requirements, limits on loans to single borrowers, and limits on the types of activities in which banks may engage restrict the ability of banks to hold high-risk portfolios or to engage in high-risk activities. Other regulations seek to restrict misconduct by bank officers. All of these regulations are enforced through bank supervision and examination.[1]

The national order is designed for crisis management as well as for crisis prevention. In the United States, Federal Deposit Insurance deters a chain reaction of deposit withdrawals by insuring small depositors. From 1933 (when the FDIC was established) until 1974, deposits of up to $20,000 were insured; since 1974 the FDIC has insured deposits of up to $40,000. The Federal Reserve has the responsibility as lender of last resort to preserve the liquidity of the system and to prevent financial panic. This it can do through loans from its discount window or through open market operations to influence the overall liquidity of the system. Although important problems remain—e.g., banks' increasing reliance on large, uninsured deposits—national banking systems benefit from a wide array of crisis management tools.

The new international activities of banks are neither as closely regulated and supervised nor as subject to crisis management as national banking activities. In the United States, regulation of competition, risk assumption, and misconduct is far more limited in international banking. There are no interest-rate ceilings and few restrictions on international branching and the formation of international subsidiaries. There are fewer constraints on the types of activities in which banks are permitted to engage, no limits on loans to any one country, and no reserve requirements. Although regulations regarding misconduct apply internationally as well as domestically, it is far more difficult to enforce such rules when a bank is engaged in far-flung international operations and linked with foreign banking networks. Indeed, international operations in general are more difficult to supervise.

Supervision of international activities is often poorly exercised, as supervisory methods designed for national systems are not adapted to banking systems which know no borders. Supervision is also incomplete. Some countries do not even examine foreign branches and offshore subsidiaries of their banks. In other instances supervision is inhibited by host-country banking laws which prevent on-site inspection or disclosure of bank records.

And, as bankers and government authorities were to discover in 1974, international banking operations had none of the crisis-control mechanisms which had been so carefully developed for national banking systems. There was no deposit insurance on foreign branches, wholly owned subsidiaries, or consortium banks. There was no defined lender of last resort responsible for confining international banking panics. Neither were national policies and responsibilities clearly defined or clearly understood outside national borders. While central bankers had been meeting for decades to discuss monetary policy, bank regulators did not even know each other, much less understand regulatory policies of other states.

The absence of management in international banking accentuates the problem of a crisis of confidence. When actors in private markets feel there are no rules of the game and that authorities may be unable to find solutions to problems, they react conservatively to any threat to banking confidence: they withdraw their uninsured deposits from all but the largest and best-known institutions or they demand higher interest rates and restrict lending to institutions which they perceive as greater credit risks. Such a reaction was an important factor in Franklin's demise. It was also an important threat to other banks in the system which, after Franklin, suffered from a loss of confidence.

Before turning to the risks growing out of the failure of Franklin National Bank, we must examine the international economic environment in which the Franklin crisis occurred.

Banks and the Environment of 1974

When the Franklin National Bank crisis erupted in May 1974, the industrial world was in the midst of an inflationary spiral and on the verge of the "deepest and most pervasive recession" since World War II.[2] Inflation, which began in 1972 with rapid growth rates, pressure on productive capacity, and raw materials shortages, rose to new heights in 1974. In the United States inflation soared to 10.3 percent, in the United Kingdom to 12.6 percent, and in Japan to 20.9 percent.[3] The fourfold increase in the price of petroleum in late 1973 accentuated already soaring costs and at the same time depressed demand. In an effort to brake inflation, governments followed stringent monetary and fiscal policies. Anti-inflationary policies and the depressing effects of the increase in the price of petroleum led to a severe recession. The coordinated impact of disruptive forces plus the interdependence of national economies led to a simultaneous decline throughout the industrialized West and the less developed countries. In 1973 the industrial countries as a group had a 6.2 percent growth in real gross national product; in 1974 their real GNP actually declined by 0.2 percent.[4]

"Stagflation" seriously weakened many banks. Restrictive monetary policies led to record high interest rates which put severe pressure on banks (see fig. 4.1). In the United States the Federal Reserve raised the discount rate to an unprecedented 8 percent in April 1974. By the middle of that summer the Federal funds rate had skyrocketed to 13.5 percent, certificates of deposit to 12.9 percent, and the prime rate to 12.1 percent.[5] In the 1960s, as we have seen, banks came to depend heavily on short-term, interest-rate-sensitive funds—certificates of deposit, Federal funds, and Eurodollars—to finance long-term loans. As interest rates skyrocketed, banks were faced with narrower, and at times negative, margins. For Franklin the rise in short-term interest rates was a crucial blow.

The economic recession also led to a deterioration in the quality of banks' assets. As businesses suffered from the economic downturn, they became less credit worthy. Cities and political subdivisions—most dramatically New York City—which had benefited from banks' increasing involvement in municipal and other financing, suffered from the combined effects of inflation, recession, increased energy costs, and inadequate fiscal planning. Real estate

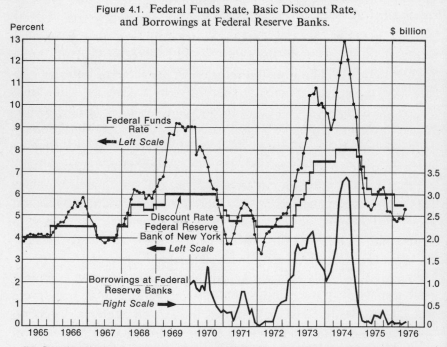

Figure 4.1. Federal Funds Rate, Basic Discount Rate, and Borrowings at Federal Reserve Banks.

Note: Data on borrowings include peak borrowings of approximately $250 million by Bank of the Commonwealth in late 1970 to early 1971 and peak borrowings of $1.7 billion by Franklin National Bank in the summer and early fall of 1974.
Source: Federal Reserve Bank of New York.

loans were particularly hard hit. Real estate investment trusts, which American banks had created in the 1960s, contributed to the down-turn by overstimulating construction and then suffered drastically from the recession. Real estate problems were also the source of the difficulties of a number of secondary British banks. Franklin's domestic customers, who were riskier to begin with, were frequently victims of the recession and an important cause of Franklin's growing loan losses.

As a result of their rapid expansion in the 1960s and early 1970s, American banks were more vulnerable to the rise in interest rates and decline in portfolio quality. From 1960 to 1970 total assets of commercial banks had increased at an average annual rate of 9 percent; from 1971 to 1973 bank assets grew more than 15 percent per year with foreign expansion accounting for one-fifth of that growth. This rapid expansion led to a decline in the ratio of assets to equity capital. Equity capital plus loan loss and valuation reserves of American commercial banks were almost 9 percent of total bank assets in 1960; by the end of 1973 the figure had fallen to about 6½ percent. Furthermore, the attenuation of capital was aggravated by leveraging of that capital through bank holding companies.[6]

Banks were also affected by international problems. Most obvious was the instability of foreign exchange markets. Those markets (responding to the multiple economic problems of the time and not under the control of the Group of Ten countries) gyrated wildly in 1973 and 1974. Virtually all important banks were heavily involved in foreign exchange trading. Many, tempted by the possibility of profits in a time when other divisions of banks were being squeezed, turned to foreign exchange speculation—and many suffered well-publicized losses. In April 1974 the Union Bank of Switzerland announced a "sizable loss" due to unauthorized trading. The loss was later estimated to have been $150 million. The Westdeutsche-Landesbank suffered foreign exchange losses of $105 million.[7] Franklin's troubles were announced in mid-May. In late June in the midst of Franklin's prolonged crisis, the most serious incident occurred: the failure of Bankhaus Herstatt. Revelations of other banks' foreign exchange losses continued throughout the year.[8]

There was also concern about the condition of Eurocurrency markets. The rapid growth of Euromarkets and the expansion of many banks into the markets in the late 1960s and early 1970s created a highly competitive situation in which interest rates declined and maturities lengthened. In January 1973 prime borrowers were paying ⅝ to ¾ of 1 percent over the six-month LIBOR rate. By January 1974 the margin for prime borrowers had narrowed to ⅜ of 1 percent. Loan maturities lengthened from a range of five to eight years in 1970 to as long as fifteen years in late 1973.[9] As world economic conditions worsened in 1974, concern developed that interest rates were too low, that the market's maturity structure was unfavorable, that the syndicated loan business had grown too rapidly, and that rapid growth had led to a deterioration of banks' capital-to-loan ratios which left them vulnerable to liquidity problems.[10]

Yet another reason for anxiety in Euromarkets was the looming problem of petrodollar recycling. As a result of the increase in the price of oil and the resultant financial surplus of oil-exporting countries, Eurobanks were accumulating large, very short-term dollar deposits from oil-producing countries. As the year wore on the ratio of short-term liabilities to bank capital reached the limits of what was considered prudent. Literally awash with dollars, banks extended long-term Euroloans to many public and private entities. The new influx of petrodollars and the oil crisis posed two problems for banks. The massive, extremely short-term petrodollar deposits made Eurobanks vulnerable to withdrawals of important percentages of their deposits. At the same time many countries, borrowers from Eurobanks, were facing unknown but potentially serious balance-of-payments crises due to the oil price increases and facing possible trouble repaying or even servicing their international loans.[11]

The year 1974 became a year of bank failures. What was especially significant about those failures was that they involved big banks.

Bank failures are not unusual events. From 1934 until 1972, 635 banks had failed in the United States. Most of these, however, were very small institutions. Until 1966 the largest bank to fail had total deposits of $48.8 million.[12]

The financial community and bank regulators themselves came to believe that large banks could not fail. Even after the Public Bank of Detroit, with $93 million in deposits, failed in 1966, confidence in big banks persisted. In 1973 and 1974, however, an important number of large banks failed. In late 1973 the U.S. National Bank of San Diego, with $932 million in deposits, failed and was merged with Crocker National Bank; the Franklin crisis erupted in May 1974; in September 1974 the American Bank and Trust Company of Orangeburg, South Carolina, with $110 million in deposits, collapsed; and authorities were well aware of other serious problem banks. Northern Ohio Bank ($96 million in deposits), Bank of the Commonwealth of Detroit ($992 million), and Security National Bank, a Long Island institution ($1.3 billion), were merged or salvaged by the FDIC in 1974.[13]

Foreign banks were also under pressure. The failure of Herstatt has already been mentioned. At the same time Westdeutsche-Landesbank and the Hessische Landesbank in West Germany were in serious trouble. The Bank of England had organized "Operation Lifeboat" to rescue a number of fringe banks faced with imminent disaster due to the collapse of the real estate market in the United Kingdom, and was faced with the failure of Israel-British Bank (see chap. 6). These failures called into question the assumption that large banks could not fail and thereby undermined banking confidence.

In sum, 1974 was a perilous time for banks. The back of the camel was weak; when the Franklin crisis erupted, it appeared as a large straw which might have broken the beast.

The International Banking Crisis of 1974

Private participants in the American and international financial markets as well as American and foreign authorities viewed the potential collapse of Franklin National Bank with alarm. Not only

Franklin's importance—its size, its links with the international banking system, and the important role of international problems in its crisis—but also the difficult financial and economic conditions of 1974 led banking authorities to fear a collapse of confidence in the United States and abroad, deposit withdrawals and disruption of domestic and international financial markets, and the threat of credit contraction and economic crisis on a worldwide scale. Franklin posed threats to the two major areas of international banking: foreign exchange markets and the Eurocurrency markets.

The effective operation of foreign exchange markets is essential for international economic interaction. Without the ability to exchange national currencies, international trade and investment would contract and disintegrate into barter. As we have seen, foreign exchange markets were very unstable in 1973 and 1974. Despite predictions by many economists, such exchange rate instability did not hinder international trade and investment. In the summer of 1974, however, the very operation of foreign exchange markets came into question, posing a threat to the entire international economy.

The source of the threat to foreign exchange markets was the failure of Bankhaus I. D. Herstatt of Cologne.[14] On June 26 at 4:00 P.M. Frankfurt time, Herstatt was ordered closed by German federal authorities. The reasons for the closing were foreign exchange losses which resulted from heavy speculation and which had been concealed by false bookkeeping entries. Herstatt, with assets of $800 million, was one of Germany's largest private banks. The Herstatt failure was a significant shock to the German banking system, but it was a far greater shock in international foreign exchange markets.

Long before the Herstatt crisis, banks had recognized the risks involved in forward foreign exchange trading—as was evidenced by the exclusion of Franklin from the forward foreign exchange markets—but had felt there were no risks in the spot market. The Herstatt episode revealed the risks in spot transactions and called into question the very mechanism of interbank payments, which was based on confidence.

The way in which Herstatt was closed disrupted the world's foreign exchange markets and actually led to their paralysis for a number of days. Andrew Brimmer, former Governor of the Federal Reserve System, has described the situation:

Normally, in a spot foreign exchange trade, the buyer and seller of a currency promise to settle with each other within two days. In the Herstatt case, German marks were sold to Herstatt on June 24, 1974, by at least a dozen banks. Settlement was due—in dollars—on June 26.

On that date, the selling banks instructed their correspondent banks in Germany to debit their mark accounts and deposit the funds in the Landes-Central Bank—the clearing house operated by the Bundesbank. The funds were then credited to Herstatt. The selling banks expected to receive dollars on the same day through London or New York clearing houses.

However, Bankhaus Herstatt was officially declared bankrupt around 4 P.M. on June 26, 1974. This was after the market had closed in Germany—but while foreign exchange was still being traded in New York. In the meantime, the Landes-Central Bank had credited Herstatt with funds in Cologne, but the latter's doors were shut before Herstatt's dollars were credited to foreign banks.

This action triggered the disruption of the foreign exchange market—since it aborted the settlement process.[15]

Among the foreign banks caught in the payments debacle were Morgan Guaranty, Seattle First National Bank, and Hill Samuel of the United Kingdom.

The failure of Herstatt to deliver on spot exchange contracts demonstrated to banks that even spot transactions carried credit and delivery risks. As banks groped for ways to cope with the risk, both forward and spot foreign exchange trading virtually ground to a halt. Traders would deal only with institutions considered to be of the highest quality. Small and medium-sized banks had great difficulty dealing in foreign exchange and, when they were able to do so, were forced to pay a premium. Confidence was at such a low ebb that the New York Clearing House banks would not make payments for correspondents until they were assured that covering receipts were in hand. Their caution further constricted the market and forced the Clearing House on July 1 to establish a special emergency rule which allowed banks to recall payments up to a day after they had been placed. The emergency procedure, which lasted until November 13,

1974, facilitated the recovery of foreign exchange trading. In subsequent weeks spot trading gradually resumed but forward markets remained thin.[16] According to one estimate foreign exchange volume declined by one-fourth to one-third.[17] According to another estimate, world foreign exchange trading declined by almost two-thirds, a drop so drastic that by 1977 total world trading had not recovered to its 1974 levels (see fig. 4.2).

The Herstatt crisis quickly spilled over into Eurocurrency markets. As we have already seen in the Franklin case, confidence in the two markets is closely linked. The Herstatt crisis made banks cautious about dealing with all but the largest and best-known banks. For a short period of time some banks were actually excluded from Eurocurrency markets and when they did regain access were forced to pay a premium over rates paid by the larger, better-known institutions.[18]

The German Central Bank defended its closing of Herstatt, arguing that the Bundesbank should not help banks floundering from unauthorized activities and that special measures by the German Central Bank to stabilize international markets in the aftermath of Herstatt were not needed. According to Brimmer, the Bundesbank rejected a Federal Reserve proposal made in July to set up a special fund to pay off Herstatt's debts to international banks growing out of the interruption of the payments transactions.[19] However, German authorities later agreed to what was essentially a political solution of the Herstatt claims which took into account international concerns. In December 1974, after the initiation of complicated legal actions by Herstatt's creditors, an agreement regarding the division of the bank's German assets was reached by creditors and approved by the Cologne District Court. Under that agreement, foreign banks were given preference over German banks and corporations. Foreign banks were eventually repaid 70 to 86 percent of their claims while German banks and corporations received from 3 to 86 percent of their claims.[20]

The dangers created by Herstatt were minor compared to the potential threat from Franklin National Bank. Herstatt's total

Figure 4.2. The Evolution of Foreign Exchange Trading.

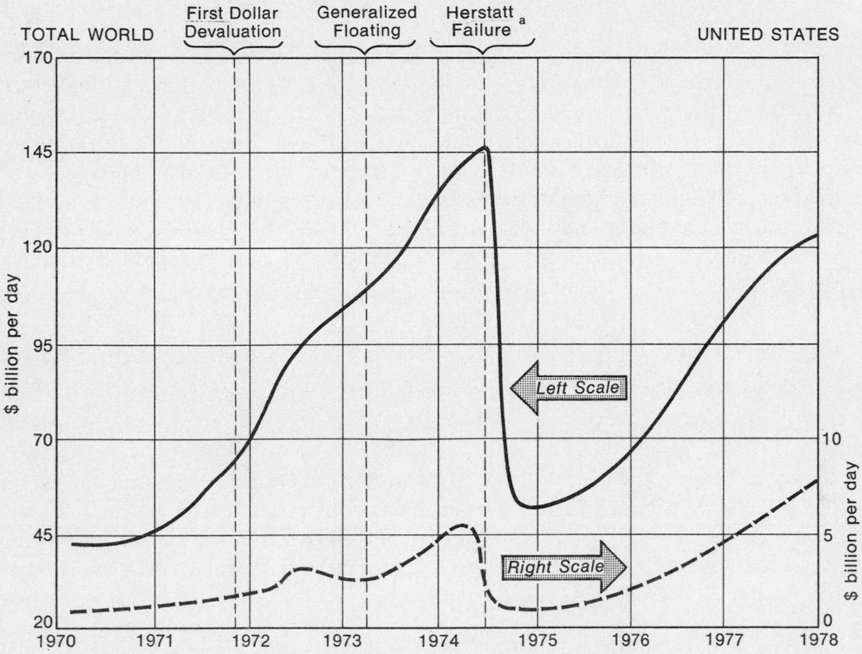

Source: Ian H. Giddy, "Measuring the World Foreign Exchange Market," *Columbia Journal of World Business*, (Fall 1979) 14(3).

aIndicative figure

foreign exchange exposure was only $200 million compared with Franklin's total foreign exchange book of almost $2 billion.[21] The collapse of Franklin National Bank and the possible consequent failure of the bank to perform on its large volume of foreign exchange contracts would certainly have seriously accentuated the crisis of confidence already existing in foreign exchange markets. Franklin's failure to perform on foreign exchange contracts could also have spilled over into Eurodollar markets and could have created a banking and economic crisis. The possible impact on foreign exchange markets and on international banking were outlined by Richard A. Debs, first vice president of the Federal Reserve Bank of New York, in September 1974:

Even under the best of international monetary conditions, failure of Franklin to perform on such a volume of international commitments could undermine foreign exchange market confidence and tarnish the reputation of United States banks in general. In today's circumstances, the consequences of such an action by Franklin would be much more serious, since confidence in interbank dealing has already been severely shaken by the losses and failures of smaller banks throughout the world, particularly the failure of the Herstatt Bank in Germany to honor its current foreign exchange commitments. Franklin's failure to honor its outstanding contracts would thus further deteriorate interbank confidence, and at the extreme, would risk producing a banking crisis with inevitable losses to depositors and creditors, disruption of funds transfers and of credit commitments, as well as consequent loss of jobs and income. The fear of this kind of risk is shared by the central banks and treasuries of most major countries, and any reasonable action that can be taken to avoid such a risk would clearly be desirable.[22]

Another foreign exchange concern was that the dollar would suffer in exchange markets just at a time when it had already undergone an important decline. As the Federal Reserve Bank of New York put it:

Earlier in the year, the failure of the Herstatt Bank in Germany to honor its current foreign exchange commitments on its closing had resulted in a shock to the foreign exchange markets and a weakening of the German mark. Similar damaging effects on the dollar could be expected if Franklin National's contracts were dishonored as a result of its insolvency.[23]

The failure of Franklin National Bank also posed an important threat to the Eurocurrency markets. The growth of that market with its reliance on short-term deposits and its interbank linkages left the system vulnerable to a problem in one part of the system. As George Blunden, then chief banking supervisor of the Bank of England, described the situation, the growth of the Eurocurrency markets

allowed many institutions, including the new banks, to obtain funds for onward lending on a scale previously quite impossible for them and . . . meant that sickness in one bank could rapidly develop into an epidemic affecting a whole range of banks, even banks which did not have direct contact with the bank where the infection had first broken out.[24]

On May 3 Franklin's foreign branches held $926 million in deposits from other banks, an estimated half of which were from foreign branches of American banks.[25] These deposits were entirely uninsured and quite volatile. Had Franklin failed precipitously, all or part of these deposits could have been lost or "blocked." The loss of confidence in Franklin could then easily have spread to weaker banks having important deposits in Franklin, to weak banks in the system generally, and even to strong but less well-known small and medium-sized banks. Banks and other investors would become even more hesitant to deal with all but the largest and best-known institutions, not only because of their presumed soundness and the availability of greater information about them, but also because of the belief that somehow governments could not allow large banks to fail.[26] Some banks would be excluded from international monetary markets, some would be limited in their access to funds, and many would be forced to pay a premium over the rate for favored institutions. Denial or limitation of funds and higher interest rates could deal a crippling blow even to viable banks. Such a disruption of financial markets in turn could lead to a contraction of credit and a threat to business activity.

Because of banking and other forms of economic interdependence, such an international financial crisis would have had potentially deeper and broader effects than earlier international financial panics such as the 1931 Credit-Anstalt crisis. The crises of a large number of banks operating in Euromarkets would have been directly transmitted to national economies. The contraction of credit would have affected a significant number of businesses and even countries dependent on Eurodollar borrowings, a dependence particularly crucial since the onset of the petrodollar crisis and the increasing reliance on Eurodollar borrowings to meet balance-of-payments deficits and to maintain economic stability. And the interdependence created by trade and investment would have transmitted the economic downturn quickly throughout the market economies, much as inflation and recession had spread internationally from 1972 to 1974.

Although it did not collapse but underwent a managed demise, Franklin National Bank's continuing problems combined with the Herstatt failure led to a crisis in Eurocurrency markets in the summer of 1974. The regular and impressive growth in those markets, which had lasted for a decade and a half, stopped (see fig. 4.3). In mid-1974 the gross size of the Eurocurrency market reached a peak of $350 billion, of which $165 billion were inter-Eurobank transactions. By the end of 1974 the gross size of the Eurocurrency market had actually fallen to $345 billion, of which $150 billion were inter-Eurobank transactions. Thus in six months the inter-Eurobank market declined by $15 billion. All of the $10 billion rise in the net size of the Eurocurrency market in the second half of 1974 was accounted for by OPEC deposits.[27] In 1973 inter-Eurobank transactions accounted for 47 percent of the gross size of the Euromarket, while in 1974 such transactions fell to 42 percent of the gross size of the market (see table 2.2).

The impact of the crisis on foreign branches of American banks reveals the seriousness of this contraction. Between May and September 1974, liabilities of these branches declined by $3.4 billion or 3.1 percent of total bank deposits in May. The withdrawal of bank

Figure 4.3. Size of the Eurocurrency Market.

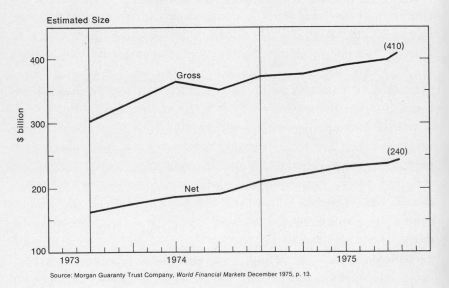

Source: Morgan Guaranty Trust Company, *World Financial Markets* December 1975, p. 13.

placements accounted for most of this decline. Banks withdrew $8.3 billion or 11.2 percent of outstanding liabilities from foreign branches of American banks. The $8.3 billion decline was offset in part by deposits from OPEC countries and by funds from American parents.[28]

The effect of this market contraction lasted well into 1975 (see table 2.3). For example, the foreign interbank market provided 48.8 percent of total liabilities of American banks in June 1974 and only 40.0 percent in June 1975. In absolute terms the decline in interbank deposits for foreign branches of American banks was $7 billion. The share of deposits by foreign nonbank depositors also declined but was offset by deposits of official institutions, primarily OPEC funds. There was an overall decline in the proportion of branch funds supplied by foreign sources which accounted for 73.3 percent of total liabilities in June 1974 and for only 65.8 percent in June 1975. Branches borrowed from their parents and from other American sources to offset this decline.[29]

As funds moved out of the Eurodollar market primarily to the United States, the premium which Eurobanks had to pay for dollars compared with banks in the United States widened (see fig. 4.4). In April the premium for three-month Eurodollar interbank rates over American CD rates was close to zero. In May the premium widened to ½ of 1 percent and at the end of June with the Herstatt shock it rose to 1¾ percent.[30]

Within the Eurocurrency market there developed a multitiered rate structure. Smaller banks, banks without the clear backing of a parent institution such as consortium banks, and banks of some of the large-deficit countries were unable to take on new commitments and had considerable difficulty obtaining refinancing in the interbank market to meet existing commitments. For two to three weeks many were unable to obtain funds. The premium unfavored banks were forced to pay rose as high as two percentage points above LIBOR, substantially above the yield they were earning on their syndicated loan portfolios. Many banks simply withdrew from the Euromarket,

Figure 4.4. Interbank Rates on Three-Month Eurocurrency Deposits and CD Rate in the United States. Wednesday Figures, in Percentages per Annum.

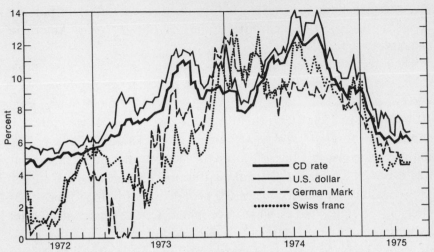

Source: Bank for International Settlements, *Annual Report, 1974–75*, Basle: Bank for International Settlements, 1975, p. 142.

some never to return, others to return several years later. The marked multitiered rate structure lasted from six to nine months.[31]

In sum, Franklin's troubles, coming in the midst of the other bank problems of 1974, posed a serious threat to the international financial system. Had the Franklin collapse been uncontrolled instead of managed, that threat would have been far more severe.

5

NATIONAL MANAGEMENT AND THE FRANKLIN CRISIS

THE LIQUIDITY CRISIS of the Franklin National Bank was the first United States banking crisis of major international proportions. From the weekend of May 10–12, 1974, when Federal authorities first confronted the possibility of a precipitous Franklin collapse, until October 8, 1974, when Franklin was declared insolvent and acquired by European American Bank, U.S. regulatory authorities developed new policies and tools for coping with the international dimensions of the Franklin problem. In the process the world's major international financial power demonstrated its ability and willingness to control international banking crises originating in the United States. It was an important precedent.

Domestic Actors

Several governmental departments and agencies were interested in the Franklin crisis, including the Treasury, the Department of

Justice, and the Securities and Exchange Commission. The responsibility for deciding what, if anything, the government should do about Franklin's liquidity crisis, however, rested primarily with three regulatory agencies.

The Office of the Comptroller of the Currency, as the primary regulator of national banks, shouldered the main supervisory responsibility for Franklin National Bank.[1] As such, the Comptroller bore much of the criticism for the failure of regulatory authorities to foresee and prevent the Franklin crisis. After the onset of the liquidity crunch, the Comptroller, James Smith, actively though ineffectively sought a resolution of the Franklin crisis. During May and June he focused on reorganizing Franklin's management—finding a new director of foreign exchange operations and a new president of the bank. He enlisted David Kennedy who persuaded Joseph Barr, former Secretary of the Treasury, to become Franklin's president. Smith also actively sought a commercial merger partner for the bank. Long after most others had abandoned the hope for a conventional merger, Comptroller Smith persisted in his quest, partly because he believed that Franklin could be saved and partly because a Franklin failure would have been—and was—most embarrassing for the Comptroller. By July 2 the Comptroller recognized that a conventional merger of Franklin with another bank would be impossible and that Franklin was certain to become insolvent. He therefore called on the FDIC to arrange an assisted merger. From July until October 8 Comptroller Smith pursued various schemes to improve Franklin's liquidity situation, all to no avail. Finally, on October 8 it was the Comptroller who made the official determination of Franklin's insolvency.

The Federal Deposit Insurance Corporation, as the insurer of Franklin and a potential receiver of the assets and liabilities of the bank, played a crucial role in the search for an assisted takeover of Franklin National Bank.[2] The FDIC assumed an active leading role in resolving the Franklin crisis in July after Comptroller Smith asked Chairman Frank Wille to pursue an assisted merger. Throughout almost all of May and June, however, the FDIC remained very much in the background. The limited involvement of the FDIC in the early days is explained by the constraints of the FDIC charter and the cautious interpretation of the responsibilities of the FDIC under the Charter by Chairman Wille. The FDIC was empowered to act only after the Comptroller informed the FDIC that Franklin National Bank was likely to become insolvent. As we have seen, it was not until July 2 that Comptroller Smith wrote to Chairman Wille requesting the FDIC to pursue an assisted merger.

Chairman Wille also explained later that his agency remained in the background in the early period in order to avoid further adverse publicity for Franklin which would have accentuated its liquidity crisis and made more difficult an unassisted solution. As he put it:

. . . public disclosure of FDIC's interest in the outcome of the Franklin National Bank situation would lead to a general conclusion that FNB's [Franklin National Bank's] failure was likely, if not imminent. . . . any public identification of FDIC's role would feed speculation in the press about the Bank's long-run ability to withstand the massive outflow of deposits it was experiencing, and in all likelihood would prevent the possible consummation of a merger or acquisition without special Government financial assistance or indemnities.[3]

Wille did, however, receive information about Franklin and proceed with contingency planning.

The third major actor was the Federal Reserve System, with the Board of Governors and the Federal Reserve Bank of New York playing occasionally divergent roles. Beginning with the weekend of May 10, when Federal authorities grappled for a way to prevent the precipitous collapse of Franklin when its doors opened on Monday, May 13, the Federal Reserve played the central role in seeking to stem the financial and economic panic which could have resulted from a Franklin collapse. The Federal Reserve Bank of New York and the Board of Governors of the Federal Reserve System had the authority and resources the Comptroller lacked to manage the liquidity crisis, and a broader responsibility to the financial and economic system than the FDIC.

As lender of last resort the Federal Reserve determines when the failure of a bank might endanger the nation's financial system and has the resources in its discount window to prevent a failure or to delay an insolvency until an acceptable solution can be found. The responsibility of the Federal Reserve for the American financial markets and national economy reflects its traditional responsibility as lender of last resort for the national economy. The lender of last resort is, as one analyst put it, "a term often used and less often defined." The classical concept involved insuring the overall liquidity of the financial system, which in application has involved liquidity support for particular institutions.[4] As James H. Oltman of the Federal Reserve Bank of New York described the domestic concerns surrounding Franklin, the Federal Reserve has "a responsibility to attempt to protect the U.S. banking system—and the national economy—from the upheaval and deterioration of confidence that can result from the failure of some banks."[5]

In the case of Franklin, the Federal Reserve also had an international concern. As we have seen, the failure of Franklin with its large interbank deposits and its large volume of foreign exchange contracts would have shaken confidence in international financial markets and could have precipitated an international banking crisis. Throughout the Franklin affair, Federal Reserve officers were sensitive to the international dimensions of the crisis. Robert Holland of the Board of Governors, for example, later testified that "the situation arose during a difficult period for financial institutions and financial markets; such a failure at that time could, in our judgement, have had serious adverse consequences for the stability of our nation's banking system, and for domestic and international financial markets in general."[6] And the Federal Reserve Bank of New York later explained that "given the general financial and economic situation at that time, such a failure would have jeopardized the stability of the United States banking system, with further serious repercussions for domestic and international financial markets in general."[7] It was this concern about international financial consequences which led the Federal Reserve to exert and expand its role as lender of last resort.

The Decision To Act:
The Crisis Weekend of May 10–12

On Friday, May 10, 1974, the management of Franklin National Bank announced that the bank had suffered foreign exchange losses, that it would recommend a suspension of dividends, and that it had requested a suspension of trading in Franklin New York Corporation shares. Over that weekend, Federal regulators and Franklin management met at the Federal Reserve Bank of New York to search for a way to prevent the collapse of the bank on the following Monday. Two principal alternatives for action emerged.

One alternative, preferred by Franklin's President Paul Luftig, and, if it had been possible, by Federal authorities, was the conventional (i.e., without subsidy) merger of Franklin with another bank. As early as May 6, before Franklin's management knew the extent of the bank's foreign exchange losses, the bank's executive committee approved a proposal by Luftig to seek a merger. Luftig informed the Federal Reserve Bank of New York and the resident examiner of the Office of the Comptroller of the Currency of his intentions during that week and received their approval.[8]

Discussions were begun with Manufacturers Hanover Trust Company, the one bank at that time willing seriously to consider a merger with Franklin. That bank was interested in Franklin's Long Island branch network, which was a rich source of deposits and was also concerned about protecting a $30 million three-year unsecured loan made to Franklin New York Corporation in April 1974. The loan was part of Franklin's effort to improve its capital base in order to gain approval for the Talcott acquisition. Manufacturers Hanover committed itself in February 1974 to a $30 million loan and to an additional $5 million to cover the costs of the Talcott merger. Franklin drew down the $30 million on April 3, 1974, but never borrowed the $5 million because the Talcott merger, as we have seen, was rejected by the Board of Governors. Just why Manufacturers Hanover made the loan to Franklin at a time when the bank's difficulties were much rumored in financial markets is hard to explain.

Part of the explanation may be inaccurate information. The bank records which Gleason, Luftig, and Carter were convicted of falsifying were used in a financial statement submitted to Manufacturers Hanover to obtain the loan (see chapter 3). On May 10 and 11, Luftig and other Franklin officers actively pursued the merger route with high-level officers of and lawyers for Manufacturers.

By the evening of Saturday, May 11, it became clear that an immediate conventional merger would not be possible. Manufacturers informed the Federal Reserve Bank of New York on Saturday noon that its preliminary financial review revealed that a conventional merger was not financially worthwhile. By Saturday evening Manufacturers informed the Reserve Bank that it was not interested because of Franklin's sizable losses and write-offs. Luftig urged the Federal Reserve to press the FDIC for Federal assistance to make a merger with Manufacturers possible, but the Federal Reserve rejected such a strategy as impossible to carry out in a short time. Other banks contacted by the Reserve Bank showed no interest in a speedy merger. Complicating matters further, Michele Sindona forcefully opposed a merger. Sindona spent Saturday and Sunday at the Reserve Bank, actively involved in negotiations. Interestingly, while the Franklin's counsel (Kaye, Scholer, Fierman, Hays, and Handler) began the weekend representing the bank, Sindona's lawyers (Mudge Rose Guthrie & Alexander) took over representation of Franklin sometime Sunday. In these discussions, Sindona proposed to save Franklin by raising $50 million of capital through a stock offering to bank shareholders and agreed that Fasco International would purchase the stock if there were no subscribers. Sindona mobilized internal bank forces against Luftig and the pro-merger group and forced his firing on Monday, May 13.[9]

With a quick merger ruled out and little time to develop other solutions, authorities turned to a second alternative: a major loan from the discount window of the Federal Reserve Bank of New York. From the outset the Federal Reserve Bank of New York and the Board of Governors agreed that Franklin National Bank should not be allowed to fail precipitously and that if necessary the Federal Reserve should prevent that failure with emergency credit assistance. Although it is impossible to identify just how and when that conclusion was reached, it seems to have emerged as a possibility during the examination of Franklin's condition in connection with the Talcott application and was considered when the Federal Reserve Bank of New York set up the Franklin task force in December 1973. The discussion on the weekend of May 10–12, when it was recognized that a loan to Franklin would be large and long-term, focused on details of what to do, not whether it was necessary to make an emergency loan.[10]

On Sunday, May 12, final agreements were negotiated. The key element was a loan from the Federal Reserve Bank of New York. George W. Mitchell, vice chairman of the Board of Governors (Chairman Burns was out of the country), in an unusual press release announced the System's support for Franklin. He commented on Franklin's recent troubles:

There is, of course, the possibility that—with many rumors about the bank—Franklin National may experience some unusual liquidity pressures in the period ahead. As with all member banks, the Federal Reserve System stands prepared to advance funds to this bank as needed, within the limits of the collateral that can be supplied. Working with Franklin National, the Federal Reserve Bank of New York has determined that there is a large amount of acceptable collateral available to support advances to the bank from the Federal Reserve discount window, if they are needed.[11]

The Federal Reserve Bank of New York later reported:

The decision to make substantial credit assistance available to Franklin National had two main purposes: first, to prevent the severe deterioration of confidence, at home and abroad, that would have resulted from an early failure of the bank and, second, to provide time to permit Franklin National itself, or if necessary the bank regulatory authorities, to achieve a more permanent solution of the bank's difficulties.[12]

The achievement of the Reserve Bank's goals was to be far more difficult than was anticipated on that hectic May weekend.

The Loan:
A New Role for the Lender of Last Resort

The loan made by the Federal Reserve Bank of New York to Franklin National Bank represented the assumption of a new role for the lender of last resort. The loan was unprecedented in size, in its use to cover outflows from Franklin's foreign branches, and in duration for an uninterrupted, large-scale loan.

Franklin's liquidity crisis proved to be more severe than the Federal Reserve had expected. Continuing revelations and rumors, centering primarily around foreign exchange losses, undermined confidence in Franklin. On May 12 Franklin issued a statement revealing to the public that the bank had realized foreign currency losses since January 31, 1974, of $2 million and that because of unauthorized trading the bank would sustain further losses of $12 million to $25 million.[13] The statement also revealed that in an effort to restore confidence Sindona had relinquished for one year his rights to vote Franklin New York Corporation stock and had delegated those rights to David Kennedy. On May 13 the firing of Paul Luftig and Peter Shaddick led to rumors that Franklin's problem's went beyond foreign exchange. On Tuesday, May 14, Franklin announced that first-quarter earnings, as well as second-quarter earnings as previously announced, would have to be revised because of foreign exchange losses.[14] For the next month rumors flew. Then on June 20 Franklin announced the results of an examination begun May 14. The examination revealed foreign exchange losses of $45.8 million, of which $26.7 million had occurred during the first quarter. As a result of foreign exchange losses plus decreased value of securities and a write-off of a tax-loss carry-forward, first-quarter losses amounted to $40.4 million and net losses for the first five months of 1974 amounted to a possible $65 million, the largest loss ever reported by an American bank.[15]

The result of these continuing revelations was a vast outflow of funds. Table 5.1 reveals the type of outflows from Franklin. The loss of Federal funds, money-market certificates of deposit, domestic

TABLE 5.1   Franklin National Bank Funds Flow ($ million)

Outflows: Decrease in Liabilities and Capital	5/8/74 through 6/30/74	7/1/74 through 10/7/74
Federal funds	$ 346	$189
Repurchase agreements	199	—
Money market CDs	322	88
Time savings—individuals, partnerships, and corporations	52	76
Other domestic time	104	3
Domestic demand	504	237
Foreign branch deposits	393	287
Foreign exchange transactions	15	8
Capital funds[a]	28	—
Total outflows	$1,963	$888

Inflows: Reduction in Assets or Increase in Liabilities	5/8/74 through 6/30/74	7/1/74 through 10/7/74
Loans	$ 93	$134
Investments	75	38
Foreign branch investments	108	90
Cash	452	109
Repurchase agreements	—	24
Reserve for losses	—	5
Total inflow	$ 728	$400
Net outflow	$1,235	$488
Increase in Federal Reserve borrowings	$1,235	$488

SOURCE: Letter from Arthur Burns to Henry Reuss, February 5, 1975, pp. 8–9.
[a]Change caused by operating losses and realized losses on securities, loans, and on foreign exchange transactions.

demand deposits, and foreign branch deposits—unsecured and for the most part uninsured and short-term liabilities—accounted for the vast majority of outflows.

Table 3.1 reveals the degree of decline over time of each of these outflows. For most items the greatest outflows took place in the first two months of the crisis. Demand deposits declined 44 percent from May 8 to July 12 and had fallen 53 percent by October 7. Money-market certificates of deposit declined 72 percent from

May 8 to July 12 and 86 percent by October 7. Unsecured Federal funds disappeared almost instantly—83 percent from May 8 to May 13 and 100 percent from May 8 to May 17. Foreign branch deposits declined 48 percent between May 8 and July 12 and 75 percent between May 8 and October 7. The decline of foreign deposits was more gradual because of the somewhat longer term of these deposits and the absence of encashment provisions. As soon as foreign deposits matured they were withdrawn. As Joseph W. Barr, the new president of Franklin National Bank, put it, Eurodollar deposits "were put to us for payment the moment they came due. Foreign banks had *no confidence* in us, and wanted out as quickly as possible." [16]

Some of these outflows were covered by a reduction of assets. Total assets declined 14 percent between May 8 and July 12 and 20 percent between May 8 and October 7 (see table 3.1). The outflows were also covered in part by the purchase of secured Federal funds from the New York Clearing House banks. The Comptroller and the Federal Reserve Bank of New York sought from the earliest days to interest the Clearing House banks in assisting Franklin by continuing to lend to that bank. These large New York banks resisted the idea of a term loan but on June 11, 1974, they succumbed to pressure from the Federal Reserve and agreed to lend Franklin jointly up to $200 million daily in Federal funds at market rates. These loans, which lasted until September 26, 1974, were secured by a first lien on collateral held by the Federal Reserve Bank of New York. In July an unsuccessful effort was made to reduce assets further and raise funds by selling the portfolio of Eurocurrency loans of the London branch (see below for the attempted sale of Franklin's Eurocurrency loans).

Franklin was unable to reduce assets sufficiently to cover outflows. The net outflow of funds was huge. As we have seen, one of the major losses was from foreign branches. On May 8 foreign branch deposits exceeded assets by $8 million; on July 12 assets exceeded liabilities by $323 million; and on October 7 assets exceeded liabilities by $465 million.

Franklin was forced to turn increasingly to the discount window to cover the net outflow (see table 3.1). On May 8 Franklin borrowed $110 million from the Federal Reserve Bank of New York; by May 13, the Monday after the crisis weekend, borrowing rose to $550 million; by May 24 it jumped to $1.13 billion; and on October 2 it reached a peak of $1.767 billion.[17] As borrowing escalated in May and June, Federal Reserve officials began to fear that Franklin would run out of collateral against which to borrow and would collapse. Fortunately, the runoff leveled after the first two months and Federal Reserve borrowings grew at a slower rate.

Borrowings from the Federal Reserve discount window covered three-fifths of Franklin's outflow from May 8 to October 7. Included in that coverage were outflows from London and Nassau. This was the first time that the discount window had been used to cover outflows at foreign branches. The Federal Reserve placed no restrictions on the transfer of funds from the United States to London and Nassau. According to former Governor Andrew Brimmer, the Federal Reserve's Board of Governors agreed after some discussion (in which there was little difference of opinion) to make no objection to the use of Federal loan funds for foreign branches.[18] (The extent of such assistance is reflected in the memo item, "Head office support of foreign branches," in table 3.1) By October 7, the day before Franklin closed, the head office was lending almost half a billion dollars to London and Nassau.

The Federal Reserve Bank loan to Franklin National Bank was unprecedented in duration.[19] Because of the difficulty encountered in finding a solution for Franklin short of insolvency and FDIC receivership, the daily loans lasted five months, from May 8 to October 7. Many factors impeded the resolution of the Franklin crisis: the unrealistic efforts of the Comptroller to find a commercial merger partner throughout June; the large size of the bank; Federal statutory restrictions against acquisition by out-of-state American banks; FDIC policy of insisting on competitive bidding for the acquisition; the efforts of Joseph Barr, the new president of Franklin, to keep an independent Franklin alive.[20] Some of the most difficult problems which impeded a rapid solution arose from Franklin's international activities.

One such problem was the purchase and assumption of the assets and liabilities of the London branch. This was the first time that an American bank with an important overseas branch was faced with a declaration of insolvency and the first time the FDIC was potentially the receiver of a bank with a large proportion of its assets overseas. This new international situation with its attendant legal and political uncertainties required discussions with the Bank of England and delayed further the resolution of the crisis (see chap. 6).

Another problem related in part to Franklin's international activities was the settlement of Franklin's huge debt to the Federal Reserve Bank of New York. The size of the loan required new solutions and complex negotiations between the FDIC and the Federal Reserve regarding the FDIC assumption of the loan. Yet another international problem was the resolution of Franklin's foreign exchange contracts.

Foreign Exchange:
Further Evolution of the Federal Reserve Role

Among the principal concerns of the Federal Reserve from the onset of the crisis were Franklin's foreign exchange contracts. These contracts played an important role in Franklin's difficulties and in the Federal authorities' delay in finding a solution for Franklin. They were also the reason for a further expansion of the role of the Federal Reserve as stabilizer of the international banking system.

Even before May 1974, as we have seen, many banks had limited or refused to enter into forward contracts with Franklin National Bank and some had limited or even refused spot transactions. After the May revelations and rumors of unauthorized foreign exchange trading, other banks refrained altogether from dealing with Franklin and crippled Franklin's ability to perform contracts. By May 8, even before the announcement of illegal trading, Franklin's situation had become so difficult that it reportedly requested Continental Illinois

Bank, with which Sindona had close connections, to engage in foreign exchange transactions on its behalf. Continental reportedly agreed on May 9. Apparently Continental withdrew from this agreement the following week.

After the May 12 announcement revealing unauthorized trading and substantial losses, Franklin's position worsened. The willingness of other banks to engage in transactions with Franklin was further undermined when they learned that on May 14 Carlo Bordoni had taken charge of Franklin's trading room. On May 14 a major New York bank informed the Federal Reserve that it would no longer deal with Franklin in foreign exchange.

The first efforts of Federal authorities were to reorganize Franklin's foreign exchange operations in order to enable Franklin to engage in foreign exchange transactions and to fulfill commitments coming due. On May 17, following a "spirited discussion" with Sindona, Comptroller Smith persuaded Edwin Reichers, former head of foreign exchange operations at First National City Bank of New York, to come to Franklin as Executive Vice President in charge of foreign exchange operations.[21] The presence of Reichers, who was respected in the market, and the removal of Bordoni enabled Franklin to renew trading. Reichers's goals were to confirm all forward contracts (i.e., to locate hidden and unauthorized contracts), to satisfy foreign exchange commitments, and to reduce the size of Franklin's open foreign exchange position.[22]

By mid-June Reichers was able to confirm all contracts. He was unable from the first, however, to purchase enough foreign exchange to fulfill Franklin's maturing contracts. Many banks continued to refuse to deal with Franklin. Foreign banks delayed foreign currency payments to Franklin until the last possible moment in order to protect themselves. One of the major problems was the inability of the London branch to deal in foreign exchange. The erosion of confidence in Franklin led other banks to exclude the branch from European foreign exchange markets. As a result, the New York office, already pressed by its own maturing contracts, was obliged to purchase currency to meet London contracts.

Unable to meet Franklin's commitments, Reichers turned to the Federal Reserve Bank of New York for assistance. The Federal Reserve Bank closely monitored Franklin's foreign exchange operations and when Franklin was unable to purchase sufficient foreign exchange to fulfill maturing contracts—which increasingly became the case—the Reserve Bank purchased currencies on its behalf. The Federal Reserve Bank felt it inappropriate to enter into forward contracts on Franklin's behalf, but from late May to September it purchased spot currencies to enable Franklin to meet its commitments.[23] Despite assistance from the Federal Reserve Bank of New York, Franklin's position deteriorated during the summer of 1974. By September Franklin was unable to carry out its own transactions and to assure timely delivery.

Although Reichers had some success in undoing contracts, the size of the foreign exchange book remained large. By late September the book amounted to what was estimated at the time as about $800 million and included approximately 300 forward contracts for purchases and sales of foreign currencies—principally in sterling, German marks, Swiss francs, and French francs, and to a lesser extent in Dutch guilders, Belgian francs, Italian lire, Canadian dollars, and Japanese yen—through August 1975. Furthermore, there was still a large forward book in many currencies which was not covered.

In the judgment of the Federal Reserve and of other central banks with which the Federal Reserve was in contact, the failure of Franklin to perform on such a volume of international commitments would lead to a crisis of confidence in foreign exchange markets and possibly to an international banking crisis.

While Reichers struggled to maintain daily operations and to reduce the book, Franklin and Federal authorities tried to sell the foreign exchange contracts. One early proposal by the Federal Reserve Bank of New York, that the New York Clearing House banks jointly assume Franklin's book, was rejected by the banks during the summer. The size of the book, its risks, and its bad reputation due to unauthorized and illegal trading and to the Sindona connection were the reasons for their refusal.

Another route, to dispose of the foreign exchange book as part of a larger merger package, was explored from May until early September. After the collapse of negotiations for a rapid merger with Manufacturers Hanover, Franklin and Federal authorities continued to seek possible merger candidates and formulas (see below). Throughout the summer Federal authorities believed that all potential purchasers with whom they were negotiating were willing to consider a purchase of Franklin which included the bank's foreign exchange contracts.

However, at a meeting held on September 4 with the Federal Reserve Bank of New York, the FDIC, and Franklin, the bidding banks announced that they were unwilling to assume the risks of loss and nonperformance as well as the inevitable "taint" associated with Franklin's foreign exchange book. The banks proposed that the FDIC and the Federal Reserve assume the book, but these authorities resisted such a solution at the meeting. The parties agreed to meet the next day.

At the September 5 meeting of senior foreign exchange officials of bidding banks, Franklin, and Federal authorities, the potential purchasers stated that they would buy Franklin's contracts only if they received an open-ended commitment from Franklin to compensate the eventual buyer whenever a closing would result in a loss. The FDIC, as receiver of Franklin's unpurchased assets and liabilities, would be left holding Franklin's commitment to indemnify purchasing banks, and the FDIC was unwilling to honor such a commitment. Chairman Wille took the position that FDIC funds could not be used to indemnify a potential purchaser against a loss due to foreign exchange.[24] Thus by September 5 the sale of the foreign exchange book to the purchaser of other Franklin assets was ruled out.

Another solution, the assumption of Franklin's foreign exchange contracts by the FDIC, was also ruled out. The FDIC took the position that as receiver it could not honor foreign exchange contracts which would lead to a loss for Franklin. In the words of Chairman Wille:

If these unexecuted contracts ended up in FDIC's hands as possible receiver, FDIC might have a fiduciary duty to FNB's creditors and owners not to honor those which were unfavorable to the Bank, and to demand performance of those which favored the Bank. We felt, accordingly, that we could give no assurances that all of these contracts would be honored by the FDIC as FNB's receiver.[25]

The FDIC also felt it had no authority as a corporation to assume and execute Franklin's foreign exchange contracts.

Had the FDIC disavowed unfavorable contracts, other contracting parties might have dishonored contracts profitable to Franklin. Such a disavowal of contracts would have seriously disrupted foreign exchange markets and potentially created the very international banking crisis which Federal authorities feared. While Chairman Wille recognized the danger of such a crisis and the need to honor Franklin's foreign exchange contracts, especially in the existing international climate, he argued that the Federal Reserve and not the FDIC had the responsibility to protect international confidence in American banks and in the international banking system itself.

Thus by September 5 it seemed that the only solution which would preserve financial stability was the acquisition by the Federal Reserve Bank of New York of the foreign exchange book of Franklin National Bank. As a bank seeking to save its loan to Franklin, the New York Bank had the authority to acquire Franklin's book; through its experience in foreign exchange transactions, it had the expertise to work out the book. Such a solution was consistent with Franklin's strategy. Franklin's new president, Joseph Barr, was pressing on Federal authorities a proposal to save Franklin by shrinking it to a Long Island bank and disposing of international and New York money market activities.[26]

The Federal Reserve Bank with the close involvement of the FDIC immediately began to explore ways in which it could assume Franklin's foreign exchange book and the financial risk that such an assumption would create. Involved in the Federal Reserve Bank's analysis were such questions as whether to include foreign exchange from proceeds of foreign denominated loans (it was decided not to), whether to reject certain questionable contracts (one was rejected), whether to assume both forward and spot contracts (yes), and how to evaluate the book and the risk.

The Federal Reserve Bank of New York, in assessing the risks involved in purchasing the Franklin foreign exchange book, estimated that assumption of Franklin's contracts could entail a loss of $15.645 million: $6.151 million due to a possible decline in market value of currencies; $3.586 million due to the risk that in some cases the other party to the contract would not perform; and $5.908 million if third parties would not confirm that they would perform on contracts with the Federal Reserve Bank of New York instead of with Franklin National Bank. In a contract agreed to September 23 and signed September 26, Franklin agreed to pay the Federal Reserve Bank of New York the amount of the estimated risk and the Federal Reserve Bank agreed to return money allocated to confirmation risk once contracts had been confirmed. The Reserve Bank also agreed to pay Franklin the difference between the estimated loss and the real loss if the real loss was less than the estimate and any gains after the execution of all contracts. Franklin in turn indemnified the Federal Reserve for any losses in excess of the estimate and backed that indemnification with collateral already held by the Federal Reserve for security against the Federal Reserve loan. Finally, at the same time, the Federal Reserve purchased Franklin's outstanding foreign exchange balances.[27]

It was agreed at the time of the purchase and confirmed by contract when Franklin was declared insolvent that the FDIC would preserve Franklin's foreign exchange contract arrangement and would indemnify the Federal Reserve Bank for any additional losses greater than the estimated risk.[28] The Federal Reserve Bank successfully worked out the foreign exchange book. With the assistance of foreign central banks, the Federal Reserve Bank was able to obtain confirmation that parties would execute contracts with the Federal Reserve Bank in place of Franklin. By October 1, 1974, when almost all third parties had confirmed, the Federal Reserve Bank released $5.908 million to Franklin.[29]

Upon acquiring the book the Federal Reserve Bank immediately purchased forward foreign exchange to cover commitments. By August 29, 1975, all contracts with the exception of 13 forward contracts with Edilcentro International, Ltd., a Sindona-affiliated entity, had been executed. The final loss on all but the Edilcentro contracts was $564,675 less than the indemnification paid by Franklin National Bank to the Federal Reserve Bank of New York. This sum was by mutual agreement applied to the FDIC debt to the Federal Reserve Bank of New York pursuant to the FDIC's assumption of Franklin's debt to the Federal Reserve Bank.[30]

The Edilcentro contracts were subjected to litigation and negotiation. Although an agreement was reached on June 18, 1975, approval of the settlement was delayed by the Italian government, which was attempting to administer foreign exchange controls to impede the outflow of currency reserves. In September 1976, following the Italian elections, governmental approval was obtained, and in January 1977 final agreement was made that a $6.75 million note would be paid by Edilcentro to the Federal Reserve Bank of New York. The first of three annual payments was made in July 1978.[31]

The Search for a Solution:
The FDIC Innovates

One of the major purposes of the Federal Reserve Bank loan to Franklin and of the Comptroller's efforts to improve Franklin's liquidity was to buy time to find a long-term managed solution to Franklin's problems. Finding such a solution, however, proved extremely difficult. Federal authorities had never confronted a situation like Franklin. The unprecedented nature of the bank's problems—its size, its international dimensions—combined with the unsteady financial markets of the time, obliged Federal authorities to innovate, and such innovation took time. Furthermore, the delay of the Comptroller in calling in the FDIC as well as the insistence of Chairman Wille that in such a situation all alternatives be thoroughly examined further slowed the process. In the end it took almost five months to find a solution for Franklin.

From May 10 until the end of June, Federal authorities sought to effect a conventional merger of Franklin with another bank or banks. After the possibility of a rapid merger with Manufacturers Hanover evaporated, Franklin, the Comptroller, and the Federal Reserve continued to seek possible merger candidates. Legal obstacles narrowed the search. The Bank Holding Company Act of 1956, which seeks to limit the accretion of financial and economic power of the banking industry by limiting geographical spread, among other things, prohibited American out-of-state bank holding companies from purchasing Franklin. As a result, the major targets of merger proposals were the large New York banks, which were legally eligible and had sufficient resources to absorb a large bank like Franklin. Even in the case of large New York banks, it should be noted, antitrust provisions might have impeded a sale. Other targets of the search were foreign banks, some of which were not subject to Bank Holding Company Act restrictions. Some foreign banks inquired about Franklin independently, and some were contacted through David Kennedy acting at the request of the Office of the Comptroller of the Currency.[32]

In the process of seeking merger candidates, Federal authorities learned that no American or foreign banks were interested in a merger without governmental assistance. On July 2 Comptroller Smith wrote Chairman Wille that it was necessary to explore the possibilities for an assisted sale. Although the FDIC soon moved into action, it was to take another three months before such a sale was achieved.

Wille felt obliged by the FDIC charter to explore all legally available solutions and to seek the least costly solution for Franklin's creditors and owners and for the FDIC. As he put it:

As a receiver of a closed bank, FDIC has a fiduciary duty to the creditors of the bank and to its owners to realize the highest price it can get for the going concern value of the closed bank's business. It also has a statutory duty to minimize its own loss.[33]

As a result, the FDIC decided to require competitive bidding for Franklin—a method found in the past to lead to more favorable results for the FDIC and the insolvent bank's creditors and owners but which took more time—and to limit the FDIC's cash contribution to a Franklin settlement to no more than $750 million, the amount estimated necessary to pay off all insured depositors.

In seeking an FDIC-assisted solution, Wille had three choices: a simple pay-out of insured depositors following a Franklin failure; a merger and consolidation of Franklin with another bank or banks with FDIC assistance; and a purchase and assumption transaction of Franklin's assets and liabilities following a Franklin insolvency, with FDIC assistance.[34] Among these solutions, the FDIC preferred the latter two because they would cause the least domestic and international financial disruption. Having set his guidelines, Wille proceeded with negotiations with potential purchasers.

During July Wille contacted twenty banking organizations headquartered or represented in New York State and asked the Board of Governors to communicate with the Bank of England, the Bank of Japan, and the Bank of Canada to determine if large banks represented in New York were interested in acquiring Franklin. Between July 5 and July 15 Wille met with sixteen potential purchasers. During these meetings Wille proposed either a conventional merger with governmental assistance, under which the purchaser would assume all of Franklin's assets and liabilities, or a purchase and assumption transaction following a Franklin insolvency. Wille's proposal for a purchase and assumption agreement at this stage included virtually all of Franklin: the assumption of all deposit and other balance sheet liabilities, including the liability of the Federal Reserve loan, and the purchase of all assets with a negotiable "put-back" provision with the FDIC. From the viewpoint of international banking, it is important to note that it was assumed by the FDIC and the potential purchasers that assumption of Franklin's deposit liabilities would include deposit liabilities of foreign branches, i.e. Eurodollar deposits. Thus, foreign liabilities were treated like domestic ones. The FDIC was willing at this point to subscribe to a capital note of the purchasing bank of at least $50 million, and to indemnify the purchaser for liabilities it did not specifically assume.

At the same time Joseph Barr was lobbying for a change in the Bank Holding Company Act to permit out-of-state banks to bid on Franklin. He proposed to permit the suspension of prohibitions on acquisitions across state lines if bank regulators and the state banking commissioner determined that an emergency existed.[35] Time and the political environment were not on Barr's side. Congress was preoccupied by Watergate. Arthur Burns opposed the measure, telling Barr he viewed the effort as a delaying tactic and that it was essential for the FDIC to negotiate an assisted merger. Barr was unable to get his proposal introduced.

Discussions with potential merger candidates revealed almost total lack of interest in a merger involving assumption of all Franklin's liabilities and assets. According to Chairman Wille, only one bank was interested in what the FDIC called the "$4 billion" proposal, i.e., assuming all of Franklin's balance sheet liabilities and most of its assets. Franklin's size, the magnitude of its problems, and the bad reputation the bank had acquired due to publicity and continuing rumors were too much for them to take on in such difficult financial times. Many banks were deterred by the size of Franklin and by the effect on their earnings and stock performance if they absorbed Franklin's low-yielding assets. Some were deterred by the managerial and capital resources which would be necessary to acquire Franklin and resolve its problems. Many pointed out that the Federal Reserve had increased standards for capital adequacy in bank holding company decisions and that the Federal Reserve pressure to improve capital positions prevented them from acquiring the burden of Franklin.

Therefore, beginning in mid-July the FDIC explored ways to reduce the size of Franklin National Bank in order to facilitate a purchase and assumption transaction. A crucial part of reducing the size of Franklin was eliminating the Federal Reserve loan from the package. On July 19 Chairman Wille wrote to Chairman Burns suggesting that Franklin's responsibility for the Federal Reserve loan be eliminated from the Franklin package offered for sale and that the acquiring bank be permitted to select Franklin National Bank assets needed to match liabilities assumed.[36] The assumption by the FDIC of a liability of a failed bank to the Federal Reserve was not unusual. In the past the FDIC had made such assumptions and immediately repaid the Federal Reserve Bank. In the Franklin case, however, the FDIC could not immediately repay the Federal Reserve Bank of New York, for to do so would have reduced its $6 billion trust fund by almost one-third and would have far surpassed the $750 million cash limit imposed by the FDIC. Thus negotiations between the Federal Reserve and the FDIC focused on conditions and terms for the FDIC repayment of the Franklin indebtedness to the Federal Reserve Bank of New York.

Under the final agreement reached on August 12, the FDIC agreed to purchase from the Federal Reserve Bank Franklin's assets remaining in the receivership estate after a Franklin insolvency and the assumption by the eventual purchaser of Franklin's other assets. The purchase price for these remaining assets would be equal to the unpaid balance of Franklin's obligations to the Federal Reserve Bank and would be paid directly to the Reserve Bank in the form of a three-year FDIC obligation to the Reserve Bank. The interest rate was set as a rate approximating the rate of return of the System Open Market Account portfolio on the day of Franklin's closing, to be compounded annually at the end of three years after the closing. The Federal Reserve Bank agreed to relinquish its security interest in that portion of Franklin's assets acquired by the eventual purchaser. In addition, the Federal Reserve turned over the remaining collateral to the FDIC for administration and agreed to pay for certain administrative and legal costs of disposing of Franklin assets.[37]

With the elimination of the Federal Reserve obligation, Wille on August 13 began discussions with officers of serious bidders (Chemical, European American, First National City, Manufacturers Hanover, First Commercial Bank of Albany, and Bank of New York were the primary potential bidders), their lawyers, and representatives of the Federal Reserve and the Comptroller to develop a common set of bidding documents. Negotiations were delayed by the demand of the potential bidders for a new examination of Franklin by the Office of the Comptroller. Another problem which had to be resolved was the purchase and assumption of assets and liabilities in the London branch (see chapter 6). Yet another impediment was the foreign exchange book, which was discussed above. The FDIC also had to arrange for a possible separation of Franklin's trust department from the bidding and for the elimination of barriers to selection among Franklin's domestic branches.

Finally, it was necessary to define the terms of the FDIC's capital assistance to the successful bidder. It was decided to offer all the capital support the FDIC termed necessary up to a maximum of $150 million. The note had a maturity of ten years for the first $100 million and eight years for the $50 million and a floating interest rate based on the yield of certain United States agency obligations.

While the potential purchasers and Federal authorities were negotiating a common set of bidding documents, Joseph Barr was developing a new proposal for Franklin. On September 16 he presented to Federal authorities a plan for the survival of Franklin as an independent, Long Island–based bank. In early October the plan, which required extensive and long-term FDIC assistance, was rejected as unworkable by all Federal regulatory authorities.

On October 7 there was a rehearsal by Federal authorities and the four banks which had agreed to bid on Franklin—Chemical, European American, First National City, and Manufacturers Hanover. On October 8 Comptroller Smith declared Franklin insolvent and appointed the FDIC receiver.[38] Waiting bank examiners immediately moved into all of Franklin's offices. On that same day Federal officials assembled in the board room of the Federal Reserve Bank of New York to open four envelopes containing bids on Franklin National Bank.

When the envelopes were opened by Frank Wille, the first reaction was a sigh of relief that the four bidding banks had made real bids which the FDIC could accept. The second response was surprise, for the highest bidder was not Manufacturers Hanover, as many expected, but European American Bank and Trust, a bank chartered in

New York State and owned by a consortium of European banks.[39] Manufacturers, as we have seen, had its eye on Franklin even before the crisis and had been expected to submit the highest bid. But European American's bid of $125 million was $2 million above that of Manufacturers Hanover.

The possible acquisition of Franklin by European American had been a concern of the Board of Governors, who were worried about the precedent of a foreign acquisition of such a large bank and about the reaction of Congress to a federally assisted purchase by a foreign owner. The representative of the Board present when the bids were opened noted the Board's concerns and raised the possibility of accepting the lower bid by Manufacturers Hanover on the argument that an American solution might be in the public interest. The rejection of the highest bid is theoretically possible under FDIC statutes if other concerns, such as antitrust considerations or an inability of the highest bidder to manage the acquisition, suggest that the acquisition by a lower bidder would be in the public interest. FDIC representatives rejected the objections raised by the Board, arguing that the only way to reject the European American bid would be to prove that the bank could not serve the community and that a brief prepared by the New York State Superintendent of Banks documented that European American could serve Franklin customers. After a telephone call to the Board to obtain approval the Board representative agreed to the European American acquisition.

The FDIC then announced to the waiting representatives of the bidding banks that European American's offer of $125 million was the winning bid. European American was to select $1,487 million of Franklin's $3,658 million in assets minus the purchase price of $125 million and to assume Franklin's deposits of $1,369 million and certain other liabilities amounting to $243 million. Included in the deposit liabilities assumed by European American were the deposits of the London branch. Franklin's remaining liabilities were assumed by the FDIC (see table 5.2).

On October 9 offices of Franklin National Bank opened as European American Bank and Trust Company. Thus it was that the

TABLE 5.2   Collapse of Franklin National Bank T-Accounts for Franklin's Deposit Assumption

Franklin National Bank of New York ($ million, as of 10/8/74)			
Assets	$3,658	Deposits	$1,369
EAB&T required to accept	(1,487)	Federal Reserve Bank of New York discount window loan	1,732
EAB&T required to reject	(2,171)	Capital and other liabilities	557
Total	$3,658		$3,658
European American Bank and Trust Company (marginal T-account, $ million)			
Assets selected from Franklin	$1,487	Deposits assumed from Franklin	$1,369
Premium paid to FDIC	125	Other liabilities assumed from Franklin	243
Total	$1,612		$1,612
Federal Deposit Insurance Corporation (marginal T-account, $ million)			
Franklin's assets rejected by EAB&T	$2,171	Federal Reserve Bank of New York discount window loan	$1,732
Less EAB&T premium paid to FDIC	− 125	Other liabilities	314
Total	$2,046		$2,046

SOURCE: Joseph F. Sinkey, Jr., "The Collapse of Franklin National Bank of New York," *Journal of Bank Research* (Summer 1976), p. 116. Used by permission.

Franklin National Bank became part of a foreign-owned bank, one of whose owners was Creditanstalt-Bankverein of Vienna, the largest bank in Austria, bearing a name similar to another Austrian bank called the Credit-Anstalt, also once the largest bank in that country, which failed in 1931 and set off the most devastating international banking crisis in history.

6

INTERNATIONAL COOPERATION AND THE FRANKLIN CRISIS

INNOVATIONS IN U.S. policy were necessary but not sufficient to cope with the international dimensions of the Franklin National Bank crisis. The satisfactory resolution of the crisis would have been impossible without the cooperation of foreign banking authorities. Management of the Franklin crisis involved a series of effective ad hoc international cooperative efforts without which the United States crisis management operation might not have succeeded. Furthermore, the banking crisis of 1974, of which the Franklin crisis was a central element, led to some important and more permanent changes in the management of international banking.

Ad Hoc International Cooperation during the Franklin Crisis

The background for ad hoc cooperation was the long collaboration among central bankers of Western Europe, North America, and Japan. Since 1960 the Chairman of the Board of Governors of the

Federal Reserve System and other high-level Federal Reserve officials had been meeting monthly with governors of other central banks at the Bank for International Settlements (BIS) in Basel, Switzerland, to discuss monetary and economic policy.[1] The result of these regular monthly meetings and of other contacts was the development of a network of high-level officials who knew each other well and who cooperated in a number of efforts to manage the international monetary system during the 1960s.[2] Until 1974, however, central bank cooperation did not involve international banking questions or bank supervisory officials. The Franklin crisis and the troubles of 1974 would change both the participants and the purview of central bank cooperation.

Exchange of Information

One of the first reactions of the Federal Reserve Bank of New York to Franklin's foreign exchange problems and looming liquidity crunch was to inform other central banks. As early as Saturday, May 11, Richard Debs of the Reserve Bank called Governor Richardson of the Bank of England and told him of the emerging crisis. By the end of that first weekend Debs had contacted all the major central banks. His purpose, as he described it, was threefold. He wanted to prepare central bankers so they could react quickly to any crisis which might develop as a result of Franklin's problems.[3] He also wanted them to understand the rationale of the Federal Reserve if it were forced to intervene to support the dollar as a result of Franklin. And, finally, he was concerned with a longer-run effort to reassure other central bankers of the Federal Reserve's assumption of responsibility so that they in turn could reassure their commercial banks, prevent panic, and maintain calm in international markets. The Federal Reserve kept other central banks informed throughout the five months of the Franklin crisis in this common effort to minimize market disruptions and to enable authorities to counteract market reactions to Franklin.[4]

This exchange of information was part of a larger concurrent effort of central banks to coordinate their interventions in exchange markets to support the dollar. United States currency, as we have seen, was under severe pressure: from January until mid-May 1974 it had dropped between nine and eleven percent against currencies in the European "snake." As we have also noted, the Federal Reserve was concerned that news about Franklin would aggravate this decline. At the May meeting of central bank officials at the BIS, Swiss, German, and American officials agreed to "concerted exchange market operations to counter excessive speculation against the dollar." Interestingly, reports of the agreement leaked to the public on May 14, just as the Franklin crisis was breaking. There was an immediate scramble to cover short dollar positions. By the next day, the German mark and the Swiss franc had fallen 4½ percent against the dollar.[5]

Foreign central banks also cooperated with the Federal Reserve in the search for a purchaser of Franklin. Because of Federal law which prevented a non–New York State American bank from acquiring Franklin and because of antitrust concerns with some potential New York State purchasers, foreign banks figured prominently in the search for a merger partner or purchaser for Franklin. Foreign central banks played a role in providing information about potential candidates. The Bank of England, for example, was consulted by Governor Mitchell of the Federal Reserve about the ability of certain British banks to join with an American bank to purchase Franklin and the position of the Bank of England on such an action. The Bank of England was also consulted on the possibility of selling or liquidating the London branch. Although the latter action was never taken, the Bank of England said it would not oppose such a solution.[6]

The Bank of England and the Federal Reserve Loan

One of the most important policy initiatives of the Federal Reserve was its massive loan to Franklin National Bank. The cooperation of the Bank of England facilitated the assistance extended by the Federal Reserve Bank of New York to Franklin.

The Federal Reserve can make loans from its discount window

only if those loans are adequately secured by government obligations or by collateral deemed satisfactory by the Reserve Bank. Because Franklin had no U.S. government obligations available for use as collateral, advances were made on other collateral such as loans, mortgages, and securities held by Franklin. The Federal Reserve Bank took into its possession all readily available assets of Franklin National Bank to secure its mushrooming loan.

The possible need to take the assets of the London branch as collateral was foreseen from the beginning of the crisis. On May 13, when Alfred Hayes, president of the Federal Reserve Bank of New York, telephoned Governor Richardson of the Bank of England to inform him of the Federal Reserve's liquidity support, Hayes asked about the possibility of taking collateral in London. Governor Richardson said the Bank of England would help in any way it could.[7] By early June the Federal Reserve was forced to take up the Bank of England on its offer. Franklin by then was borrowing over $1.2 billion, and was reaching the limits of its collateral available in the United States to secure its loan. If a larger sum were needed, the Federal Reserve Bank would have to obtain the quite substantial collateral of Franklin's London branch in order to continue to keep Franklin alive.

One of the major problems facing the Federal Reserve Bank was taking the London collateral without informing the public. Reserve Bank officials felt that if the public knew of the collateral being pledged by Franklin, the amount of its support to Franklin would also become known and that public knowledge of the extent of its massive support to Franklin would aggravate deposit withdrawals and the liquidity crisis.

The problem of public knowledge of the taking of collateral centered on nonassignable securities, i.e., those assets which required the consent of the other party or legal registration for the Federal Reserve to assure or "perfect" its first claim on the asset. Because of its concern the Federal Reserve did not publicly record its security in much of the collateral it took in the United States. It took physical possession of the documents but refrained from taking the public steps necessary to perfect its claim.

The concern and the procedure followed in England were similar. With the help of Freshfields, the law firm frequently retained by the Bank of England, the Federal Reserve Bank of New York took assignable assets but did not notify other parties. For assets requiring consent it set up a trust under which the Reserve Bank acquired title, albeit not perfect title. Because British law allowed such trusts to last for only 21 days without a public filing, this trust agreement was renewed every 20 days.

In order to better assure its control over the London branch collateral, the Federal Reserve Bank of New York deposited the documents with the Bank of England. That latter bank agreed to hold Franklin's collateral for the Reserve Bank—i.e., to assure the Reserve Bank's physical possession of the assets. On June 14 an officer of the Federal Reserve Bank of New York received Franklin's notes and documents and placed them in safekeeping with the Bank of England in a locked box. The London branch collateral was to prove crucial to the Federal Reserve Bank of New York loan. One-fourth of the collateral pledged for the Reserve Bank advance as of October 8, 1974, was foreign branch loans and placements.[8]

Foreign Central Banks and Foreign Exchange

Foreign central bank cooperation was also essential in the Federal Reserve's support for Franklin's foreign exchange trading during the crisis and in enabling the Federal Reserve Bank of New York to manage the Franklin book effectively after the September 26 purchase.

Much as the Federal Reserve Bank acted as Franklin's agent in purchasing foreign exchange, so other central banks acted as the Federal Reserve's agent in acquiring foreign exchange. When Franklin was unable to purchase foreign currencies needed to fulfill maturing contracts, the Federal Reserve Bank turned to other central banks who sold their currency to the Federal Reserve.

Foreign central banks also played a crucial role after the Federal Reserve purchased Franklin's foreign exchange contracts. One of the major problems in purchasing the book and thereby stabilizing exchange markets was the possibility that parties to foreign exchange contracts with Franklin would renege on unfavorable contracts, arguing that they had made the contract with Franklin National Bank and were under no legal obligation to perform when that contract was transferred to the Federal Reserve Bank of New York. Even a few such actions could have been highly destabilizing in a market already severely shaken by Franklin and Herstatt, and by continuing foreign exchange losses by other banks.

Such market destabilization was prevented by the cooperation of foreign central banks. Those banks pressed their commercial banks which had outstanding contracts with Franklin to agree to the transfer of those contracts to the Federal Reserve Bank of New York. As one official of the Bank of England described it, the Bank of England called United Kingdom banks and "made clear they understood the position of the Bank of England."[9] In England such an act constitutes a command. Other central banks took similar steps. Thus, when the Federal Reserve Bank of New York cabled commercial banks requesting confirmation of the transfer of contracts, it received a confirmation from virtually all parties to contracts with Franklin National Bank. Without foreign central bank cooperation, the situation, as one Federal Reserve official put it, "would have been impossible."[10]

During the year in which the Federal Reserve Bank of New York worked out the Franklin book, foreign central banks continued to cooperate in the sale of foreign exchange.

Closing the London Branch

Franklin's London branch, as we have seen, held a large part, and many of the best, of the bank's assets. Franklin's Eurodollar loans were among the highest quality and highest yielding in the bank's portfolio and were considered by the FDIC a significant part of the assets a successful bidder might select to balance the liabilities assumed in acquiring Franklin National. Without the London branch assets, the FDIC felt that the price the bidding banks would have been willing to pay would have been lower and, indeed, they might not have been willing to bid at all.[11]

Throughout July and August the FDIC negotiated with the potential bidders on the assumption that London assets would be part of the bidding package. Then its English counsel informed the FDIC that the London branch assets might prove an important stumbling block. It was possible that a separate liquidation proceeding would be required in London, which would delay the transfer of London assets. Approval for transfer was also required under the United Kingdom's Foreign Exchange Controls Act. It was possible that if there were any delay in transferring the London assets to the United States, creditors of Franklin's London branch might institute legal proceedings to seize those assets to satisfy the liabilities of the branch. The acquisition of the assets was complicated by the fact that the Federal Reserve, because of its concern about publicity, had not perfected its claim to the assets.

The cooperation of the Bank of England was essential in resolving these important problems. Its approval was required under the Foreign Exchange Controls Act, which it administered for the Treasury. It also held the London branch assets on behalf of the Federal Reserve Bank of New York and could have blocked the transfer of those assets had it wished. Its position posed a potential political problem for the Bank of England. If it cooperated with the FDIC in transferring the London branch assets, it could have been criticized by British creditors of the London branch who in turn might pressure Ministers or Parliament and thus damage the reputation of the Bank and the City of London.[12] A different potential political problem, it seems, was the presence of European American Bank and Trust Company as one of the bidding banks. Some of European American shareholders operated in Rhodesia, which was subject to a United Kingdom economic boycott. If European American acquired Franklin—as in fact it did—and the Bank of England allowed the transfer of assets from London to European American, the Bank might also have faced political reaction.

Governor Burns used his good offices to arrange a meeting between the FDIC and the Bank of England. On September 20 Frank Wille, Chairman of the FDIC, H. David Willey of the Federal Reserve Bank of New York, Governor Richardson of the Bank of England, and Rodney Galpin of the Bank of England's Banking and Money Market Supervision Section met on Threadneedle Street to confront the problem of the London branch. Governor Richardson, stressing his fear that an unsuccessful settlement of the Franklin crisis would lead to further disturbances in international banking, was sympathetic and encouraging to the FDIC proposals. On advice of counsel the Bank of England agreed that a separate liquidation in the United Kingdom was probably not necessary and that as long as all Franklin's tax liabilities were met there was little risk of a separate liquidation. The Bank of England agreed to make the necessary approvals for the immediate transfer of Franklin's London assets to the FDIC. It was agreed that the Bank would be informed immediately before the public announcement of Franklin's insolvency and that it would then immediately give the necessary authorizations for transfer of the London assets. This agreement and advance arrangement were crucial to the willingness of banks to bid on Franklin and to the settlement, at long last, of the crisis.

The plan worked like clockwork. As Frank Wille later put it: "When Franklin National Bank was in fact declared insolvent and the FDIC appointed receiver, the necessary approvals for transfer of the Bank's London assets to the FDIC were immediately forthcoming under the English Foreign Exchange Controls Act, and other necessary governmental approvals were cleared expeditiously"[13]

Toward International Management

In addition to ad hoc cooperation, the banking crisis of 1974 (of which the Franklin crisis was a central element) led to important innovations in the management of international banking. New international cooperative mechanisms developed at three levels: central bank governors meeting together at the BIS; top level bank regulatory and supervisory authorities from twelve major countries meeting in a newly formed international committee; and national regulatory and supervisory authorities acting both on their own initiative and cooperatively with their foreign counterparts.

Central Bank Governors

Central bank cooperation to avert and manage international financial crises is not a new phenomenon. Such cooperation was a stabilizing force in the interwar monetary system and rose to prominence again after 1960.[14] Beginning in that year, governors and high officials from the central banks of the Group of Ten countries gathered monthly at the Bank for International Settlements at Basel, Switzerland, and conferred frequently between meetings on monetary and economic problems. As a result there developed a close personal network and a high degree of consultation and cooperation among central bankers.[15] This experience was the essential base on which international financial consultation and cooperation were expanded to international banking.

Despite the dramatic growth in international operations, there was little concern among central bankers before 1974 about crisis prevention or crisis management in international banking. Bank regulation and supervision were perceived as relatively unimportant issues which, in any case, were of national and not international concern. Similarly, crisis management issues such as lender of last resort policies were seen as problems of primarily historical interest and, again, ones with national not international dimensions. As one high official of the Bank of England put it:

For some years . . . international developments went largely unheeded by the main national supervisory authorities, for the good reason that they had no immediate cause for concern. . . . it was not until the end of 1973 that the potential weaknesses of the system began to become clear.[16]

The crisis of 1974 forced central bankers seriously to consider the problems raised by the internationalization of banking. The first joint effort of central bankers was their attempt to prevent the further erosion of confidence in international banks during the summer and autumn of 1974. The central bank governors sought to shore up confidence by convincing the world that they were ready and able to act as lenders of last resort in international banking.

The regular monthly meeting at the BIS in July 1974 took place less than two weeks after the Herstatt collapse, during the Franklin crisis, and in the midst of great instability in foreign exchange and Eurodollar markets and great concerns about bank liquidity. At that meeting the bankers agreed in principle to provide emergency assistance to financially troubled banks wherever necessary to avert a crisis of confidence in the international banking system.

This commitment, however, was very vague. It was not officially announced but instead leaked to the press. The nature of the commitment was kept unclear. According to Andrew Brimmer, who at the time was a member of the Board of Governors of the Federal Reserve System, the decision was in fact a compromise between the Federal Reserve, which argued for an explicit commitment by central banks to act as lenders of last resort, and the Bundesbank, which did not want to be committed to intervene when banks engaged in unauthorized or illegal activities.[17] Banks did not commit themselves to helping troubled institutions but only to preventing a general liquidity crisis. Thus it remained uncertain just which illiquid institutions would be helped. The determination of lending in actual situations was presumably left to national authorities, perhaps with some international consultation. And the assignment of responsibility for different forms of foreign banking institutions was either not made or not announced. It was understood, as the Franklin events demonstrated, that national authorities would be responsible for foreign branches because they were considered integral parts of the parent. Responsibility for consortium banks and for foreign subsidiaries, however, remained unclear. Such subsidiaries are owned by foreign banks but incorporated in the host country. They are thus legally separate from the parent and from the home lender of last resort. However, morally and for reasons of their own reputations parents may feel responsible for such subsidiaries and home authorities may thus be confronted with the issue of support.

The July agreement did little to arrest the erosion of confidence in international markets. Depositors continued to flock to large banks of major countries which they, correctly, believed authorities could not allow to fail. Smaller institutions such as regional banks and those from countries with weak balances of payments such as Italy and Japan were increasingly squeezed. Particularly hard hit were consortium banks and foreign subsidiaries which were unable to acquire funds or were forced to pay high interest rates.

In September, therefore, the central bank governors took the unusual step of issuing a communiqué following their monthly meeting. The statement made specific reference to the problem of lender of last resort:

The governors had an exchange of views on the problem of lender of last resort in the Euromarket. They recognized that it would not be practical to lay down in advance detailed rules and procedures for the provision of temporary liquidity. But they were satisfied that means are available for that purpose and will be used if and when necessary.[18]

The commitment—although now public—was still left ambiguous. This ambiguity was due in part to the persistent dilemma facing lenders of last resort: the problem of trying to make depositors feel confident without making bankers feel complacent. In seeking to ensure the liquidity of the system the lender of last resort must inevitably prevent the failure of specific banks, but if banks feel the lender of last resort will come to their rescue they may be encouraged to undertake riskier ventures.[19] Henry C. Wallich, a member of the Board of Governors of the Federal Reserve System, testifying in the Senate, described the September statement and United States policy and explained why emergency lending commitments had not been made specific:

There are dangers in trying to define and publicize specific rules for emergency assistance to troubled banks, notably the possibility of causing undue reliance on such facilities and possible relaxation of needed caution on the part of all market participants. Therefore, the Federal Reserve has always avoided comprehensive statements of conditions for its assistance to member banks. Emergency assistance is inherently a process of negotiation and judgment, with a range of possible actions varying with circumstances and need. Therefore, a predetermined set of conditions for emergency lending would be inappropriate.[20]

Another reason for the vague nature of the BIS commitment was the real differences in the capabilities and policies of various national lenders of last resort. In West Germany and Luxemburg there were no official lenders of last resort. In addition, there were great differences of opinion between home and host countries regarding responsibility for subsidiaries and consortium banks.

As the host central bank for the largest concentration of foreign bank institutions in the world, the Bank of England pressed for international rules which would restrict its responsibilities and force other states to assume responsibility for nonbranch affiliates of their banks. George Blunden, the head of banking supervision of the Bank of England, described the policy of the British central bank in a speech in March 1975:

Our contentions . . . are: first, that branches of overseas banks here are integral parts of the banks to which they belong and are thus primarily the concern, not of us as the central bank of the host country, but of their parents and of their parents' central bank or other supervisory authorities for both supervision and support; second, that . . . for banks registered here but owned overseas, such ownership entails responsibility for support, whether the bank concerned is wholly owned or is owned by a consortium. . . .[21]

The Bank of England has made several attempts to persuade other central banks to adopt this position. When the Israel British Bank, a subsidiary of an Israeli bank incorporated in the United Kingdom, went into receivership in August 1974 because of illegal activities, the Bank of England insisted that it had no responsibility as lender of last resort for a wholly owned subsidiary of a foreign bank. Israeli banking authorities, on the other hand, argued that Israel was not responsible for a British corporation. The two governments jousted for over one year. Eventually, under pressure from the United States, Israel agreed to pool the assets of the parent bank and the British subsidiary while the Bank of England, in a concession it insisted was not a precedent but a magnanimous gesture, contributed £3 million to the pool of assets. The Bank of England had held to its principle although the events reveal there is little international agreement on the subject.

In September 1974 the Bank of England sought a commitment to its policy by sending a letter to the owners of consortium banks operating in London asking that they acknowledge "moral responsibility" for their investments in London. Moral responsibility was defined as "responsibility to support those investments beyond the narrow limits laid down by laws of limited liability and, above all, as responsibility to protect depositors with those banks."[22] When the Bank received such confirmations, it then wrote to the parents of subsidiary banks asking for a similar commitment, which it received.

In the view of the Bank of England, acquiescence to its actions suggests most central banks agree with the interpretations of the Old Lady of Threadneedle Street. As Mr. Blunden put it: " . . . we have clarified with banks in London associated with overseas banks, with their shareholder banks and with other central banks, where responsibilities for support lie. Our contentions . . . have been generally accepted by those banks."[23]

Acceptance, however, is not so widespread and clearcut as Mr. Blunden suggests. The Federal Reserve, a crucial actor in the system, has taken the position that although American banks responded with a moral commitment, the Federal Reserve is not bound by these "comfort letters."

Nonetheless, the Board of Governors has taken steps to deal with the problem of risks in foreign joint ventures of American banks. In a policy statement on February 12, 1976, the Board announced that in determining whether to approve an application of an American banking organization to invest in a foreign joint venture it would, "as a matter of policy," take into account:

1. The possibility that the venture might need additional financial support.
2. The possibility that the additional support might be significantly larger than the original equity investment in the joint venture.[24]

While not acquiescing to the Bank of England's interpretation, the Federal Reserve has sought to protect against a testing of its support for foreign joint ventures. Thus, just what the letters of assurance mean will not be known unless and until they are tested.

Not only is the division of responsibility unclear, the policies of central banks toward intervention in crises also differ greatly. The Federal Reserve, as demonstrated in the Franklin National Bank case, believes in early intervention to manage crises, while the Deutschebundesbank continues to defend its policy of nonintervention in the Herstatt case. Thus there remains great uncertainty as to what national policies will actually be in the event of a crisis.

In sum, even though the issue of the lender of last resort in Euromarkets has been raised to the level of central bank consultation, important national differences and thus important gaps remain.

Another result of the 1974 crisis was that central bank governors expanded their purview to bank supervision. While discussion previously centered on monetary and economic policy and is still heavily focused on those issues, bank supervisory and regulatory policy has become a more prominent subject of discussion at the monthly meetings and in more informal encounters than before. The September 1974 communiqué stressed this new focus:

At their regular meeting in Basel on 9th September, the central bank governors from the countries of the Group of 10 and Switzerland discussed the working of the international banking system. They took stock of the existing mechanisms for supervision and regulation and noted recent improvement made in these fields in a number of major countries.

They agreed to intensify the exchange of information between central banks on the activities of banks operating in international markets and, where appropriate, to tighten further the regulations governing foreign-exchange positions.[25]

Not only have central bank governors directly discussed supervisory problems, they have also created a Standing Committee on Banking Regulations and Supervisory Practices within the BIS, the so-called Blunden (now Cooke) Committee.

The Standing (Blunden-Cooke) Committee

The Standing Committee on Banking Regulations and Supervisory Practices was a direct outgrowth of the 1974 banking crisis. As a result of the Franklin and Herstatt episodes and other bank failures and losses, supervisory activities came to be seen in a new and more important light. As W. Peter Cooke, the present chairman of the Standing Committee, put it:

Although the international character of major banks had developed enormously, there was absolutely no parallel development of international supervisory machinery. This left large gaps through which many imprudent activities could be driven. The events of 1974 highlighted the problem. People were aware of the problem before 1974 but the crisis impelled them to move.[26]

The initiative for the formation of a Standing Committee came from Governor Richardson of the Bank of England. As host for the major center for Euromarket operations and the largest concentration of foreign branches, subsidiaries, and consortium banks, the Bank of England took the lead in pressing for supervisory cooperation, much as it had pressed for agreement on the responsibility of the lender of last resort. Richardson's main concerns were direct responses to the events of 1974. He wanted an improvement in bank supervision and regulation of foreign exchange trading and an international early warning system which would sound the alarm before another crisis erupted. Thus in the fall of 1974 Governor Richardson proposed that the Group of Ten governors establish a Standing Committee on regulatory and supervisory practices.

There was a precedent for such cooperation. Since 1972 bank

supervisors within the EEC had been meeting in the Groupe de Contact. This informal gathering of regulatory officials was the response of central bank supervisors to movement within the EEC to develop an economic and monetary union and to harmonize banking laws. It had no official status; participants did not attend as national representatives but as informal members of an unofficial club. Its meetings, which took place three times a year, were very informal, involving no interpreters, no minutes, no secretariat. Its discussions centered on such problems as banking secrecy, national regulatory systems, and new problems posed by international banking. Importantly, the Groupe de Contact also served as a method for exchanging confidential information on the situation of banking and banks within the EEC.

Governor Richardson's proposal that a new, broader, and formally institutionalized body be created fell on receptive ears. The United States, as the other power in international banking, was particularly interested. Pressure was building within the Federal Reserve System for improvement in the regulation and supervision of international banking. Within the Federal Reserve System a Steering Committee on International Banking Regulation had been established, with Governor George Mitchell as chairman. It considered the status and position of foreign banks in the United States and American regulatory policies governing the activities of American banks abroad.[27] Governor Mitchell was interested in encouraging international cooperation among supervisors and had independently invited the Group of Ten supervisors to a meeting in Washington in 1975.

As a result of Richardson's efforts, the Group of Ten central bank governors in autumn 1974 established the Standing Committee on Banking Regulations and Supervisory Practices. The Standing Committee is composed of representatives from the Group of Ten countries plus Luxemburg and Switzerland—the countries where the principal international markets are located and whose banks are most active in those markets. George Blunden (until June 30, 1977) and Peter Cooke have attended in the capacity as chairman. The Standing Committee meetings are more formal than the gatherings of the Groupe de Contact. Interpreters are present; minutes are kept; papers are presented. The Standing Committee also has a secretariat, a function performed by the BIS.

The purpose of the Standing Committee is to prevent international financial disruptions resulting from banking failures. The actual agenda is set by the Committee itself within the broad terms of reference set by the central bank governors and subject to their further instructions. It was specifically charged by the governors to develop international early warning systems to identify problems in national banking systems which might have international repercussions. It has also been authorized to examine the health of the international banking system, supervision across national frontiers, and other international banking problems as they arise. The governors, however, did not want the problem of lender of last resort discussed in the Committee, and reserved it for themselves.

The role of the formal meetings of the Standing Committee is primarily consultative. At the first meeting there was some talk of creating a new international body with supervisory power. However, as George Blunden put it:

The Committee quickly reached the conclusion that it would not be practicable to establish a separate reporting system, operated by an international body, to cover all international banking operations and to provide early warnings by identifying potential danger spots. Such arrangements would inevitably, in large part, wastefully duplicate existing national arrangements, would in many countries be incompatible with existing legislation, and would be very difficult to co-ordinate because of differences in individual banking and political systems.[28]

The Committee has thus focused on improving national supervisory systems and on developing cooperation among national authorities through a consultative process.

One important type of consultation has been the regular study of supervisory techniques and innovations in the member countries. Before the formation of the Standing Committee, supervisors had very little knowledge of supervisory responsibilities and methods in other countries. As a result of national reports in the Committee and of comparative studies made by the BIS secretariat, they are now well informed about foreign practices. The purpose of this exchange of information is not only to educate supervisors about foreign systems but also to encourage national change by making authorities aware of weaknesses in their own systems and of possible models for improving them. Thus, studies have focused not only on general analysis and comparison of supervisory systems but also on specific problem areas: attitudes of member countries on the role of loan capital in a bank's balance sheet, requirements for endowment capital for foreign branches, arrangements for bank audits, control over potential clashes of interest.

The Standing Committee has given special attention to supervisory problems created by international banking. It has sought to develop some common understanding and guidelines on a variety of international problems. Its initial concern was the problem of foreign exchange. The Committee discussed foreign exchange supervision and examined the experience of the Federal Reserve Bank of New York in acquiring the foreign exchange book of Franklin National Bank and the international problems involved in working out that book. Although the Committee began by emphasizing foreign exchange and although it is still concerned with some of the more specialized aspects of foreign exchange, such as the legal status of foreign exchange contracts and relationships between banks and foreign exchange brokers, it has moved on to other areas of supervision of foreign activities: guidelines for judging capital adequacy for foreign branches, desirable maturity spreads, overgearing and imprudent lending, internal control systems within banks.

The Committee has also sought to identify and fill gaps in the supervision of foreign banking. It has had some success in identifying responsibilities of home and host countries. There has been agreement that the host supervisory authority has primary authority for supervising foreign subsidiaries and joint ventures, and that parent authorities have primary responsibility for foreign branches. The Committee has pressed for the right of parent supervisory authorities to make direct inspections of or at least to have access to information about the foreign affiliates of their banks.

The Committee has also examined problems arising from differences in auditing and accounting practices between countries. The Committee's studies of cases such as the Israel-British case showed that such differences contributed to the failure of supervisory authorities, auditors, and lending banks to identify bank problems. There has been general agreement within the Committee that auditing and accounting practices can be improved and harmonized. To this end the Committee has commissioned the International Accounting Standards Committee to study and develop proposals for the harmonization of national accounting and auditing standards.

In all these studies and discussions the Committee's goal is not, as George Blunden put it; "a massive harmonisation of our approaches to supervision. The legislative backgrounds against which we operate, the banking systems which we supervise, and the political structures—for example unified or federative—of our different countries, are all so vastly different that we could not operate a unified system." Rather, the goal, he said is to "learn from each other and adapt the best features of each other's systems for inclusion in our own systems."[29]

Members of the Committee point out that it does act as an important catalyst for national reform. It subjects national policy to international examination, offers suggestions and models for national change. Such suggestions have been effective because they have come at a time when national banking problems have led to widespread national reforms in bank supervision and regulation. The Committee can also serve as a pressure group for national change. George Blunden, for example, suggested that its support for greater access by home supervisory authorities contributed to greater openness by host authorities:

It is interesting to note that, since these recommendations on the desirability of increased co-operation were made, a number of countries have already taken powers under legislation, or have the taking of such legislative powers in prospect, to permit the passing of information gleaned for supervisory purposes to supervisory authorities in other countries.[30]

There is another important dimension to the work of the Standing Committee: its informal activities. One of the major consequences of the Committee has been the creation of an international network of high-level supervisory authorities who know each other well, trust each other, and are able to communicate confidentially with each other. Before the creation of the Committee this international network simply did not exist. Except for those supervisory authorities who had begun to meet in the Groupe de Contact, high-level officials had never met. Now they have close contacts.

This contact and trust have made possible an informal but important international early warning system for international banking. The formal structure of the Committee has created links which enable the members to engage in informal discussion both in the corridors and between meetings. As George Blunden put it, the group has established "among ourselves such a degree of personal contact and trust that we can help to forestall troubles in the international system by working closely together."[31] The subjects of these discussions are the "facts and gossip" of bank supervision which national supervisors feel it is important for other supervisors to know. U.S. bank regulators feel confident enough now to reveal to their counterparts in Standing Committee countries information about activities of banks from those countries operating in the United States. West German and Luxemburg authorities have arranged for German authorities to receive information on the operations of German banks in Luxemburg. This exchange better enables national authorities to control their own banks.

The face-to-face contact of the Committee has also made it easier for supervisory authorities to work together during a banking crisis. One case of international cooperation which was discussed by the Committee was that of American Bank and Trust Company of New York and Banque de l'Amérique du Sud of Belgium (BAS). This case was not handled within the Standing Committee network because it involved a nonmember, the New York State Banking Commission. But the case did reflect the new efforts at international cooperation in the wake of 1974.

American Bank and Trust Company, (ABT) (chartered by New York State and owned by Swiss-Israel Trade Bank of Geneva, which was in turn controlled by a Chilean citizen) had close links with BAS, owned by the Graiver family of Argentina. The two banks, it seems, were being used for an international looting scheme designed to benefit the Graivers. Cooperation between New York State and Belgian banking authorities made possible the uncovering of the scheme and led to the closing of both banks. The New York State Banking Commission uncovered suspicious activities involving transactions between ABT and BAS which it could not evaluate without evidence from Belgian authorities. New York authorities contacted Belgian authorities who then came to the United States, received information about the mysterious transactions, and returned armed with accounts and names. The transactions matched and the fraud was confirmed. Once the scheme was uncovered authorities continued to keep each other informed and to coordinate the closing of the two banks. The international exchange of information, exchange of views about the situation and about what each was doing and planned to do enabled both Americans and Belgians to manage the domestic banking problem more effectively. After it was all over, Herman Baeyens, Director of the Belgian Banking Commission, gave a presentation of the case to the Standing Committee.[32]

The Standing Committee and other BIS cooperation, such as the collection of Eurocurrency data, have paved the way for the formation of other groups within the BIS to discuss international banking problems. One such problem has been the growing debt of certain countries, particularly underdeveloped countries. A surge in Eurodollar borrowing of Third World countries in the late 1960s and early 1970s plus the recent borrowing to finance oil-induced deficits has led to a significant increase in Third World indebtedness and in the indebtedness of certain countries. Just how that debt is distributed, however, remains a mystery. Complete and uniform data for Eurobank loans are simply not available. Information exists for United States banks and their foreign branches and for head offices of banks in Europe and Japan. But European and Japanese authorities have not collected data on loans of their foreign branches around the world. Furthermore, because the type of reporting required by different national authorities varies significantly, available data are often not comparable or capable of being aggregated. Finally, there has been no aggregation of data beyond rudimentary national efforts.

In July 1976 at their monthly meeting the central bank governors established a group within the BIS to gather better and more complete data on the geographical distribution of international lending. The group began meeting in September 1976. Its data-gathering effort, now in process, is the first step toward an international evaluation of the problem of country risk.

The Standing Committee network is also developing external links. There has been concern within the Committee that its control does not extend beyond the twelve member states and that the limit of its scope might be a problem in preventing and controlling future problems. Thus, while the Group of Ten plus Switzerland and Luxemburg remain the only members of the Committee on Banking Regulations and Supervisory Practices, the Committee has developed relations with banking authorities in other countries. Such links broaden the pressure for reform, the early warning network, and could prove vitally important in the event of a bank crisis which required cooperation of authorities outside the Committee membership group.

A Separate Network

From 1975 to March 1978, the Comptroller—the principal supervisor of national banks and of their overseas branches—was not invited to attend the Standing Committee meetings. In part, the exclusion of the administrator of national banks grew out of the historical origins of the Standing Committee: it began as a concern of the central bank governors and was established as part of the BIS, which is an organization of central banks. Nonetheless a number of other central banks—those of Belgium, Canada, France, Luxemburg, and West Germany—had invited their national banking supervisory authorities to participate in the Committee meetings.

A more important explanation for the exclusion of the Comptroller was the politics of bank supervision and monetary policy in the United States. In the fragmented American regulatory and supervisory system, the Office of the Comptroller has great responsibility but less power and status than the Federal Reserve. Furthermore, the Comptroller is a department, although a very independent one, of the Treasury. The rivalry between the Federal Reserve and the Treasury in policymaking is a long and powerful one. The Federal Reserve, long on the defensive against the rising power of the Treasury, has jealously guarded its prerogatives. The management of international financial relations is terrain which the Federal Reserve has annexed and which it carefully guards. Inviting the Comptroller may have been seen as opening a door to the Treasury. Finally, from June 1976 to May 1977 the Office of the Comptroller was headed by an Acting Comptroller, who was not in a position to press for participation. Thus, until March 1978, the Federal Reserve made no effort to include the Comptroller in its international dialogue, and the Comptroller did not have the power to oblige the Federal Reserve to invite it to participate. The Comptroller was merely kept informed of the Standing Committee's activities.

The Comptroller, however, was not completely excluded from international interaction. Since 1967, when the International Division was established, the Comptroller's office has developed a series of bilateral relations with supervisory authorities in countries having branches of American banks. This network of bilateral relations involves regular visits, an exchange of information on methods of examining banks, data sharing, and in some cases joint examination of American branches abroad with foreign supervisory authorities.[33]

In 1978 when John G. Heimann became the new Comptroller of the Currency he pushed for inclusion on the Standing Committee. Heimann, who had a special interest in and concern about international banking, argued that it was irrational for the administrator of national banks not to be on the Committee, especially since bank supervisory authorities from other member states were included. Once Heimann raised and pushed the issue, there was no resistance from the Federal Reserve. In March 1978 the national administrator of banks was included in the Standing Committee network.

National Changes

Finally, the crisis of 1974 has led to a revision of national supervisory and regulatory law and policy as they apply to international banking. The most concerned country and the most active in adapting national policy has been the United States. Partly because of the Franklin experience, partly because of the increasing involvement of American banks in international banking, and partly because of a long tradition of close supervision of banks, the United States has taken the lead in monitoring more closely the new risks of international banking. Following the foreign exchange losses of 1974, the Comptroller and the Federal Reserve pressed banks to develop internal control systems for foreign exchange operations. They also began regularly to monitor foreign exchange trading, an activity facilitated by legislation requiring reporting of foreign exchange transactions. At the same time the Federal Reserve adopted more conservative policies regarding foreign expansion by American banks, establishing more stringent capital and liquidity requirements for new ventures. Regulatory authorities have also worked independently and together to develop an evaluation and review process for international loans which is designed to monitor a country's risk.[34] Finally, in 1978 Congress passed and the President signed the International Banking Act which brings foreign banks operating in the United States under federal control.[35]

The crisis of 1974 also led to important reforms in West Germany. In October 1974, a little over three months after the Herstatt debacle, federal authorities established detailed limits on foreign exchange trading by German banks, limiting various open positions to fixed percentages of bank capital. The government also moved toward a lender of last resort capability by establishing the Liquiditäts

Konsortialbank. This bank, with capital of DM 1 billion of which 30 percent is contributed by the Bundesbank, can help banks with temporary liquidity problems. In October 1974 the government also introduced a new banking bill. Finally enacted in May 1976, the so-called Lex Herstatt establishes limits on large loans as a percentage of bank capital and increases the supervisory powers of the Federal Banking Supervisory Office and Bundesbank.[36] In 1978 the Federal Banking Supervisory office sought to fill an important gap in its purview by seeking greater information on Luxemburg operations of German banks. This it has tried to do through parent banks and through cooperation with the Luxemburg Banking Control Commission.

Yet another major supervisory reform but one not specifically directed at international banking has been implemented in the United Kingdom. Partly in response to pressure from the EEC to harmonize banking legislation and partly in response to the domestic and international banking crises of 1973-74, the bank revised its practices in 1975, and in 1976 the government issued a White Paper on the revision of bank supervision. These changes enacted by Parliament in 1979 expand the supervisory role in general of the Bank of England and formalize and make more frequent reporting procedures.[37]

Other Standing Committee countries have instituted more limited reforms. Luxemburg has developed a lender of last resort facility. All are now supervising foreign exchange activities more carefully and insisting on tighter internal controls within banks on foreign exchange operations. All are developing new principles for assuring capital adequacy and liquidity which will take foreign operations into account. And pressure is building in part through the BIS for greater national supervision of offshore activities of national banks through increased data collection.

In this context of national change, international interaction takes on greater importance. The exchange of information and the development of new data through the Standing Committee and the Groupe de Contact and the pressure for change arising from these groups arrive at a time when national authorities are in quest of new ideas. In this process of national change, the input of the policies and practices of other countries through the Standing Committee and the Groupe de Contact will have an influence.

7

PAST, PRESENT, AND FUTURE CHALLENGES FOR THE INTERNATIONAL BANKING SYSTEM

IN 1974 THE international financial system faced its most serious crisis since the 1930s. The stresses and shocks of that year including the failure of the Franklin National Bank led to a crisis of confidence which brought the international banking system dangerously close to disaster. Fortunately the crisis of 1974 did not become the crash of 1974, in part because of the resilience of the system and in part because central bankers were able to manage and contain the crisis.

The events of 1974 and the Franklin National Bank have now passed into history. But agonizing questions remain: Can it happen again? Are international banks and the international banking system vulnerable to crisis? And if a crisis erupts will the system be pulled back from the brink as it was in 1974? Is there sufficient political capability to prevent or control another international financial crisis? The lessons of the Franklin crisis and the experience in the intervening years suggest some answers to these questions.

The Vulnerability of International Banking

Liquidity and Solvency of Individual Banks

The problems which led to the demise of the Franklin National Bank were, in some ways, unique. The incompetence of management, the influence of Sindona, the degree of fraud—all made Franklin a special case. But more widespread systemic problems not unique to Franklin also played a crucial role in the collapse of that bank and the crisis of 1974. Changes in the nature of banking which made institutions more susceptible to liquidity and solvency problems, and difficulties in the international economic system which placed important stresses on banks, played a crucial role in the Franklin and international banking crises. The systemic problems in the banking business and in the international economy which made banks vulnerable in 1974 have been partially eliminated, but they have not disappeared.

As we have seen, the business of commercial banking changed profoundly in the 1960s and 1970s. Pressed by market forces and supported by regulatory policy, banks including Franklin National became more competitive and aggressive, more eager to seek growth and profits, and more willing to assume risks. They adopted more liberal lending policies and moved into new and often riskier activities. The sources of their financing also became riskier. They increasingly funded their lending with short-term uninsured liabilities, which led to a decline in capital/asset ratios and left them sensitive to interest rate changes and to deposit runoffs.[1]

One of the important new growth areas was international banking. International operations expanded dramatically and came to account for an important part of bank assets, liabilities, and earnings. In some ways, the risks banks encountered in international ventures were no different from risks encountered in new domestic activities. Thus, for example, Franklin's foreign exchange trading and Eurodollar operations resembled its new domestic ventures in the New York wholesale market, in which the bank's lack of experience and knowledge and its perceived need to carve a position in a competitive market increased risk. Similarly, reliance on short-term, uninsured Eurodollar placements to fund long-term loans was not uniquely an international risk, but rather one dimension of the larger phenomenon of liability management which included the use of domestic Federal funds and certificates of deposit.

In other ways, however, the risks in international banking are quite different from those encountered in domestic activities. Information costs are higher than in domestic banking. At home, banks have the advantages of familiarity with social, political, and business practices which they do not have abroad. In domestic banking in the United States they have access to more accurate and complete information, which enables them to evaluate the ability of a potential borrower to repay a loan. In international banking the dearth of information makes it difficult to calculate credit worthiness. Many countries do not require disclosure of information by businesses. It is virtually impossible to acquire information on total outstanding debt and maturity structure of that debt of many international borrowers, especially multinational corporations and foreign governments, which borrow in many states and under many different guises. Furthermore, the cost of acquiring even this inadequate information is so high for all but the biggest banks that smaller banks joining in international syndications rely on the research and evaluation of large lead banks. Some analysts suggest that this follow-the-leader process not only enhances the power and advantages of the big banks but also increases the danger of miscalculation by one or more of the large international banks.[2]

In making cross-border loans, banks also encounter the problem of country risk, in which the change in the economic or political situation in the country of the foreign borrower may alter the credit risk. Even a credit-worthy borrower, for example, may be prevented from servicing a loan if a government imposes foreign exchange controls or if political authorities decide to repudiate debts for whatever reasons.[3]

Yet another problem with special international significance is that of deposit withdrawal. As we have seen in the Franklin case, long-term Eurodollar loans are funded almost entirely with short-term, uninsured liabilities (largely placements of other banks) for which banks are not required to hold reserves. The character of these deposits makes international banks especially vulnerable to a liquidity squeeze arising from massive, unexpected Eurocurrency deposit withdrawals.

Another important difference between domestic and foreign risk is solvency regulation. National regulatory systems designed to assure that banks will remain solvent are directed at domestic and not at international banking. There is far more limited regulation of competition, risk assumption, and misconduct in international banking. For United States banks there are no interest rate ceilings or geographical restrictions on international branching. There are fewer constraints on the types of activities in which banks are permitted to engage, and no reserve requirements. Furthermore, international operations are more difficult to supervise. As a result, international banking is highly competitive, more risk prone, and possibly more vulnerable to misconduct than domestic banking.

Banks, motivated by the new goals of growth and profit and responding to the competitive environment, have taken advantage of the international opportunities offered by this system. Such a permissive international regulatory environment may increase risk and endanger stability. Banks may make wise decisions in managing their new international activities—and, indeed, until now, figures for losses on international loans are better than on domestic loans[4]—but they may also assume dangerous risks.

The problem of excessive risk assumption deriving from the competitive and risk-prone environment of international banking was revealed by the Franklin crisis and the troubles of 1974. In the highly competitive Eurocurrency market of the early 1970s, banks increased loans, narrowed interest rate spreads, and lengthened maturities while continuing to rely on short-term Eurodollar placements to fund credits. We have seen that Franklin's Eurodollar operation grew from virtually nothing to nearly a billion dollars—

one-fifth of the bank's assets and liabilities—in the space of two years, that the Eurodollar operation was a drain on the bank's earnings, and that the transformation problem in the Euromarket played a critical role in Franklin's liquidity crisis. Within the Euromarkets more broadly, dangerous maturity structures and low profitability led to great uneasiness which provided a fertile environment for the crisis of confidence of 1974.

For a while it seemed that, as a result of the 1974 shock, banks had learned an important lesson about risk assumption in Euromarkets. Beginning in the summer of that year, spreads widened and maturities shortened. By 1977, however, conditions again resembled those of 1973–74. Increasing liquidity in the Eurocurrency market plus limited loan demand from prime borrowers led to intense competition.[5] The results, once again, were narrower spreads, longer maturities, increasing size of loans, and a willingness to lend to higher-risk borrowers (see table 7.1). Many analysts felt that the margins did not accurately reflect the risks banks were assuming in such loans.[6]

In sum, the more limited regulation of competition, risk assumption, and misconduct in international banking enhances the possibility of bank solvency problems.

Not only changes in banking but also changes in the international economic environment have created problems for bank stability. One such change, clearly revealed in the Franklin National Bank episode, is the emergence of a floating exchange rate regime. Banks, of course, have long operated in foreign exchange markets as part of their regular international business, and many have for a variety of reasons maintained open foreign exchange positions. When banks maintain such open positions, some inevitably make a profit while others inevitably suffer losses. Under a fixed exchange rate regime, however, the possibility of loss from trading was minimized by official intervention which, except in times of devaluation or revaluation, maintained exchange rates within narrow bands.[7]

Under a floating regime, these bands have by and large disappeared and currency fluctuations have become large and often erratic.

TABLE 7.1 Average Loan Rate Spreads on New Eurocurrency Bank Credits to Governments and State Enterprises in Selected Countries (spreads in percentage points over LIBOR)

	1977				1978	
	QI	*QII*	*QIII*	*QIV*	*QI*	*QII*
Industrial countries:						
Denmark	1.32	1.19	—	0.96	0.75	0.72
Finland	—	1.09	—	—	0.71	0.75
France	0.92	0.94	—	0.69	0.57	0.56
Ireland	1.41	—	—	0.88	—	0.75
Italy	—	1.38	1.34	1.19	1.12	1.01
Spain	1.63	1.39	1.54	1.00	0.94	0.87
Sweden	0.93	—	0.99	0.88	—	0.70
Non-oil LDCs:						
Argentina	1.65	1.70	1.56	—	1.57	1.22
Brazil	1.93	1.88	2.00	2.08	1.97	1.63
Korea	1.88	1.44	1.89	1.72	1.13	0.88
Malaysia	1.13	0.88	—	—	0.78	0.70
Mexico	1.57	1.53	1.70	—	1.30	1.11
Philippines	1.75	1.75	1.63	1.63	1.32	1.00
OPEC countries:						
Algeria	1.63	1.63	1.63	1.57	1.44	1.41
Indonesia	—	—	1.70	1.38	1.38	0.88
Iran	1.13	0.95	0.88	0.92	0.80	0.71
Venezuela	1.00	—	0.88	—	0.75	0.79
Communist countries:						
Bulgaria	—	1.13	1.13	1.08	—	0.85
East Germany	1.25	1.19	1.25	1.13	1.08	0.75
Hungary	—	—	1.05	1.00	—	0.70
Weighted averages:						
7 industrial countries	0.99	1.17	1.35	0.92	0.85	0.78
6 non-oil LDCs	1.76	1.61	1.76	1.99	1.30	1.22
4 OPEC countries	1.04	1.18	1.15	1.31	0.98	0.95
3 Communist countries	1.25	1.18	1.15	1.10	1.08	0.75
Total: 20 selected countries	1.21	1.32	1.52	1.22	1.09	1.03

SOURCE: Morgan Guaranty Trust Company, *World Financial Markets* (June 1978), p. 5. Used by permission.

Note: Average loan rate spreads over LIBOR are calculated by weighting the average spread on each loan by the size of the loan. The average spread on an individual loan with a split spread is calculated by weighting each spread by the number of years it is in effect. *Q* followed by roman numeral indicates quarter of the year.

Wide movements in foreign exchange rates increase the range of possible gains—and losses—on the same volume of bank foreign exchange trading, while erratic movements increase the possibility of miscalculation. Furthermore, as we have seen, banks have not traded the same volume of foreign exchange. The needs of customers plus possibilities for profits under floating exchange rates have led many banks to increase their foreign exchange trading significantly. Trading by twelve major American banks more than doubled from 1971 to 1974, and foreign banks were reputed to be even more active in exchange markets than these American banks.[8] In these circumstances profits and losses, especially at times of extreme exchange rate fluctuations, may be significant.

Even before the well-publicized foreign exchange losses of 1974, many banks recognized the dangers inherent in foreign exchange trading and established limits on foreign exchange exposure and controls on foreign exchange traders to minimize risk. After the Franklin and Herstatt experiences, banks on their own initiative and with encouragement from regulators tightened up their surveillance systems. Although the likelihood of significant losses has been reduced through such controls and through official monitoring of foreign exchange trading by banks, it is still possible that controls could fail or, as in the case of Franklin, be evaded through fraud and the collusion of bank management.[9]

Economic recession, which placed great strains on banks in 1974, remains a potential threat to the international banking system. For nearly three decades following World War II, it seemed that the problems of cyclical growth and recession had been solved by the political implementation of economic prescriptions. Bankers, along with many others, came to believe in the inevitability of a prosperous economic environment and made decisions accordingly. In the late 1960s and early 1970s banks were caught up in the euphoria of the world economic boom. Responding to business demands, banks— especially banks like Franklin National—increased loan portfolios and ventured into riskier activities without expanding their capital proportionately.

In 1974 the bubble burst. The combined effects of the energy crisis, the excessive and unsustainable earlier expansion, and deflationary public policy led to a deep recession. Economic contraction weakened the value of bank assets, led to the deterioration of the credit standing of important borrowing sectors (and to a resultant increase in classified and criticized loans), and to a rise in the number of problem banks. The assets affected by the recession of 1974 were primarily domestic. While, as we have seen, there was concern about the profitability and maturity structure of Eurocurrency loans, there was little concern about the credit worthiness of international borrowers. Indeed, in the Franklin case international loans were considered among the most desirable in the bank's portfolio.

Economic conditions have improved markedly since the depths of 1974. Economic activity in both industrial and developing countries has picked up and unemployment rates have declined. However, the problem of maintaining growth—especially growth without inflation—is far from being solved. Economic analysts remain perplexed and political leaders are unable to agree at a national or international level on the correct way to realize national adjustment and to achieve stable economic growth. In such circumstances, another economic downswing is entirely possible. Indeed, many analysts are once again convinced of the inevitable cyclical nature of economic activity. Should a recession occur and should it approach the severity of 1974, it could place an important stress on banks. As in 1974, the deterioration of the credit standing of a major borrowing sector would pose a severe threat to bank prosperity and even viability.

One sector potentially vulnerable to renewed recession is an international one: loans to less developed countries (LDCs). For a variety of reasons, loans to developing countries have grown dramatically in the 1970s.[10] From 1970 to 1976, the external public debt of non-oil LDCs to private financial markets rose from $7.7 billion to $47.9 billion.[11] These loans are highly concentrated as to borrowers (Brazil and Mexico account for one-half of U.S. bank claims on non-oil LDCs) and as to lenders (most of the LDC lending is done by a small number of large banks). An economic recession which led to a decline in export revenues and thereby threatened the ability of one or more LDC borrowers to service or amortize their loans would pose a serious threat to international banks. The recent difficulties of Peru, Zaïre, and Turkey in servicing international loans arose in large part from economic problems which undermined expected sources of foreign earnings or transfer payments.[12] While the system thus far has been able to manage the debt problems of individual countries, a worldwide recession which led to widespread debt repayment problems or a recession which affected the ability of an important borrower to service its debt might overload the system and cause a crisis.

Inflation is another systemic problem with potential dangers for international banking. As political authorities have tried to walk the tightrope between recession and inflation, they have manipulated interest rates, at times with stressful consequences for banks. Unanticipated and extreme rises in interest rates can undermine loan profitability and overall bank earnings. The unprecedented and unanticipated rise in interest rates in 1974 placed a squeeze on banks, which were caught between long-term loan commitments made at times of lower rates and the need to borrow money to fund those loans at new, high rates. The narrow spreads in the Eurodollar market in the early 1970s accentuated this problem and actually led to negative margins when interest rates soared in 1974. Beginning in mid-1974, spreads for new Eurocurrency loans widened to reflect both risk and inflation factors, but, as we have noted, by 1977 they had once again narrowed. If interest rates should once again rise precipitously, banks could be faced for a time with little or no profit on their Eurocurrency loans. Furthermore, inflation has led to rising costs which eat away at the already narrow margin of profit on Euroloans.

Yet another change affecting banks is the massive financial disequilibrium caused by the rise in the price of oil. On the one hand, a few oil-exporting countries have accumulated massive financial surpluses which they have placed to a great extent in the Euromarket. The importance of these deposits has raised a question about the risks of deposit concentration and what would happen if, for whatever reasons, oil-surplus countries should decide to withdraw funds from one or more Eurobanks or from the system as a whole. The initial concern about the manipulation of deposits has, with reason, subsided. Analysts now realize that depositors would themselves suffer the most from international financial turbulence. Furthermore, should such depositors withdraw funds from one bank or group of banks they would be forced to redeposit those funds with other financial institutions which could then recycle funds through the Euromarket to the losing banks—the result being simply a tiering of interest rates as in 1974. Despite these important questions about OPEC motivation and the impossibility of withdrawing funds from the system as a whole, the potential disturbance and challenge to confidence which could arise from a movement of funds remains an important danger.

A more serious challenge arising from the oil-induced international financial disequilibrium is the problem of oil-importing deficit countries. Unable to increase exports, to deflate their economies sufficiently to reduce imports, or to finance their deficits through public international institutions, many LDCs have turned to multinational banks to finance their deficits. The banks, awash with petrodollar deposits and facing competitive pressures and a decline in domestic loan demand, made massive loans to governments, central banks, and state entities in deficit countries. These loans came on top of existing important loans to LDCs made in the early 1970s.

Loans to Third World countries, which are particularly vulnerable to economic and political instability, pose some special risks. Economic problems, particularly a decline in export earnings, could lead to problems in servicing debt. Other difficulties could arise if a government decided it was unwilling to repay its debt for purely political reasons.

The seriousness of these risks is a much and hotly debated topic.[13] Analysts' positions on the issues depend on their calculation of future OPEC surpluses and LDC deficits, on the likelihood of economic problems and political disruption in individual borrowing countries, on the importance of such potential problems for individual banks, and on the ability of banks and public authorities to manage possible crises. Whether one concludes that the risk is more or less serious, there is little doubt that in assuming a new role in Third World financing, international banks have incurred significant new risks.

In sum, the lessons of Franklin and of recent experience in international banking are that liquidity and solvency problems of international banks are not inevitable, but that they are more likely now and in the future than they were in the recent past. The important question raised by this possibility is what it means for the stability of the banking system as a whole.

The Stability of the International Banking System

One of the most important lessons of the failure of the Franklin National Bank is that the international banking system is potentially vulnerable to a weakness in one of its parts. The combination of the new interdependence of the world's banking system and the absence of an order to manage that interdependence make the system susceptible to a crisis of confidence.

We have seen that the growth of international banking in the 1960s and 1970s coincided with the development of the Euro-currency and foreign exchange markets which link banks together through a network of mutual deposits, credits, and foreign exchange contracts. Because of the direct linkages of banks through these markets and because of the intangible but very real indirect linkage of bank confidence throughout the system, problems in one bank can spread in a domino fashion throughout the system. A crisis in one bank—whether that crisis arises from international or domestic problems and whether that bank is large or small—can lead to a chain reaction of deposit withdrawals, exclusion from exchange markets, or interest rate and exchange rate discrimination which affects institutions throughout the international banking system. Because of the significance of interbank liabilities and foreign exchange transactions to bank operations, such withdrawals, exclusion, or rate discrimination could impose serious damage even on healthy banks.

In 1974, the contraction of the inter-Eurobank portion of the Eurocurrency market, the paralysis of foreign exchange markets, and the tiering of both markets clearly demonstrated the vulnerability of banks to problems in other banks operating in the same market and to the dangers of this spread effect. Since 1974 interbank linkages have continued to grow (see Table 2.2). In 1977 inter-Eurobank transactions amounted to $280 billion, up from $155 billion in 1974. That figure, it should be noted, represented a slightly smaller percentage of the gross size of the Euromarket than the year before. In 1976 inter-Eurobank transactions accounted for 45 percent of the gross size of the market, while in 1977 they accounted for only 42 percent.

While we do not have comparable yearly estimates of the size of foreign exchange markets, we know that they too have grown. According to a study made by the Federal Reserve Bank of New York, gross foreign currency transactions in the United States foreign exchange market during April 1977 totaled $106.4 billion, or over $5 billion each business day. A similar survey by the Reserve Bank in March 1969 showed total transactions of $17 billion, or less than $1 billion each business day. Interbank trading accounts for almost all of these transactions.[14] Another study yielded even more startling results. According to its findings the average daily volume for all world foreign exchange trading in 1977 was $120 billion, which amounts to an annual volume of about $30 trillion. Of this amount about 95 percent were interbank transactions.[15]

The absence of an order or system of management to prevent or control crises of confidence accentuates the inherent fragility of the international banking system. The stability of domestic banking systems is enhanced by solvency regulations, deposit insurance, and the existence of a lender of last resort, all of which seek to assure solvency, instill public confidence, and prevent panic. The international banking system does not benefit from such an order. As we have seen, the absence of solvency regulation in international banking leaves the system highly competitive, risk prone, and without the protection of obligatory reserves. American deposit insurance does not cover foreign branches and in any case would not cover large deposits such as international certificates of deposit and Eurodollar placements. Finally, there are important gaps in the lender of last resort responsibility which lower the level of confidence.

Aggravating the problem of order is that of information. While there is no comprehensive international order, there are various national orders which to a certain degree protect international banks. However, the lack of understanding of these orders outside national boundaries and the resultant uncertainty about national policy undermines confidence.

Given these important weaknesses in the international banking system, severe strains on that system can overburden it and create a crisis of confidence. The crisis of 1974 developed from the coincidence of a number of difficulties: a precarious international economic environment shaken by inflation, recession, international monetary instability, and the oil crisis; a vulnerable international banking system weakened by policies implemented in the euphoric 1960s and early 1970s; and the shock of the failure of several banks and serious losses in a number of other banks. It is possible that a combination of strains could again render the system fragile. Should the world economy enter another cyclical decline and should the banks have placed themselves in a vulnerable position through unwise policies, a shock could once again trigger a crisis of confidence. That shock could arise from a bank failure as in 1974 or from some other strain such as the default of a major international borrower or a war in the Middle East leading to an oil embargo or to a politically motivated shift in the financial assets held by Middle East oil producers.

If, under certain conditions, it *can* happen again, it is essential that public authorities have the capability to minimize the possibility of crisis and to contain a crisis if and when it should develop.

The Management of International Banking

The international banking crisis of 1974 was a milestone in the public management of international banking. The crisis altered the perception of public authorities about the stability of the international banking system. Before 1974 it was generally believed that the problem of financial crisis had long ago been solved. After 1974 no one could be confident of the inherent stability of the system. As a result of their changed perceptions, authorities began to adapt regulatory systems to enable them to control, and if possible to prevent, international banking crises.

The Franklin Experience: Failures and Successes

The Franklin episode revealed both the weaknesses and the strengths of the United States regulatory system as it applies to international banking.

Regulators were ineffective in preventing the Franklin crisis. Supervisory laxity and failure to adapt to the revolution in banking set the stage for Franklin's failure. Supervision of Franklin by the Office of the Comptroller of the Currency was extremely weak. In most instances supervisors discovered Franklin's problems but relied on assurances of Franklin's management, and not on actual observation, that problems were being solved—which they were not. Nowhere was this more true than in foreign exchange. Despite findings of inadequate controls and reports of heavy trading, the supervisors took no action. The Comptroller also made no efforts to stem Franklin's growth, including its international expansion. While the Comptroller's endorsement of the Nassau branch was routine, the London branch endorsement was given despite Franklin's having been placed on the problem bank list and despite an initial decision to recommend that the Board of Governors deny Franklin's request. When the Comptroller's office recommended against the London branch, a little pressure and promises from Franklin sufficed to overcome the initial hesitation. There is also no evidence that the

Comptroller's office sought to enforce the Board of Governors' requirement that the size of the London branch operation be limited.

The Federal Reserve, although not the primary supervisor of Franklin, did have responsibility for regulating and supervising Franklin New York Corporation, the Franklin holding company, and for approving foreign branch expansion. At three points the Federal Reserve might have used its powers to constrain Franklin, and in all but one case it failed to do so. In the case of foreign branch approval, the Board of Governors, despite its own doubts, followed the advice of the Comptroller regarding Franklin's strength and approved the bank's applications. That approval seems justified for a Nassau shell branch but questionable for the London branch. Again, although the Board hedged its London approval by stating that Franklin should limit the size of its London operation, there is no evidence of any further Board surveillance of London activities.

The Federal Reserve also failed to act on the Sindona acquisition of a controlling interest in Franklin New York Corporation. Legal questions, Franklin's pressure to take no action, and the absence of pressure within the Federal Reserve System to act led to the Board's failure to declare Fasco a bank holding company. Evidence suggests, however, that the Board could have made such a finding and thereby enhanced its supervision and regulation of the Sindona connection. Had Fasco been declared a bank holding company the Board might even have prevented the Sindona purchase of a controlling interest in Franklin New York Corporation. Only on the Talcott acquisition did the Board of Governors decide to take action to constrain Franklin. By then, unfortunately, it was too late. At one other point—when Morgan Guaranty officers informed Federal Reserve Bank of New York officers of their mounting concerns about Franklin—the Federal Reserve Bank might have been more persistent in uncovering Franklin's rumored excessive foreign exchange trading. Whether such persistence would have been effective in light of the cover-up by Franklin officers is questionable.

In an environment of supervisory permissiveness, Franklin's

management was left to pursue its reckless and illegal policies. As a study of the Comptroller by the House of Representatives Committee on Government Operations concluded, the failure of Franklin National bank "brought to a conclusion half a decade of financial mismanagement and regulatory neglect."[16]

While authorities were unable to prevent or anticipate the Franklin crisis, they were able to respond effectively once the crisis erupted. The massive Federal Reserve loan and the use of that loan to cover foreign branch outflows, the assistance in managing foreign exchange operations and the eventual purchase of Franklin's foreign exchange book, and the FDIC sale of a large bank like Franklin with foreign branches required creative innovation. That innovation and the concomitant interagency bargaining took time. The five months of the Franklin crisis, however, may have served as a learning experience which will enable authorities to manage the next crisis more rapidly.

International cooperation was also effective in the Franklin crisis. The Federal Reserve loan, the management of the foreign exchange book, and the disposal of Franklin, as we have seen, were greatly facilitated by the existing institutional and informal framework of central bank cooperation in monetary and economic problems. Without international cooperation, the crisis would certainly have lasted longer and very well might have had more serious effects.

Since Franklin

The shock of 1974 forced regulators to recognize the vulnerability of the international banking system and led to some efforts to contain and prevent international financial crises.

A number of changes have taken place at the national level, many of which have important consequences for international banking. The action of the Federal Reserve in the Franklin National Bank crisis demonstrated that the world's most important banking power is willing and able to take action to contain financial crises. The eventual participation of the Bank of England in the settlement of the Israel British failure and even the favorable treatment to foreign creditors in the Herstatt case demonstrate the recognition by important banking authorities of the special needs for crisis prevention in international financial markets.

Changes have also taken place in supervisory and regulatory law and practice which move in the direction of crisis prevention. In the United States the Federal Reserve has been more conservative in approving foreign expansion of American banks and has required greater attention to capital and liquidity positions. New supervisory methods have been introduced by the Comptroller of the Currency in an effort to prevent the kind of laxity which let Franklin National Bank slip through the supervisory net. On the international side, bank supervisors now pay greater attention to risks such as foreign exchange trading and country loan concentration. Federal control has been extended to foreign banking institutions operating in the United States.[17]

Outside the United States there have also been changes. Reforms in national banking laws which would limit risks banks assume, extend supervisory authority over banks, and facilitate the international exchange of information about banking problems have been proposed in many countries and enacted in some. Some states have created new lending facilities to aid illiquid banks and many states are considering deposit insurance schemes. Efforts have also been made to make national supervisory systems more sensitive to the new nature of banking, including special attention to such international problems as foreign exchange trading and country risk.

These national changes enhance the ability of national authorities to manage crises and to identify and prevent national problems which might escalate into international difficulties. They also narrow some of the gaps in international banking supervision by broadening national supervision. But changes at the national level, however far-reaching they may be, are inadequate to deal with some of the most important problems of international banking—those gray areas where responsibility for crisis management and crisis prevention remain undefined. Dealing with the large gray area can only be achieved through international cooperation.

Some steps toward international management have been taken

since 1974. The central mechanism of management of international banking is not an institution or a constitution but a series of international consultative processes. As a result of the crisis of 1974, central bank governors broadened the purview of their ongoing dialogue to include lender of last resort problems as well as issues of supervision and regulation in international banking. The governors also established the Standing Committee on Banking Regulations and Supervisory Practices, which regularly discusses important technical issues of bank regulation and supervision.

The results of the new, institutionalized consultative processes are threefold. First, governors and supervisors have been able to establish certain formal rules of the game. They have reached some agreement on lender of last resort and supervisory responsibility in international banking, although important gaps remain. There have also been efforts to harmonize auditing and accounting standards. Where agreement has not been reached on formal rules, there is the possibility that general principles will eventually be established through the continuing dialogue.

Second, the dialogue is itself an important management mechanism. The consultative process at the governor level, for example, may serve as a substitute for formal agreement on the lender of last resort's responsibility. Although the governors will probably be unable to establish firm rules defining who is responsible for what and when, they may very well be able to develop ad hoc agreements in specific cases involving lending to illiquid institutions and containment of international banking crises. Informal management also exists at the level of the Standing (Cooke) Committee. While supervisors found they were unable to create a formal international early warning system, they were able to develop an informal network of close contact with each other which serves as an informal early warning system to identify national bank problems which might have international ramifications. And although it is impossible to harmonize national supervisory and regulatory systems, the exchange of information on national systems and policies makes better coordination of those systems possible. The dialogue also contributes to international confidence and stability by disseminating knowledge of national systems and policies and thereby improving the predictability of the behavior of other actors. Finally, the dialogue and the network create the possibility of influencing the behavior of national actors, especially in a crisis situation. In sum, the international consultative processes provide an informal steering mechanism for the international banking system.

Third, the work of the Standing (Cooke) Committee and of the central bank governors to whom the members report has served as an initiator of national change. The Committee's practice of subjecting national supervisory systems to international discussion, of developing broad principles or guidelines for supervisory reform, and of offering models for that reform has had an effect on national supervisory and regulatory policy. At a time when many national authorities are seeking to reform their systems, the initiatives of the Committee and the Governors fall on fertile ground. Furthermore, the very process of discussing reform in the Committee acts as a pressure for maintaining national interest in regulatory reform. How national reform would have proceeded without the international consultative process is impossible to determine, but it probably would have been slower.

International cooperation in banking is proceeding independently in the European Economic Community. In December 1977 the Commission of the European Community adopted the EEC's first directive on the coordination of banking legislation. The Commission had originally proposed a directive which called for sweeping harmonization of member countries' supervisory and regulatory systems. The Bank of England, however, argued decisively against such a sweeping policy and persuaded the Commission, instead, to adopt the more gradual method of the Standing Committee. Thus the directive set out several principles and established an Advisory Committee of bank supervisory authorities to work toward cooperation among national authorities and the EEC.[18] The work of the Community will be complemented by the continuing work of the Groupe de Contact. Future EEC harmonization and supervisory cooperation in the Groupe de Contact might facilitate coordination through the Standing Committee.

A number of forces are encouraging the further development of international management. The changed perceptions of regulators—the fear of a world financial crisis, the recognition that in an interdependent banking system a crisis cannot be prevented without some level of cooperation—provide rational motives for cooperation. Pressure from the leading international banking powers, the United States and the United Kingdom, for some minimal level of consultation gives force to these rational interests. And international consultative mechanisms provide a forum and further pressure for cooperation.

But equally important forces are working against management. Despite the interdependence of the world's banking systems, there remain important national differences. Different methods of supervision (the Bank of England's informal consultations and the United States multi-agency system of formal reporting and inspection; different laws governing the activities of banks; the integration of deposit institutions and investment banking in many European countries and their separation in the United States) and different concepts of the role of public management of banking (the FDIC and the broad interpretation of the lender of last resort responsibility in the United States and the absence of deposit insurance in most European countries along with a more narrow view of the role of the lender of last resort) all pose difficult obstacles to the establishment of any uniform regulatory system for international banking. Furthermore, the control of the banking remains a central element of national economic management and a prerogative which states are not yet ready to relinquish or adapt to international as opposed to national needs.

An important competitive element in international banking also undermines international cooperation. Most regulatory authorities—and certainly the authorities whose banks are most active in international markets—are eager to enable their banks to compete effectively in international banking. In addition, some countries seek to encourage international banking centers in their territory by imposing few requirements on such activities. As long as some states (for whatever reasons) impose few regulations on international banking in their territory or on the activities of their national banks, there will be the incentive for all banking authorities to allow their banks to compete on equal terms. More stringent regulation would impose costs which, argue bankers and regulators, would make national banks less able to compete internationally. Such an attitude has motivated the United States policy of imposing fewer restrictions on the international activities of American banks than on their domestic activities. As a result, regulation of international banking sinks to the level of the lowest common denominator.

Because of national differences and the competitive dynamic of international banking, international management remains limited to informal consultative processes such as that of the central bank governors and the Standing (Cooke) Committee network. To be sure, such mechanisms are an important advance over the pre-1974 system. Through international consultation and greater national attention, it is now more likely that international banking problems will be identified and dealt with at an early stage. It is even possible that greater national attention to international banking may prevent some problems in the first place. But the management of international banking has a long way to go. Important gaps—in the lender of last resort responsibility, in policies of states in lending to illiquid or insolvent banks, in supervisory responsibility, and in the supervision of international risk—still exist. Whether those gaps will be filled remains to be seen. And if they are not filled, it remains to be seen whether existing mechanisms will be able to prevent or manage a future international banking crisis.

NOTES

Abbreviations

The following abbreviations have been used in the notes.

BGFRS: Board of Governors of the Federal Reserve System, files on Franklin National Bank and Franklin New York Corporation (Washington, D.C.).

FDIC: Federal Deposit Insurance Corporation, files on Franklin National Bank (New York).

FRBNY: Federal Reserve Bank of New York, legal department, files on Franklin National Bank and Franklin New York Corporation (New York).

OCC: Office of the Comptroller of the Currency, files on Franklin National Bank (Washington, D.C.).

SEC: Securities and Exchange Commission, files on Franklin New York Corporation (Washington, D.C.).

USDC: U.S. District Court.

1. International Banking, International Stability, and the Franklin National Bank

1. U.S. House, Committee on Banking, Currency and Housing, "U.S. Banks Abroad," in *FINE: Financial Institutions and the National Economy, Compendium of papers prepared for the FINE Study,* Book II, p. 812. (Hereafter cited as "U.S. Banks Abroad.")

2. Salomon Brothers, *United States Multinational Banking: Current and Prospective Strategies,* p. 13.

3. Morgan Guaranty Trust Company, *World Financial Markets,* various issues. Figures are for net size, i.e., exclusive of inter-Eurobank transactions.

4. "U.S. Banks Abroad," p. 878. The twelve banks are Bank of America, Bankers Trust, Chase Manhattan, Chemical Bank, Continental Illinois National Bank, First National Bank of Boston, First National Bank of Chicago, First National City Bank, Manufacturers Hanover Trust, Marine Midland, Morgan Guaranty Trust, and Wells Fargo Bank.

5. Morgan Guaranty Trust Company, *World Financial Markets* (September 1978), p. 12.

6. See for example U.S. Senate, Committee on Foreign Relations, *Multinational Corporations in the Dollar Devaluation Crisis.* Milton Friedman, "The Euro-dollar Market: Some First Principles," pp. 1-11; Fred H. Klopstock, "Money Creation in the Euro-Dollar Market—a Note on Professor Freidman's Views," pp. 130-38; Jonathan David Aronson, *Money and Power.*

7. The historical literature on bank and financial crises is extensive. See for example F. W. Hirst, *The Six Panics and Other Essays;* H. M. Hyndman, *Commercial Crises of the Nineteenth Century;* Susan Estabrook Kennedy, *The Banking Crisis of 1933;* Charles P. Kindleberger, *Manias, Panics, and Crises;* E. Ray McCartney, *Crisis of 1873;* U.S. Senate, National Monetary Commission, *History of Crises under the National Banking System;* George Washington Van Vleck, *The Panic of 1857: An Analytical Study.* On the theory of financial crises see Hyman P. Minsky, "Financial Instability Revisited: The Economics of Disaster," pp. 95-136; Wesley C. Mitchell, *Business Cycles: The Problem and Its Setting;* Oskar Morgenstern, *International Financial Transactions and Business Cycles.*

8. John Cooper, "How Foreign Exchange Operations Can Go Wrong," pp. 4-7; Samuel I. Katz, "Managed Floating as an Interim International Exchange Rate Regime, 1973-1975"; U.S. Congress, Joint Economic Committee, *How Well Are Fluctuating Exchange Rates Working?*

9. See for example U.S. House, Committee on Banking, Finance and Urban Affairs, *International Banking Operations;* U.S. Senate, Committee on Foreign Relations, *International Debt, the Banks, and U.S. Foreign Policy;* David O. Beim, "Rescuing the LDCs," pp. 717-31; Harold Van B. Cleveland and W. H. Bruce Brittain, "Are the LDCs in Over Their Heads?" pp. 732-50; Richard Portes, "East Europe's Debt to the West: Interdependence Is a Two-Way Street," pp. 751-82; Albert Fishlow, "Debt Remains a Problem," pp. 133-43; Richard S. Weinert, "Why the Banks Did It," pp. 143-48; Marina v. N. Whitman, "Bridging the Gap," pp. 148-56; Declan Duff and Ian Peacock, "Refinancing of Sovereign Debt," pp. 69-75. Robert Solomon, "A Perspective on the Debt of Developing Countries," pp. 479-501.

10. U.S. Congress, Senate, Committee on Banking, Housing and Urban Affairs, *Multinational Banking,* p. 5. The problem was the subject of a best-selling novel by Paul Erdman, *The Crash of '79.*

11. Andrew F. Brimmer and Frederick R. Dahl, "Growth of American International Banking: Implications for Public Policy," pp. 341-63; Robert C. Holland, "Public Policy Issues in U.S. Banking Abroad"; Arthur F. Burns, "Maintaining the Soundness of Our Banking System," pp. 263-67; U.S. House, Committee on

Banking, Finance and Urban Affairs, *Banking Operations,* statement by Henry C. Wallich, pp. 3–9.

12. *Ibid.*

2. The Internationalization of the Franklin National Bank

1. Andrew F. Brimmer and Frederick R. Dahl, "Growth of American International Banking," p. 347.

2. Edge Act corporations, named for Senator Walter Edge, who sponsored the 1919 legislation which made such entities possible, are subsidiaries of U.S. national banks operating abroad which are authorized to engage in a broader range of activities and to make overseas investments that are not permitted in domestic banking activities. Agreement corporations are similar subsidiaries of state-chartered banks.

3. Robert Z. Aliber, "International Banking: Growth and Regulation," p. 10.

4. Andrew F. Brimmer, "International Finance and the Management of Bank Failure: Herstatt vs. Franklin National," p. 7 (mimeo). See also "U.S. Banks Abroad," p. 810.

5. "U.S. Banks Abroad," p. 891. For a list of the banks, see ch. 1, note 4.

6. *Ibid.,* p. 892.

7. Morgan Guaranty Trust Company, *World Financial Markets,* various issues. Figures are for net size, i.e., exclusive of inter-Eurobank transactions.

8. Transactions also take place in such places as Nassau and Singapore.

9. The London Interbank Offered Rate (LIBOR) is the interest rate on Eurodollars in the London interbank market.

10. Brimmer and Dahl, "Growth of American International Banking," p. 356.

11. Many deposits recorded in the net size of the Eurocurrency market are between banks.

12. "U.S. Banks Abroad," pp. 878, 879.

13. Federal Reserve Bank of New York, News Release no. 1202, July 12, 1977. See also Roger M. Kubarych, *Foreign Exchange Markets in the United States.*

14. Ian H. Giddy, "Measuring the World Foreign Exchange Market." I am grateful to Professor Giddy for making his findings available to me.

15. Retail banking is the servicing of individuals and small businesses.

16. Franklin National Bank, *Annual Reports.*

17. Wholesale banking is the servicing of large businesses and financial entities.

18. Resolution adopted by Board of Directors, Franklin National Bank, September 21, 1961, sent by George H. Becht, Assistant Vice President and Cashier, to the Office of the Comptroller of the Currency; letter from H. S. Haggard, Deputy Comptroller of the Currency, to George H. Becht, November 13, 1961.

19. See U.S. House, Committee on Government Operations, *Oversight Hearings into the Effectiveness of Federal Bank Regulation (Franklin National Bank Failure),* pp. 237–38 (hereafter cited as *Oversight Hearings*); Brimmer, "International Finance and the Management of Bank Failures;" p. 220.

20. Letter from Franklin National Bank to Board of Governors of the Federal Reserve System (BGFRS), August 16, 1968.

21. Franklin International Corporation's main holdings were American Swiss Credit Corporation and a 7 percent interest in Banque Vernes et Commerciale de Paris.

22. Letters from Franklin National Bank to the Board of Governors of the Federal Reserve System (BGFRS), August 16, 1968, and November 4, 1970.

23. In 1969, when credit became tight in the United States, the Eurodollar market also became attractive as a source of funds for domestic financing; see Brimmer and Dahl, "Growth of American International Banking," p. 349.

24. Interview with Rodney Galpin, Bank of England.

25. Letter from Franklin National Bank to Board of Governors of the Federal Reserve System (BGFRS), August 16, 1968.

26. Letter from Franklin National Bank to Board of Governors of the Federal Reserve System (BGFRS), November 4, 1970. In 1973 the bank had established a representative office in Singapore and, at the time the Franklin crisis erupted, planned to open others in Mexico City and Tokyo.

27. *Oversight Hearings,* p. 234.

28. One somewhat extreme example was the opening of La Banque Continentale in 1965, a plush branch on Fifth Avenue and 60th Street offering the privileges and services of a private club to its carefully selected and limited group of depositors who were required to maintain a $25,000 minimum balance. The Banque Continentale alone cost $750,000. *Burroughs Clearing House,* (September 1965), 49:19.

29. See Brimmer and Dahl, "Growth of American International Banking," p. 349.

30. Confidential source. See Janet Kelly, *Bankers and Borders: The Case of American Banks in Britain,* pp. 33–37, on the general trend.

31. Interviews with Raymond Hoffman, Federal Deposit Insurance Corporation, and James Q. Hall, Loeb Rhoades Hornblower and Company. The practice of accepting a minimal fee or no fee for managing a syndication organized by an investment banking firm was not exclusive to Franklin in the highly competitive days of the early 1970s.

32. For further details see U.S. Congress, Joint Economic Committee, "A Progress Report on the Federal Reserve Foreign Credit Restraint Programs," pp. 163–68.

33. Brimmer and Dahl, "Growth of American International Banking," p. 347.

34. Letter from Franklin National Bank to Board of Governors of the Federal Reserve System (BGFRS), August 16, 1968.

35. *Ibid.*

36. Howard D. Crosse, "Restraint of Trade in International Banking." p. 1 (mimeo; in FRBNY).

37. This capability was ended just about the time of Crosse's memorandum, when reserve requirements were imposed on deposits "lent" by overseas branches to head offices.

38. Crosse, "Restraint of Trade," p. 1.

39. *Ibid*, p. 2.

40. Law and regulatory policy also enabled banks to engage in a broader range of activities abroad than at home. By forming Edge Act corporations, as Franklin did in 1967, they could engage in commercial activities forbidden under the Glass-Steagall Act at home. Under section 213.3(b) of Regulation M, foreign branches were given broader powers than domestic branches, which are prohibited from guaranteeing the debts of customers, underwriting foreign government obligations, and acting as an insurance agent or broker.

41. Brimmer and Dahl, "Growth of American International Banking," p. 342.

42. On New York law see "Bank Expansion in New York State: The 1971 State-wide Branching Law," pp. 266–74. The Stephens Act divided New York State into nine banking districts and permitted branching only within districts. Manhattan, the Bronx, and Richmond (Staten Island) constituted one district while Brooklyn, Queens, Nassau, and Suffolk constituted another. Thus large New York City banks located in Manhattan were blocked from moving to Long Island and Long Island banks were excluded from Manhattan.

43. Kelly, *Bankers and Borders,* pp. 88–90. While many hailed the Comptroller for modernizing the banking system, which had changed little since the 1930s and which no longer served the needs of the U.S. economy, others, particularly Chairman Burns of the Board of Governors of the Federal Reserve System, charged that the Comptroller was lax in the supervision of banks. See Arthur F. Burns, "Maintaining the Soundness of Our Banking System," pp. 263–67.

44. Cited in "U.S. Banks Abroad," p. 867.

45. *Ibid.,* p. 868.

46. The Federal Reserve also examines foreign branches of state member banks.

47. Cited in "U.S. Banks Abroad," p. 869.

48. *Oversight Hearings,* pp. 229–31, 257.

49. Letter from Board of Governors of the Federal Reserve System to Franklin National Bank (BGFRS), February 20, 1969.

50. *Oversight Hearings,* p. 233.

51. Letter from Board of Governors of the Federal Reserve System to Franklin National Bank (BGFRS), December 10, 1971.

52. *Ibid.*

53. Kelly, *Bankers and Borders,* pp. 57–82.

54. *Oversight Hearings,* pp. 233, 234.

55. Interview with Rodney Galpin, Bank of England.

56. Unless otherwise noted, information about Michele Sindona comes from the following sources: Dun and Bradstreet International Report, March 7, 1972; Letter from Andrew O. Miller, Esq., White & Case, to Federal Reserve Bank of New York, July 11, 1972; Securities and Exchange Commission, Schedule 13-D, Information to be included in Statements filed pursuant to Rule 13d-1, Franklin New York Corporation (Name of issuer), Fasco International Holding S.A. (Name of person filing statement), July 11, 1972; Securities and Exchange Commission, Michele Sindona, Fasco, A.G. and Fasco International Holding, S.A., Amendment No. 1 to Schedule 13-D, Filed Pursuant to Rule 13d-1 of Regulation 13-D of the General Rules and Regulations Under the Securities Exchange Act of 1934, October 25, 1972; USDC, Southern District of New York, Securities and Exchange Commission Plaintiff v. Franklin New York Corporation, Harold V. Gleason, Paul Luftig, Peter R. Shaddick, Michele Sindona, Carlo Bordoni, Howard D. Crosse, Andrew N. Garofalo, Donald H. Emrich, Robert C. Panepinto Defendants, 74 Civil Action, File No. 4557, Filed October 17, 1974; USDC, Southern District of New York, In the Matter of the Requested Extradition of Michele Sindona by the Republic of Italy, 76 Cr. Misc. 1; *USDC, Southern District of New York, U.S. v. Gleason, Luftig and Carter,* Trial transcript, December 1978–January 1979. Interviews.

57. "The Italian Connection," pp. 56–57.

58. "Hambros at the Helm," p. 49; "A Sicilian Financier Takes Aim at the U.S.," pp. 34–35; "Italy's Establishment Fights an Outsider," p. 26.

59. "Italy's Establishment Fights an Outsider," p. 35.

60. "The Italian Connection," p. 56.

61. *U.S. v. Gleason et al.,* trial transcript, testimony of David M. Kennedy, pp. 2642–68.

62. Letter from Wright Patman to Arthur F. Burns (BGFRS) July 19, 1972.

63. Years later, after the failure of the Franklin National Bank, the FDIC filed a suit charging Laurence Tisch and Loews Corporation with a breach of fiduciary duties in the sale. The FDIC claimed that Tisch should have investigated Sindona's background before selling shares of Franklin New York Corporation to him. Sindona also filed a suit against Tisch seeking the return of his $40 million plus punitive damages (see *New York Times,* July 13, 1978).

64. Letter from Andrew O. Miller, Esq., White & Case, to Federal Reserve Bank of New York, July 11, 1972.

65. White & Case resigned because of what Mudge Rose Guthrie & Alexander described as a possible conflict of interest. Interestingly, Mudge, Rose, Guthrie and Alexander had been the law firm of President Nixon and Attorney General John Mitchell.

66. Letter from Randolph H. Guthrie (of Mudge Rose Guthrie & Alexander) to Ben Stackhouse, Bank Applications Department, Federal Reserve Bank of New York, September 22, 1972.

67. Letter from Arthur F. Burns, Chairman, Board of Governors of the Federal Reserve System to Wright Patman, Chairman, Committee on Banking and Currency, House of Representatives (BGFRS) August 2, 1972.

68. U.S. House, Committee on Banking, Currency and Housing, *Bank Failures. Regulatory Reform. Financial Privacy,* p. 761.

69. Burns to Patman (BGFRS) June 5, 1974.

70. See Italy, Camera Dei Deputati, *Bolletino Delle Giunte e Delle Commissioni Parlamentari,* 7 novembre 1974, pp. 1-11.

71. *Oversight Hearings,* p. 292. This is also the thesis of Rose, "What Really Went Wrong at Franklin National," pp. 118-21ff.

72. Rose, "What Really Went Wrong at Franklin National," p. 233.

73. See *U.S. v. Gleason et al.,* trial transcripts, pp. 869-70 and chapter 3.

74. *Ibid,* pp. 597-608.

75. Rose, "What Really Went Wrong at Franklin National," p. 233.

76. *Oversight Hearings,* p. 140.

77. *Ibid.,* p. 269.

78. Haskins and Sells, "Observations and Comments concerning Special Review of Franklin National Bank," in *ibid.,* pp. 225-65.

79. Memorandum from David E. Bodner to Federal Reserve Bank of New York, November 30, 1973, in *ibid.,* pp. 291-93.

3. *The Franklin Crisis*

1. House Committee on Government Operations, *Oversight Hearings,* p. 251.

2. *Ibid.,* p. 121.

3. *Ibid.,* p. 251.

4. There were provisions for encashment of United States CDs but not for CDs issued in London.

5. Franklin New York Corporation, *Annual Report 1973,* p. 19.

6. *Oversight Hearings,* pp. 238, 259.

7. Michael C. Jensen, "Loans Assessed at Charter Banks—Fed Report Says Portfolio of 1974 Lending Showed Sharp Deterioration," *New York Times,* January 26, 1976 in U.S. Senate, Committee on Banking, Housing and Urban Affairs, *Problem Banks,* pp. 318-20.

8. *Oversight Hearings,* p. 248.

9. Rose, "What Really Went Wrong at Franklin National," p. 1.

10. *U.S. v. Gleason et al.,* trial transcript, pp. 3370-71.

11. *Oversight Hearings,* pp. 243, 136, 253; draft outline of talk by H. David Willey, Federal Reserve Bank of New York (FRBNY), September 30, 1975.

12. International Monetary Fund, *Annual Report 1975,* p. 26.

13. Bank for International Settlements, *Annual Report 1974-1975,* p. 121; International Monetary Fund, *Annual Report 1974,* p. 16; *ibid.,* 1975, p. 26; Federal Reserve Bank of New York, *Annual Report 1974,* pp. 15-16.

14. *Oversight Hearings,* p. 235.

15. *U.S. v. Gleason et al.* trial transcript, pp. 696-714, 606-612, 877, 869-70.

16. *Oversight Hearings,* p. 235.

17. *Ibid.,* pp. 298-99.

18. *Ibid.,* p. 236; and U.S. House, Committee on Government Operations, *Adequacy of the Office of the Comptroller of the Currency's Supervision of Franklin National Bank,* p. 33. (Hereafter cited as *Report on the Adequacy of the Comptroller.*)

19. *U.S. v. Gleason et al.,* trial transcript, p. 437.

20. USDC, Southern District of New York, U.S. v. Carlo Bordoni, Peter R. Shaddick, Andrew Garofalo, Arthur Slutzky, Donald Emrich, Martin Keroes, Michael Romersa and Paul Sabatella, defendants, Indictment S. 75 Cr. 948. All but Bordoni pleaded guilty in 1975. Bordoni fled to Venezuela, where he fought extradition for two years. In 1978 he lost his battle, was returned to the United States, and pleaded guilty in September 1978 (see also *Oversight Hearings,* pp. 273-81).

21. *U.S. v. Gleason et al.,* trial transcript, p. 459.

22. *U.S. v. Bordoni, Shaddick, et al.* pp. 1 and 39-59.

23. *U.S. v. Gleason et al.,* trial transcript, pp. 650-58, passim.

24. *Report on the Adequacy of the Comptroller.*

25. *Oversight Hearings,* pp. 110, 293.

26. *U.S. v. Gleason et al.,* trial transcript, pp. 667-73. Morgan Guaranty officers continued to express concern to Franklin officials right up until May. Gleason at one point invited Morgan authorities to audit Franklin's foreign exchange operation.

27. *Oversight Hearings,* p. 291.

28. Interview with Benedict Rafanello, Federal Reserve Bank of New York. Testimony of Benedict Rafanello, *U.S. v. Gleason et al.,* trial transcript, pp. 2346-76.

29. *Oversight Hearings,* pp. 291-92.

30. *Ibid.,* p. 292.

31. *Ibid.,* p. 293. At other meetings Franklin officials questioned about foreign exchange trading denied excessive trading and potential losses and attributed loss of confidence to false rumors. To counteract such rumors senior Franklin officials held meetings with officers of other banks (interviews).

32. *Oversight Hearings,* p. 235.

33. International Monetary Fund, *Annual Report 1975,* p. 26.

34. The Federal Reserve Bank of New York took a different position from that of the Board of Governors (interviews).

35. *U.S. v. Gleason et al.,* trial transcript, pp. 2126-27, 2146-52, 2346-76. Letter from Paul Luftig to Brenton Leavitt, Program Director for Banking Structure, Board of Governors of the Federal Reserve System (USDC), January 3, 1974.

36. *Federal Reserve Bulletin* (June 1974), 60 (6):459.

37. Andrew Brimmer, "International Finance and the Management of Bank Failures, Herstatt vs. Franklin National," pp. 43-44.

38. *Ibid.,* pp. 42-44.

39. *Oversight Hearings,* p. 137, and interview with Paul Luftig.

40. *Wall Street Journal,* April 30-May 10, 1974.

41. Franklin National Bank press release (FRBNY), May 10, 1974.

42. Federal Reserve Bank of New York, *Annual Report 1974,* p. 22.

43. FRBNY.

44. FDIC.

45. Bank of England, *Bulletin* (1975), 14(1), table 28.

46. FDIC.

47. *Ibid.*

48. Interview with Raymond Hoffman, Federal Deposit Insurance Corporation.

49. Thomas H. Hanley, *Eurolending Profitability: Gradual Improvement in 1979,* p. 9.

50. *Oversight Hearings,* pp. 125-26.

51. Memo, FRBNY.

52. FDIC.

53. Franklin National Bank call reports for London branch (FRBNY).

54. *Oversight Hearings,* p. 291.

55. *Ibid.,* p. 292.

56. USDC, Southern District of New York, *U.S. v. Michele Sindona and Carlo Bordoni,* Indictment 79 Cr., pp. 10 and 11.

57. USDC, Southern District of New York, *Securities and Exchange Commission Plaintiff v. Franklin New York Corporation, Harold v. Gleason, Paul Luftig, Peter R. Shaddick, Michele Sindona, Carlo Bordoni, Howard D. Crosse, Andrew N. Garofalo, Donald H. Emrich, Robert C. Panepinto, Defendants,* 74 Civil Action, File No. 4557, pp. 8-10, *U.S. v. Sindona,* p. 11.

58. *U.S. v. Sindona,* pp. 10-11, 13; *U.S. v. Gleason et al.,* trial transcript, pp. 858-60, 996-1007.

59. *U.S. v. Sindona,* pp. 10, 12 and 14. *U.S. v. Gleason et al.* trial transcript, pp. 1110-12, 1167-72.

60. See USDC, Southern District of New York, in the Matter of the Requested Extradition of Michele Sindona by the Republic of Italy, Supplemental Memorandum of Law and Fact in Support of the Requested Extradition of Michele Sindona, 65 Cr. Misc. 1, p. 123.

61. USDC, Southern District of New York, *Securities and Exchange Commission Plaintiff v. Franklin New York Corporation, U.S. v. Gleason et al.,* trial transcript, pp. 2582-85, 2636.

62. Interview with Silvano Montanaro and Francesco Buono of the Bank of Italy.

63. On the problems of Sindona's Italian banks see: Italy, Camera Dei Deputati, *Bollettino Delle Giunte e Delle Commissioni Parlamentari,* 7 novembre 1974, pp. 1-11.

4. *The Franklin National Bank and the International Banking System*

1. For regulatory policy and criticisms of the need for regulation see Robert Charles Clark, "The Soundness of Financial Intermediaries," pp. 1-102; and Franklin R. Edwards and James Scott, "Regulating the Solvency of Depository Institutions: A Perspective for Deregulation."

2. Bank for International Settlements, *Annual Report, 1974-1975,* p. 2.

3. International Monetary Fund, *Annual Report, 1975,* p. 4.

4. *Ibid.,* p. 3.

5. Bank for International Settlements, *Annual Report, 1974-1975,* p. 11.

6. See Arthur F. Burns, "Maintaining the Soundness of Our Banking System," pp. 264-65.

7. "Losers' League Table," p. 1284.

8. Foreign exchange losses of $77 million were suffered by Lloyds Bank International, Lugano, and losses estimated at $16-$39 million were incurred by the Banque de Bruxelles (*ibid.*).

9. Brimmer, "International Finance and the Management of Bank Failures," p. 11.

10. Bank for International Settlements, *Annual Report, 1974-1975,* p. 133.

11. See chapter 1, notes 9, 10. On problems of 1974 in general see for example Edward I. Altman and Arnold W. Sametz, eds., *Financial Crises: Institutions and Markets in a Fragile Environment.*

12. George J. Benston, "How We Can Learn from Past Bank Failures," p. 20; Paul Horvitz, "Failures of Large Banks: Implications for Banking Supervision and Deposit Insurance," pp. 589-601.

13. Horvitz, "Failures of Large Banks," p. 589.

14. See Brimmer, "International Finance and the Management of Bank Failures," pp. 20-23.

15. *Ibid.,* p. 22.

16. Charles A. Coombs, "Treasury and Federal Reserve Foreign Exchange Operations," pp. 637-38: and Brimmer, "International Finance," p. 25.

17. "U.S. Banks Abroad," p. 877.

18. See below, and Coombs, "Treasury and Federal Reserve Foreign Exchange Operations," p. 638.

19. Brimmer, "International Finance," pp. 27–28.

20. *Ibid.*, pp. 31–33, and Joseph D. Becker, "International Insolvency: The Case of Herstatt," pp. 1290–95.

21. "U.S. Banks Abroad," p. 876, and *Oversight Hearings,* p. 97.

22. Letter from Richard A. Debs to Board of Governors of the Federal Reserve System (FRBNY), September 25, 1974.

23. Federal Reserve Bank of New York, *Annual Report, 1974,* p. 25.

24. George Blunden, "The Supervision of the UK Banking System," p. 190.

25. Information submitted by Chairman Burns for the record of the hearing of the Joint Economic Committee on October 10, 1974, U.S. Senate, Committee on Banking, Currency and Housing, *An Act to Lower Interest Rates and Allocate Credit,* p. 223.

26. Paul M. Horvitz, "Bank Risks in the New International Financial Structure— Lessons from Bank Failures," p. 161.

27. Bank for International Settlements, *Annual Report, 1974–1975,* p. 131.

28. "U.S. Banks Abroad," p. 821.

29. *Ibid.,* pp. 821–22.

30. Bank for International Settlements, *Annual Report, 1974–1975,* pp. 142–43.

31. *Ibid.,* p. 131.

5. *National Management and the Franklin Crisis*

1. See *Oversight Hearings.*

2. On the FDIC generally see Frank Wille, "The FDIC and Franklin National Bank: A Report to the Congress and All FDIC-Insured Banks." Information in this chapter is also based on interviews with Mr. Wille and with Edward Bransilver and Robert E. Barnett.

3. Wille, "The FDIC and Franklin National Bank," p. 7.

4. Allen B. Frankel, "The Lender of Last Resort Facility in the Context of Multinational Banking," p. 120; Thomas M. Humphrey, "The Classical Concept of the Lender of Last Resort," pp. 2–9.

5. James H. Oltman, "Failing Banks—The Role of the Fed," p. 319.

6. U.S. House, Committee on Banking, Housing and Currency, *Bank Failures; Regulatory Reform; Financial Privacy,* Part 2, p. 729.

7. Federal Reserve Bank of New York. *Annual Report, 1974,* p. 23.

8. *Oversight Hearings,* p. 137.

9. Paul Luftig contended that the Federal Reserve and the FDIC could have made a merger with Manufacturers Hanover possible if they had agreed at an early date to an assisted merger. Interview with Paul Luftig.

10. One concern, for example, was whether the Board should issue a public letter. Another concern was the procedure for taking collateral for the loan.

11. Board of Governors of the Federal Reserve system (BGFRS), press release, May 12, 1974.

12. Federal Reserve Bank of New York, *Annual Report, 1974,* p. 23.

13. Franklin National Bank press release (FRBNY), May 12, 1974. Actually the statement was incorrect, for Franklin had incurred losses in the first as well as the second quarter. The statement also incorrectly contended that the losses were insured.

14. Franklin National Bank press release (FRBNY), May 14, 1974.

15. Franklin National Bank press release (FRBNY), June 20, 1974.

16. Joseph W. Barr, "The Last Days of Franklin National Bank," p. 310.

17. October 2 figure from Franklin National Bank, Call Report, (FRBNY), October 2.

18. Brimmer, "International Finance and the Management of Bank Failures," pp. 49-50.

19. One issue raised by the duration of the loan was the rate of interest charged to Franklin. One study estimated that the Federal Reserve interest rate subsidy to Franklin amounted to $25 million. Joseph F. Sinkey, Jr., "The Collapse of Franklin National Bank of New York," p. 118. From May 8 to September 26 Franklin was charged the discount rate, which ranged from 8 to 8.5 percent. Later, however, reacting to the nature of the loan and to the criticism of the rate as in fact a public subsidy of Franklin National, the Federal Reserve altered its regulations and established a new special discount rate for advances for "protracted assistance where there are exceptional circumstances or practices involving only a particular member bank" (Regulation A, 12 CFR 201.2[C][2]). That rate for Franklin from September 27 to October 7 was set at 10 percent.

20. See Barr, "Last Days of Franklin National Bank"; Wille, "The FDIC and Franklin National Bank."

21. *Oversight Hearings,* p. 166.

22. Debs to Board of Governors, September 25, 1974.

23. Burns to Reuss, February 5, 1975, pp. 19-20.

24. Wille, "The FDIC and Franklin National Bank," p. 27.

25. *Ibid.*

26. Letter from Joseph W. Barr, Chairman of the Board, President, and Chief Executive Officer of the Franklin National Bank, to Frank Wille, Chairman of the Federal Deposit Insurance Corporation (FRBNY), September 16, 1974. See also FDIC press releases (FDIC), "FDIC Costs Out Management Plan for Independent Franklin National Bank," October 3, 1974, and "FDIC Rejects Request for Assistance from Franklin National Bank," October 7, 1974; letter from William A. Anderson, Jr., Senior Vice President, Blyth Eastman Dillon &

Company to James E. Smith, Comptroller of the Currency, (FRBNY), October 3, 1974; memorandum from Henry S. Fujarski, Jr., and H. David Willey to Alfred Hayes, Federal Reserve Bank of New York, (FRBNY), October 4, 1974.

27. Contract for Sale of Foreign Exchange Contracts and Foreign Currency Balances, between Franklin National Bank and Federal Reserve Bank of New York (FRBNY), made as of September 26, 1974.

28. Burns to Reuss, February 5, 1975, p. 19; interviews.

29. Letter from H. David Willey, Vice President, Federal Bank of New York to Mr. Arthur L. Broida, Secretary, Federal Open Market Committee, Board of Governors of the Federal Reserve System (FRBNY), October 1, 1974.

30. Letter from H. David Willey, Federal Reserve Bank of New York to the Federal Deposit Insurance Corporation (FRBNY), September 11, 1975.

31. Interview with Leopold S. Rassnick and John C. Junek, Federal Reserve Bank of New York. The Edilcentro payments are being transferred to the FDIC under terms of the agreements between the Federal Reserve Bank of New York on the one hand and Franklin National Bank and the FDIC on the other hand (see notes 27 and 37, this chapter).

32. On the latter see *Oversight Hearings*, p. 169 and *U.S. v. Gleason et al.*, trial transcript, pp. 2642–68.

33. Wille, "The FDIC and Franklin National Bank," pp. 10–11.

34. In late May the possibility of a direct FDIC loan to Franklin was discussed by Federal authorities, including the FDIC. Under its charter, the FDIC has certain authority to prevent an immediate insolvency. Section 13(c) of the Federal Deposit Insurance Act gives the FDIC authority to provide direct financial aid to an operating bank in danger of closing when the continued operation of that bank is essential to provide adequate banking service in the community. Chairman Wille was unwilling, however, to give direct aid to Franklin. In his opinion, it would have been difficult to argue that Franklin's services were needed in the highly competitive urban New York markets. Furthermore, to grant such aid would threaten the FDIC trust, whose entire assets amounted to only $6 billion. The establishment of a Deposit Insurance National Bank was also ruled out because it, too, would have required a finding that continued operation of Franklin was essential to provide adequate banking service for its community.

35. Barr, "Last Days of Franklin National Bank," pp. 308-9.

36. Letter from Frank Wille, Chairman, FDIC, to Arthur A. Burns, Chairman of the Board of Governors of the Federal Reserve system (BGFRS), July 19, 1974.

37. Letter from Frank Wille to Arthur A. Burns (BGFRS), August 8, 1974. Agreement of Assumption of Indebtedness between Federal Reserve Bank of New York and Federal Deposit Insurance Corporation (FRBNY), October 8, 1974. The trustee in bankruptcy for Franklin New York Corporation subsequently sued the FDIC and the Federal Reserve Bank of New York charging that the interest rate paid by the FDIC was unfair and excessive. See USDC, Eastern District of New York, *Corbin v. Federal Reserve Bank of New York*, 458 F. Supp. 143, 1978.

38. Even at this point the regulatory agencies squabbled over whether technically Franklin had become insolvent because it was so declared by the Comptroller of the Currency or because the Federal Reserve Bank of New York terminated its loan.

39. The shareholding banks of European American are: Amsterdam-Rotterdam Bank N.V., with head offices in Amsterdam and Rotterdam; Creditanstalt-Bankverein, with head office in Vienna; Deutsche Bank A.G. with head office in Frankfurt; Midland Bank Limited, with head office in London; Societé Générale de Banque S.A., with head office in Brussels; and Société Générale (France), with head office in Paris.

6. International Cooperation and the Franklin Crisis

1. See Stephen V. O. Clarke, *Central Bank Cooperation 1924-1931* on an earlier period.

2. Robert W. Russell, "Transgovernmental Interaction in the International Monetary System, 1960-1972," pp. 431-64.

3. The Bank of England was also kept informed of developments in the London branch by George Roberts, the head of the branch.

4. Interview with Richard A. Debs.

5. Charles A. Coombs, "Treasury and Federal Reserve Foreign Exchange Operations," p. 637.

6. Interview with Rodney Galpin, Bank of England.

7. *Ibid.*

8. Letter from Arthur F. Burns to Fernand J. St. Germain, Chairman, Subcommittee on Financial Institutions Supervision, Regulation and Insurance of the Committee on Banking, Currency and Housing, House of Representatives (BGFRS), September 8, 1975.

9. Interview with Rodney Galpin.

10. Interview with Frederick R. Dahl.

11. See Wille, "The FDIC and Franklin National Bank," pp. 31-33. Ironically, in the end European American Bank chose few of the London branch assets, largely because it already had a significant international portfolio and preferred Franklin's domestic assets.

12. Interview with Rodney Galpin.

13. Wille, "The FDIC and Franklin National Bank," p. 33.

14. Clarke, *Central Bank Cooperation 1924-1931.*

15. The Group of Ten included the major industrial countries (see Russell, "Transgovernmental Interaction in the International Monetary System").

16. George Blunden, "International Cooperation in Banking Supervision," p. 325.

17. Andrew F. Brimmer, "International Finance and the Management of Bank Failures," pp. 28-29.

18. *New York Times,* September 11, 1974, p. 64, col. 1.

19. See, for example, Fred Hirsch, "The Bagehot Problem," pp. 241–57.

20. *Federal Reserve Bulletin,* (November 1974), 60(11):760.

21. George Blunden, "The Supervision of the U.K. Banking System," p. 1192.

22. *Ibid.*

23. *Ibid.*

24. *Federal Reserve Bulletin,* (February 1976), 62(2):185.

25. *New York Times,* September 11, 1974.

26. Interview with Peter Cooke. Information on Standing Committee based on interviews with members: Rodney Galpin, Peter Cooke, Silvano Montanaro, H. David Willey, Frederick Dahl, Robert Gemmill, John G. Heimann, and his assistant Robert A. Baer, Jr. Also useful was Blunden, "International Co-operation in Banking Supervision," pp. 325–29.

27. See George W. Mitchell, "How the Fed Sees Multinational Bank Regulation," pp. 759–60.

28. Blunden, "International Co-operation in Banking Supervision," p. 327.

29. Blunden, "Supervision of the U.K. Banking System," p. 193.

30. Blunden, "International Co-operation in Banking Supervision," p. 328.

31. Blunden, "The Supervision of the U.K. Banking System," p. 193.

32. Interview with John G. Heimann. See also: Richard Karp, "Sleeping Watchdogs: How the American Bank and Trust Company Went Broke," pp. 3ff and Karp "Hands Across the Sea: Millions Were Looted from the American Bank and Trust," pp. 3ff. New York State, Supreme Court, County of New York, Affidavit in the Matter of the Application of John G. Heimann, as Superintendent of Banks of the State of New York, and Federal Deposit Insurance Corporation, for approval, pursuant to the provisions of Banking Law No. 618, of the purchase of assets and assumption of liabilities of American Bank & Trust Company, New York, New York, September 25, 1975.

33. Interview with Robert Bench.

34. "A New Supervisory Approach to Foreign Lending," pp. 1–6; Harold D. Schuler, "Evaluation of Risk in International Lending: A Bank Examiner's Perspective," pp. 5–7 (mimeo; OCC).

35. *International Banking Act of 1978,* Public Law 95-369. Among other provisions, the act limits interstate deposit taking by foreign banks, applies restrictions on their nonbanking activities, allows foreigners to be directors of American banks, provides for voluntary membership of foreign banks in the FDIC, and makes possible federal supervision of foreign banks. It also alters the regulation of Edge Act Corporations and thereby alters permissible activities of U.S. banks. U.S. Senate, Committee on Banking, Housing and Urban Affairs, *International Banking Act of 1978; Federal Institutions Regulatory and Investment Rate Control Act of 1978,* Public Law 95-630, which, among other things, broadens the power of regulatory authorities to remove bank directors, and enhances regulatory control over persons acquiring control of banks and bank holding

companies, and also has implications for regulation of foreign directors and owners.

36. Rolf E. Breuer, "Banking Law," p. 105.

37. Blunden, "The Supervision of the U.K. Banking System"; Chancellor of the Exchequer, *The Licensing and Supervision of Deposit-Taking Institutions,* White Paper, August 1976.

7. Past, Present, and Future Challenges for the International Banking System

1. See Paul M. Horvitz, "Bank Risks in the New International Financial Structure," pp. 145–63; Paul M. Horvitz, "Failures of Large Banks," pp. 589–601; Thomas Mayer, "Should Large Banks Be Allowed To Fail," pp. 603–10; R. Alton Gilbert, "Bank Failures and Public Policy," pp. 7–15.

2. I am grateful to Andrew A. Beveridge and Philip A. Wellons for this latter insight.

3. Since World War II only one country, Ghana, actually repudiated a loan. It did so because of alleged bribery in the making of the loan.

4. See U.S. House, Committee on Banking, Finance and Urban Affairs, *International Banking Operations*, p. 215.

5. In 1977–78 the Eurocurrency market became quite liquid for a variety of reasons: the continuing surpluses of the oil-producing states which were to a great extent deposited in the Eurocurrency market; the easing of capital controls in the oil-importing countries; and the U.S. balance-of-payments deficit, and continuing economic problems in the developed countries resulting in depressed loan demand.

6. See Bank for International Settlements, *Annual Report 1977-1978,* (Basel: BIS, 1978), pp. 86–91; speech by Gordon Richardson, Governor of the Bank of England, before the Association of Foreign Banks in Switzerland (reprinted in *The Banker,* suppl. [July 1978], pp. ii–iii); "The Health of International Banking—The Great Debate," *Euromoney* (May 1977), pp. 17–27.

7. Robert C. Bradshaw, "Foreign Exchange Operations of U.S. Banks," in *Conference on Bank Structure and Competition,* pp. 113–23; John Cooper, "How Foreign Exchange Operations Can Go Wrong," pp. 4–28.

8. "U.S. Banks Abroad," p. 879.

9. There is also a foreign exchange risk associated with international loans denominated in foreign currencies.

10. See below on the role of the oil crisis. See also U.S. Senate, Committee on Foreign Relations, *International Debt, the Banks and U.S. Foreign Policy.*

11. *World Bank, World Debt Tables* (October 20, 1978), 1:134.

12. Peru lost export revenues from anchovies and copper and did not produce oil as expected. Zaïre was hurt by the fall in the price of copper and Turkey by the loss of transfer payments from foreign workers.

13. For the debate on international lending see David O. Beim, "Rescuing the LDC's," pp. 717–31; Harold van B. Cleveland and W. H. Bruce Brittain, "Are the

LDCs in Over Their Heads?" pp. 732–70; Albert Fishlow, "Debt Remains a Problem," pp. 133–43; Richard W. Weinert, "Why the Banks Did It," pp. 148–56; David C. Beek, "Commercial Bank Lending to the Developing Countries," pp. 1–8; Irving S. Friedman, *The Emerging Role of Private Banks in the Developing World;* Robert Solomon, "A Perspective on the Debt of Developing Countries, pp. 479–510.

14. Federal Reserve Bank of New York, news release no. 1202, July 12, 1977.

15. Ian H. Giddy, "Measuring the World Foreign Exchange Market."

16. U.S. House, *Adequacy of the Office of the Comptroller of the Currency's Supervision of Franklin National Bank,* p. 1.

17. See *International Banking Act of 1978,* Public Law 95-369; *Federal Reserve Bulletin* (December 1978), 64(12):990–92.

18. *Bulletin of the European Communities,* (1977), no. 11, p. 32. Europe: Agence International d'Information pour la Presse, Summary, no. 2333 (n.s.), pp. 8–9.

BIBLIOGRAPHY

Interviews

Informants are listed either by their titles at the time of the interview or by their titles during the Franklin events, in which case they are noted as "former."

Federal Reserve Bank of New York

Paul A. Volcker	President, former Under Secretary of the Treasury for Monetary Affairs
Richard A. Debs	Former First Vice President
Thomas M. Timlen	First Vice President
Alan R. Holmes	Executive Vice President, Foreign Open Market Operations and Treasury Issues
Fred W. Piderit, Jr.	Senior Vice President, Bank Supervision
H. David Willey	Vice President, Foreign Central Bank Accounts and International Institutions
David E. Bodner	Former Vice President, Foreign Department
Frederick C. Schadrack	Vice President, Bank Supervision
Suzanne Cutler	Assistant Vice President, Loans and Credits

Henry S. Fujarski, Jr.	Assistant Vice President, Accounting Department and Operations Analysis
Benedict Rafanello	Assistant Vice President, Bank Supervision
James H. Oltman	Deputy General Counsel
Leopold S. Rassnick	Assistant General Counsel
Ernest T. Patrikis	Assistant Counsel
Donald L. Bittker	Assistant Counsel
Walker F. Todd	Attorney
John C. Junek	Attorney
A. John Maher	Chief Examiner, Bank Examinations Department
William Milusich	Supervising Examiner, International Examinations Division
Walter W. Zunic	Supervising Examiner, Bank Examinations Department

Board of Governors of the Federal Reserve System

George Mitchell	Former Vice Chairman
Ralph Bryant	Former Director, Division of International Finance
John E. Ryan	Director, Banking Supervision and Regulation
Frederick R. Dahl	Associate Director, Banking Supervision and Regulation
Robert F. Gemmill	Associate Director, Division of International Finance
Henry S. Terrell	Section Chief, International Banking Section
Kay J. Auerbach	Financial Analyst

Federal Deposit Insurance Corporation

Frank Wille	Former Chairman
Robert E. Barnett	Acting Chairman, Former Deputy to the Chairman
Edward Bransilver	Former General Counsel

George W. Hill   Chief, Division of Liquidation

Raymond H. Hoffman   Liquidator in charge of Franklin National
                            Bank Liquidation

C. F. Muckenfuss III   Former Assistant to Director
                            George A. Le Maistre

Office of the Comptroller of the Currency

John G. Heimann   Comptroller of the Currency

Robert Bloom   Acting Comptroller of the Currency

Robert R. Bench   Associate Deputy Comptroller,
                            International Division

Timothy M. Sullivan   Assistant Director, International
                            Examinations Division

Leon S. Tarrant   Assistant Director, International
                            Examinations Division

Robert A. Baer, Jr.   Special Assistant

Bank of England

W. Peter Cooke   Head of Banking Supervision

Rodney D. Galpin   Deputy Chief Cashier, Banking and
                            Money Market Supervision

Bank of Italy

Silvano Montanaro   Director of Bank Supervision

Francesco Buono   Supervisor, Liquidation of Banca Privata

Giuseppe Catalano   Foreign Exchange Regulation

Bankers and Lawyers

Paul Luftig   Former President, Franklin National
                            Bank of New York

André C. Jacques   Director and Vice Chairman, European American Bank and Trust Company

Hamilton F. Potter, Jr.   Partner, Sullivan and Cromwell, counsel for European American Bank and Trust Company, member of the Board of Directors, European American Bank and Trust Company

George B. Balamut   Partner, Simpson Thacher and Bartlett, counsel for Manufacturers Hanover Trust Company

Robert J. McKean, Jr.   Partner, Simpson Thacher and Bartlett, counsel for Manufacturers Hanover Trust Company

James Q. Hall   Vice President, Loeb Rhoades Hornblower and Company

Mario Ardito   Partner, Studio Legale Ardito, Rome

J. K. Grieves   Partner, Freshfields, Solicitors, London

Archival And Governmental Sources

Board of Governors of the Federal Reserve System. Files on Franklin National Bank and Franklin New York Corporation. Washington, D.C.

Federal Deposit Insurance Corporation. Files on Franklin National Bank. New York.

Federal Reserve Bank of New York. Legal Department. Files on Franklin National Bank and Franklin New York Corporation. New York.

Office of the Comptroller of the Currency. Files on Franklin National Bank. Washington, D.C.

Securities and Exchange Commission. Files on Franklin New York Corporation. Washington, D.C.

United States District Court. Eastern District of New York. *Corbin v. Federal Reserve Bank of New York,* 458 F. Supp. 143, 1978.

United States District Court, Southern District of New York. *Securities and Exchange Commission, Plaintiff v. Franklin New York Corporation, Harold V. Gleason, Paul Luftig, Peter R. Shaddick, Michele Sindona, Carlo Bordoni, Howard D. Crosse, Andrew N. Garofalo, Donald H. Emrich, Robert C. Parepinto, Defendants,* 74 Civil Action, File No. 4557.

United States District Court, Southern District of New York, *U.S. v. Carlo Bordoni, Peter R. Shaddick, Andrew Garofalo, Arthur Slutzky, Donald Emrich, Martin Keroes, Michael Romersa and Paul Sabatella,* Indictment S. 75 Cr. 948.

United States District Court, Southern District of New York, *U.S. v. Harold V. Gleason, Paul Luftig, and J. Michael Carter,* Indictment 78 Cr.

United States District Court, Southern District of New York, *U.S. v. Harold V. Gleason, Paul Luftig, and J. Michael Carter,* Trial Transcript, December 1978–January 1979.

United States District Court, Southern District of New York, *U.S. v. Michele Sindona and Carlo Bordoni,* Indictment 79 Cr.

United States District Court, Southern District of New York, *Requested Extradition of Michele Sindona by the Republic of Italy,* Supplemental Memorandum of Law and Fact in Support of the Requested Extradition of Michele Sindona, 65 Cr. Misc. 1.

General Sources

Aharoni, Yair, ed. *The Emerging International Monetary Order and the Banking System.* Tel Aviv: University Publishing Projects, 1976.

Aliber, Robert Z. "International Banking: Growth and Regulation," *Columbia Journal of World Business* (Winter 1975), 10(4):9–15.

——. "Towards a Theory of International Banking," Federal Reserve Bank of San Francisco, *Monthly Review* (Spring 1976), pp. 5–8.

Altman, Edward I. and Arnold W. Sametz, eds. *Financial Crises: Institutions and Markets in a Fragile Environment.* New York: Wiley, 1977.

Aronson, Jonathan David. *Money and Power: Banks and the World Monetary System.* Beverly Hills, Calif: Sage, 1978.

Bagehot, Walter. *Lombard Street: A Description of the Money Market.* New York: Scribner's, 1912.

Balamut, George B. "A Morality Tale: Everything's Got a Moral If Only You Can Find It," *Administrative Law Review* (Fall 1975), 27(4):342–56.

"Bank Expansion in New York State: The 1971 Statewide Branching Law," Federal Reserve Bank of New York, *Monthly Review* (November 1971), 53(11):266–74.

Bank for International Settlements, *Annual Report.* Basel: BIS, various years.

Barr, Joseph W. "The Last Days of Franklin National Bank," *Administrative Law Review* (Fall 1975), 27(4):301–14.

Becker, Joseph D. "International Insolvency: The Case of Herstatt," *American Bar Association Journal* (October 1976), 62:1290–95.

Beek, David C. "Commercial Bank Lending to the Developing Countries," Federal Reserve Bank of New York, *Quarterly Review* (Summer 1977), 2:1–8.

Beim, David O. "Rescuing the LDC's," *Foreign Affairs* (July 1977), 55(4):717–31.

Benston, George J. "How We Can Learn From Past Bank Failures," *Bankers Magazine* (Winter 1975), 158(1):19–24.

Blunden, George. "Control and Supervision of the Foreign Operations of Banks," in J. E. Wadsworth, J. S. G. Wilson, and H. Fournier, eds., *The Development of Financial Institutions in Europe 1956-1976,* pp. 193–213. Netherlands: Sijthoff, 1977.

——. "International Cooperation in Banking Supervision," Bank of England *Quarterly Bulletin* (September 1977), 17(3):325–29.

——. "The Supervision of the UK Banking System," *Bank of England Quarterly Bulletin* (June 1975), 15(2):188–94.

Bradshaw, Robert C. "Foreign Exchange Operations of US Banks," in *Conference on Bank Structure and Competition,* pp. 113–23. Chicago: Federal Reserve Bank of Chicago, May 1975.

Bransilver, Edward. "Failing Banks—FDIC's Options and Constraints," *Administrative Law Review* (Fall 1975), 27(4):327–41.

Breuer, Rolf E. "Banking Law," *Euromoney* (July 1976), p. 105.

Brimmer, Andrew F. "International Finance and the Management of Bank Failure: Herstatt v. Franklin National." Paper prepared for presentation before a joint session of the American Economic Association and the American Finance Association. Atlantic City, New Jersey, September 16, 1976.

Brimmer, Andrew F. and Frederick R. Dahl. "Growth of American International Banking: Implications for Public Policy," *Journal of Finance* (May 1975), 30(2):341–63.

Burns, Arthur F. "Maintaining the Soundness of Our Banking System," Federal Reserve Bank of New York, *Monthly Review* (November 1974), 56(11):263–67.

Carswell, John. *The South Sea Bubble* (Stanford, Calif.: Stanford University Press, 1960).

Clark, Robert Charles. "The Soundness of Financial Intermediaries," *The Yale Law Journal* (November 1976), 86(1):1–102.

Clarke, Stephen V. O. *Central Bank Cooperation 1924-1931.* New York: Federal Reserve Bank of New York, 1967.

"The Central Bankers Gather," *Euromoney* (April 1975), p. 3.

Cleveland, Harold van B. and W. H. Bruce Brittain. "Are the LDCs in Over Their Heads?" *Foreign Affairs* (July 1977), 55(4):732–50.

Coombs, Charles A. "Treasury and Federal Reserve Foreign Exchange Operations," *Federal Reserve Bulletin* (September 1974), 60:636–50.

Cooper, John. "How Foreign Exchange Operations Can Go Wrong," *Euromoney* (May 1974), pp. 4–7.

Debs, Richard A. "International Banking," Federal Reserve Bank of New York, *Monthly Review* (June 1975), 57(6):722–29.

Dondelinger, Albert. "How to Improve International Banking Supervision," *Euromoney* (June 1975), p. 98.

Duff, Declan and Ian Peacock. "Refinancing of Sovereign Debt," *The Banker* (January 1978), 128(623):69–75.

Edwards, Franklin R. and James Scott. "Regulating the Solvency of Depository Institutions: A Perspective For Deregulation," Columbia University Graduate School of Business Research Papers, no. 210. New York: Columbia University, November 1977.

Erdman, Paul. *The Crash of '79*. New York: Simon & Schuster, 1976.

Evans, John R. "Disclosure Through a Glass Darkly," *Administrative Law Review* (Fall 1975), 27(4):357–66.

Fishlow, Albert, "Debt Remains a Problem," *Foreign Policy* (Spring 1978), no. 30, pp. 133–43.

Frankel, Allen B. "The Lender of Last Resort Facility in the Context of Multinational Banking," *Columbia Journal of World Business* (Winter 1975), 10(4):120–27.

Franklin New York Corporation, *Annual Report*. New York: Franklin New York Corporation, various years.

Friedman, Irving S. *The Emerging Role of Private Banks in the Developing World*. New York: Citicorp, 1977.

Friedman, Milton. "The Euro-Dollar Market: Some First Principles," *The Morgan Guaranty Survey* (October 1969), pp. 1–11.

Giddy, Ian H. "Measuring the World Foreign Exchange Market," *Columbia Journal of World Business* (Fall 1979), 14(3).

Gilbert, R. Alton. "Bank Failures and Public Policy," Federal Reserve Bank of St. Louis, *Review* (November 1975), 57(11):7–15.

"Hambros at the Helm," *Fortune* (September 1971), 84(3):49.

Hanley, Thomas H. *Eurolending Profitability: Gradual Improvement in 1979*. New York: Salomon Brothers, 1978.

Hawtrey, R. G. *The Art of Central Banking.* New York: Augustus Kelley Reprints of Economics Classics, 1965.

Hirsch, Fred. "The Bagehot Problem," *The Manchester School* (September 1977), 45(3):241-57.

Hirst, F. W. *The Six Panics and Other Essays.* London: Methuen, 1913.

Holland, Robert C. "Public Policy Issues in U.S. Banking Abroad." Remarks at the 53d Annual Meeting of the Bankers Association for Foreign Trade, April 8, 1975. Mimeo.

Horvitz, Paul M. "Bank Risks in the New International Financial Structure—Lessons from Bank Failures," in Yair Aharoni, ed., *The Emerging International Monetary Order and the Banking System,* pp. 145-63. Tel Aviv: University Publishing Projects, 1976.

——. "Failures of Large Banks: Implications for Banking Supervision and Deposit Insurance," *Journal of Finance and Quantitative Analysis* (November 1975), 10(4):589-601.

Humphrey, Thomas M. "The Classical Concept of the Lender of Last Resort," Federal Reserve Bank of Richmond *Economic Review* (January/February 1975), 61:2-9.

Hyndman, H. M. *Commercial Crises of the Nineteenth Century.* London: Allen & Unwin, 1892.

International Monetary Fund. *Annual Report* (various years) Washington, D.C.: IMF.

"The Italian Connection," *Forbes* (December 1972), 110(11):56-57.

Italy, Camera Dei Deputati, *Bolletino Delle Giunte e Delle Commissioni Parlamentari,* November 7, 1974, pp. 1-11.

"Italy's Establishment Fights an Outsider," *Business Week* (September 18, 1971), 2194:26.

Jensen, Michael C. "Loans Assessed at Charter Banks—Fed Report Says Portfolio of 1974 Lending Showed Sharp Deterioration," *New York Times,* January 1, 1976, reprinted in U.S. Congress, Senate, *Problem Banks,* Hearing Before the Committee on Banking, Housing and Urban Affairs, 94th Congress, 2d Session, 1976, pp. 318-20.

Johnston, Robert. "Proposals for Federal Control of Foreign Banks," Federal Reserve Bank of San Francisco, *Economic Review* (Spring 1976), pp. 32-39.

Karp, Richard. "Hands Across the Sea: Millions Were Looted from the American Bank and Trust," *Barron's,* December 27, 1977, pp. 3ff.

——. "Sleeping Watchdogs: How the American Bank and Trust Company Went Broke," *Barron's,* December 20, 1976, pp. 3ff.

Katz, Samuel I. "Managed Floating as an Interim International Exchange Rate Regime, 1973–75," *The Bulletin* (1975), no. 3.

Kelly, Janet. *Bankers and Borders: The Case of American Banks in Britain*. Cambridge, Mass: Ballinger, 1977.

Kennedy, Susan Estabrook. *The Banking Crisis of 1933*. Lexington, Ky.: University Press of Kentucky, 1973.

Kindleberger, Charles P. *Manias, Panics, Crises*. New York: Basic Books, 1978.

Klebener, Benjamin J. *Commercial Banking in the U.S.: A History*. Hinsdale, Ill.: Dryden, 1974.

Klopstock, Fred H. "Money Creation in the Euro-Dollar Market—a Note on Professor Friedman's Views," in Federal Reserve Bank of New York, *Monthly Review* (July 1968), pp. 130–38.

Kubarych, Roger M. *Foreign Exchange Markets in the United States*. New York: Federal Reserve Bank of New York, 1978.

"Losers' League Table," *The Banker* (November 1974), 124(595):1284.

Mayer, Thomas. "Should Large Banks be Allowed to Fail?" *Journal of Financial & Quantitative Analysis*, (November 1975), 10(4):603–10.

McCartney, E. Ray. *Crisis of 1873*. Minneapolis, Minn.: Burgess, May 1935.

Minsky, Hyman P. "Financial Instability Revisited: The Economics of Disaster," Board of Governors of the Federal Reserve System, *Reappraisal of the Federal Reserve Discount Mechanism* (June 1972), 3:95–136.

Mitchell, George W. "How the Fed Sees Multinational Bank Regulation," *The Banker* (July 1974), 124(581):757–60.

Mitchell, Wesley C. *Business Cycles: The Problem and Its Setting*. New York: National Bureau of Economic Research, 1927.

Morgenstern, Oskar. *International Financial Transactions and Business Cycles*. Princeton, N.J.: Princeton University Press, 1959.

"A New Supervisory Approach to Foreign Lending," Federal Reserve Bank of New York, *Quarterly Bulletin* (Spring 1978), 3(1):1–6.

New York State. Supreme Court, County of New York. Affidavit in the Matter of the Application of John G. Heimann, as Superintendent of Banks of the State of New York, and Federal Deposit Insurance Corporation, for approval, pursuant to the provisions of Banking Law No. 618, of the purchase of assets and assumption of liabilities of American Bank & Trust Company. New York, N.Y., September 25, 1975.

Oltman, James H. "Failing Banks—The Role of the Fed," *Administrative Law Review* (Fall 1975), 27(4):317–25.

Panerai, Paolo and Maurizio De Luca. *Il Crack: Sindona, La DC, Il Vaticano E Gli Altri Amici.* Italy: Panorama, 1975.

Portes, Richard. "East Europe's Debt to the West: Interdependence is a Two-Way Street," *Foreign Affairs* (July 1977), 55(4):751–82.

Robertson, Ross M. *The Comptroller and Bank Supervision.* Washington, D.C.: Office of the Comptroller of the Currency, 1968.

Rose, Sanford. "What Really Went Wrong at Franklin National," *Fortune* (October 1974), 90(4):118–21ff.

Russell, Robert W. "Transgovernmental Interaction in the International Monetary System 1960–72," *International Organization* (Autumn 1973), 27(4):431–64.

Salomon Brothers, *U.S. Multinational Banking: Current and Prospective Strategies.* New York: Salomon Brothers, 1976.

Schuler, Harold D. "Evaluation of Risk in International Lending: A Bank Examiner's Perspective," remarks at Federal Reserve Bank of Boston Conference on Key Issues in International Banking, October 5–7, 1977. Mimeo.

Schumpeter, Joseph A. *Business Cycles, A Theoretical, Historical and Statistical Analysis of the Capitalistic Process.* New York: McGraw-Hill, 1939.

"A Sicilian Financier Takes Aim at the U.S.," *Business Week* (April 29, 1972), 2226:34–35.

Sinkey, Joseph F., Jr., "The Collapse of Franklin National Bank of New York," *Journal of Bank Research* (Summer 1976), 7(2):113–22.

——. "Franklin National Bank of New York: A Portfolio and Performance Analysis of our Largest Bank Failure," Federal Deposit Insurance Corporation, Financial and Economic Research Section, Division of Research, Working Papers, No. 75-10, 1975.

Solomon, Robert. "A Perspective on the Debt of Developing Countries," in *Brookings Papers on Economic Activity,* 2:479–501. Arthur M. Okun and George L. Perry, eds. Washington, D.C.: Brookings Institution, 1977.

Stem, Carl H. "Some Eurocurrency Problems: Credit Expansion, The Regulatory Framework, Liquidity, and Petrodollars." In Carl H. Stem, John H. Makin, and Dennis E. Logue, *Eurocurrencies and the International Monetary System.* Washington, D.C.: American Enterprise Institute, 1976, pp. 283–332.

"Supervising the Euromarket Dinosaur," *The Banker* (August 1978), 128(630):77–83.

Trescott, Paul B. *Financing American Enterprise: The Story of Commercial Banking.* New York: Harper & Row, 1963.

United Kingdom. Bank of England. *Quarterly Bulletin,* various issues.

——. Chancellor of the Exchequer. *The Licensing and Supervision of Deposit Taking Institutions.* White Paper (August 1976).

United States Board of Governors of the Federal Reserve System. *Annual Report.* Washington, D.C.: Board of Governors, various issues.

——. *Annual Statistical Digest.* Washington, D.C.: Board of Governors, various years.

——. *Banking and Monetary Statistics, 1941-1976.* Washington, D.C.: Board of Governors, 1976.

——. *Federal Reserve Bulletin,* various issues.

——. *Reappraisal of the Federal Reserve Discount Mechanism,* vol. 3. Washington, D.C.: Board of Governors, 1972.

U.S. Congress. *Federal Institutions Regulatory and Investment Rate Control Act of 1978.* Public Law 95-630.

——. *International Banking Act of 1978.* Public Law 95-369.

——. Joint Economic Committee. *How Well Are Fluctuating Exchange Rates Working,* Hearings before the Subcommittee on International Economics. 93d Congress, 1st sess., 1973.

——. *A Review of Balance of Payments Policies,* "A Progress Report on the Federal Reserve Foreign Credit Restraint Programs," by Andrew F. Brimmer, Hearing before the Subcommittee on International Exchange & Payments, 91st Cong., 1st sess., 1969.

United States Congress, House. Committee on Banking, Currency, and Housing. *An Act to Lower Interest Rates and Allocate Credit,* Hearings before the Subcommittee on Domestic Monetary Policy. 94th Cong., 1st sess., 1975.

——. *Bank Failures, Regulatory Reform, Financial Privacy,* Part II, Hearings before the Subcommittee on Financial Institutions Supervision, Regulation & Insurance. 93d Cong., 2d sess., 1974.

——. *Bank Failures, Regulatory Reform, Financial Privacy,* Hearings before the Subcommittee on Financial Institutions Supervision, Regulation, & Insurance. 94th Cong., 1st sess., 1975.

——. *FINE: Financial Institutions & the National Economy,* a compendium of papers prepared for the FINE Study, Book II, "Foreign Bank Activities in the United States" and "U.S. Banks Abroad," by Jane D'Arista. 94th Cong., 2d sess., 1976, pp. 732-937.

——. *Financial Institutions and the Nation's Economy (FINE): Discussion Principles,* prepared for the Subcommittee on Financial Institutions Supervision, Regulation and Insurance. 94th Cong., 1st and 2d sess., 1975-1976.

——. *International Banking: A Supplement to a Compendium of Papers Prepared for the FINE Study.* Staff Report, 94th Congress, 2d session, 1976.

——. Committee on Banking, Finance, and Urban Affairs. *International Banking Operations,* Hearings before the Subcommittee on Financial Institutions Supervision, Regulation, and Insurance. 95th Cong., 1st sess., 1977.

——. Committee on Government Operations. *Adequacy of the Office of the Comptroller of the Currency's Supervision of Franklin National Bank,* House Report 94-1669. 94th Cong., 2d sess., 1976.

——. *Oversight Hearings into the Effectiveness of Federal Bank Regulation (Franklin National Bank Failure),* Hearings before a Subcommittee on Government Operations. 94th Cong., 2d sess., 1976.

United States Congress, Senate. Committee on Banking, Currency, and Housing. *An Act to Lower Interest Rates and Allocate Credit,* Hearings before the Subcommittee on Domestic Monetary Policy. 94th Cong., 1st sess., 1975.

——. *Apartment Loans by Savings and Loan Associations,* Hearings before a Subcommittee. 86th Cong., 2nd Sess., 1962.

——. Committee on Banking, Housing, and Urban Affairs. *Compendium of Major Issues in Bank Regulation,* 94th Congress, 1st session, 1975.

——. *The International Banking Act of 1978,* Report of the Committee on Banking, Housing, and Urban Affairs to Accompany HR 10899. 95th Cong., 2d sess., 1978.

——. *Multinational Banking,* Outline of a Study by the Staff of the Committee on Banking, Housing, and Urban Affairs. 94th Cong., 2nd sess., 1976.

——. *Problem Banks,* Hearings. 94th Cong., 2d sess., 1976.

——. Committee on Foreign Relations. *International Debt, the Banks and U.S. Foreign Policy,* Staff Report Prepared for the Use of the Subcommittee on Foreign Economic Policy. 95th Cong., 1st sess., 1977.

——. *Multinational Corporations in the Dollar Devaluation Crisis: Report on a Questionnaire,* Staff Report for the Subcommittee on Multinational Corporations. 94th Cong., 1st sess., 1975.

——. Committee on Governmental Affairs. *Inquiry into Certain Matters Relating to T. Bertram Lance and Various Financial Institutions,* Hearings, 95th Cong., 1st sess., 1977.

——. National Monetary Commission. *History of Crises Under the National Banking System,* by O. M. W. Sprague. 61st Cong., 2d session, 1910.

United States Federal Reserve Bank of New York. *Annual Report 1974.* New York: Federal Reserve Bank of New York, 1975.

——. *Monthly Review,* various issues.

——. *Quarterly Review,* various issues.

Van Vleck, George Washington. *The Panic of 1857: An Analytical Study.* New York: Columbia University Press, 1943.

Weinert, Richard W. "Why the Banks Did It," *Foreign Policy* (Spring 1978), no. 30, pp. 148–56.

Whitman, Marina v.N., "Bridging the Gap," *Foreign Policy* (Spring 1977), no. 30, pp. 148–56.

Wille, Frank. *The FDIC and Franklin National Bank: A Report to the Congress and All FDIC Insured Banks,* presented before 81st Annual Convention of the Savings Banks of New York State, Boca Ration, Fla., November 23, 1974. Mimeo.

INDEX

Agreement corporations, 16; defined,
    195n2
Agreements to repurchase, 70, 71
American Bank and Trust Company of New
    York: closing of, 164–65
American Bank and Trust Company of
    Orangeburg, S.C.: failure of, 109
Amincor Bank, A.G., 53, 81–82, 83, 95–96
Amsterdam-Rotterdam Bank N.V., 206n39
Antitrust laws, 137, 147
Argus Corporation, 57, 59
Assets (banks): affected by recession, 178;
    deterioration in quality of, 106–7; of Edge
    Act and Agreement corporations, 16; of
    foreign banks in U.S., 16–17; of foreign
    branches of U.S. banks, 16, 17, 24T; of
    Franklin National Bank, 90, 150–51, 152
Auditing and accounting practices, 163, 188

BIS. *See* Bank for International Settlements
Baeyens, Herman, 165
Bahamas, 8, 45; "shell" branches in, 43.
    See also Nassau, the Bahamas
Balance-of-payments, 4, 115; and oil price
    increase, 86, 108; policies, U.S., 42
Banca de Messina, Messina, 53
Banca di Roma, 98
Banca Privata Finanziaria, Milan, 53, 65,
    96; deposit withdrawals from, 98; merged
    with Banca Unione, 98

Banca Privata Italiana, 98; declared
    insolvent, 99
Banca Unione, S.P.A., Milan, 53, 59, 65,
    81–82, 83, 95–96; deposit withdrawals
    from, 98; merged with Banca Privata
    Finanziaria, 98
Banco Nationale de Costa Rica, 41
Bank and tax havens, 8, 53
Bank failures, 102, 108–9
Bank for International Settlements (BIS),
    10, 146, 161, 166, 169; central bank
    governors' and officials' meetings at, 153;
    cooperative efforts in, 165; secretariat for
    Standing Committee, 161. *See also*
    Standing Committee on Banking
    Regulations and Supervisory Practices.
Bank holding companies, 7, 47, 107; defined,
    58; determination of control of, 60–61;
    foreign activities of, 7
Bank Holding Company Act, 57, 63, 137;
    proposed changes in, 139; Federal
    Reserve and Fasco under, 57–60
Bank of Canada, 138
Bank of England, 9, 130, 138, 153;
    cooperation of, in Franklin crisis, 147,
    149, 150, 151, 152; and EEC directive,
    189; and Federal Reserve loan to
    Franklin National, 147–49; and Franklin
    National's application for London
    branch, 51–52, 57, 62, 97–98; in Israel-

225

INSTITUTE OF WAR AND PEACE STUDIES
of the School of International Affairs
of Columbia University

The Failure of the Franklin National Bank is one of a series of studies sponsored by the Institute of War and Peace Studies of Columbia University. The research program of the Institute has two parts. One deals with international security policy, including American foreign and military policy, strategic studies, and arms control policy. The other deals with general international relations, including theories of international politics, comparative foreign policy, and the political, economic, and institutional aspects of international order. Institute publications dealing with general international relations are *Theoretical Aspects of International Relations* edited by William T. R. Fox; *The Structure of Nations and Empires* by Reinhold Niebuhr; *Political Power: USA/USSR* by Zbigniew Brzezinski and Samuel P. Huntington, jointly sponsored with the Russian Institute, Columbia University; *Political Unification: A Comparative Study of Leaders and Forces by Amitai Etzioni*; *Foreign Policy and Democratic Politics* by Kenneth N. Waltz, jointly sponsored with the Center for International Affairs, Harvard University; *A World of Nations* by Dankwart A. Rustow, jointly sponsored with the Brookings Institution; *Western European Perspectives on International Affairs* by Donald J. Puchala and Richard L. Merritt, jointly sponsored with the Yale Political Data Program; *The American Study of International Relations* by William T. R. Fox; *How Nations Behave* by Louis Henkin, jointly sponsored with the Council on Foreign Relations; *Soviet Perspectives on International Relations, 1956–1967* by William Zimmerman, jointly sponsored with the Russian Institute, Columbia University; *Philosophers and Kings: Studies in Leadership* edited by Dankwart A. Rustow, jointly sponsored with the American Academy of Arts and Sciences; *Charter of the United Nations: Commentary and Documents* by Leland M. Goodrich, Edward Hambro and Anne Simons; *Dag Hammarskjold's United Nations* by Mark Zacher; *The New Nations in the United Nations* by David A. Kay; *Dominance and Diversity: The International*

Hierarchy by Steven L. Spiegel; *Planning, Prediction and Policy-making in Foreign Affairs* by Robert L. Rothstein; *International Organization: Politics and Process* edited by Leland M. Goodrich and David A. Kay; *The United Nations in a Changing World* by Leland M. Goodrich; *The Crouching Future: International Politics and U.S. Foreign Policy—a Forecast* by Roger Hilsman; *Canada and the United States: Transnational and Transgovernmental Relations* edited by Annette Baker Fox, Alfred O. Hero, Jr., and Joseph S. Nye, Jr.; *The Politics of Attraction: Four Middle Powers and the United States* by Annette Baker Fox; *Technology, World Politics, and American Policy* by Victor Basiuk; and *The Weak in the World of the Strong: The Developing Countries in the International System* by Robert L. Rothstein.